Second production Typhoon R8199, *at Langley in 1942. Issued to No 56 Squadron (presentation aircraft* Borough of Sutton & Cheam*), it was shot down accidentally over the Channel by 401 Squadron Spitfires while on its second operation on June 1 1942.*

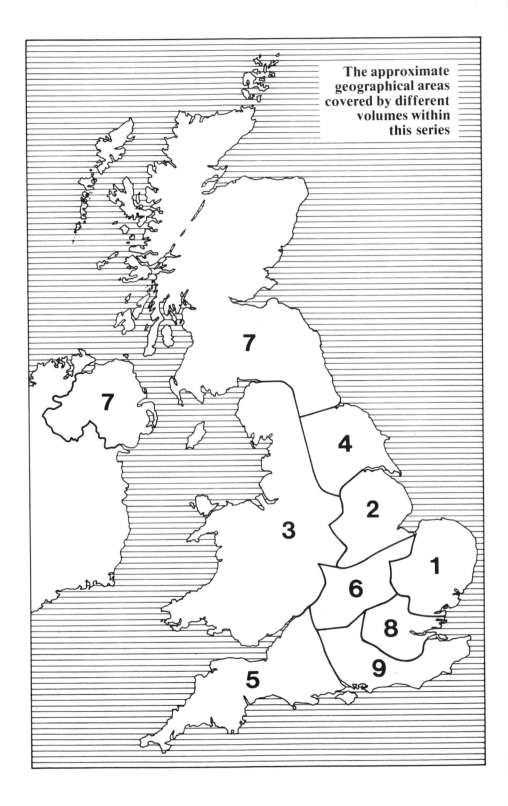

The approximate geographical areas covered by different volumes within this series

ACTION STATIONS

8. Military airfields of Greater London

Bruce Barrymore Halpenny

PSL Patrick Stephens, Cambridge

Title page *Ground crews are important everywhere, especially in Fighter Command where they must work fast. This crew with 403 'Wolf' Squadron could refuel and rearm a Spitfire in three or four minutes. Left to right: LAC Hugh Bebbington of Winnipeg; Corporal John Buxton of Moncton; Corporal Jim Cleaver of Winnipeg; LAC Brankbyrne of Bristol; Pilot Officer Willie Lane of Sudbury, Ontario, and LAC Pete Morley of Peterborough, Ontario. Kenley, April 21 1943.*

First published in 1984

British Library Cataloguing in Publication Data

Action Stations.
  8: Military airfields of Greater London
  1. Air bases—Great Britain—History
  I. Halpenny, Bruce Barrymore
  358.4'17'0941   UG635.G7

  ISBN 0-85059-585-1

Photoset in 9 pt and 10 on 11 pt Times by Manuset Limited, Baldock, Herts. Printed in Great Britain on 100 gsm Fineblade coated cartridge, and bound, by The Garden City Press, Letchworth, Herts, for the publishers, Patrick Stephens Limited, Bar Hill, Cambridge, CB3 8EL, England.

Contents

Introduction

Having written *Action Stations 2** and *Action Stations 4†*, which were about bomber country, I now turn to *Action Stations 8*, covering Greater London, which was fighter country, the home of the Hurricane and Spitfire. There is a vast difference between the fighter and bomber crews. As in *Action Stations 4*, I have listed at the end of the airfields some non-airfields, in order to make this a comprehensive volume, for these sites too had an important part to play in one way or another and some are still very active today.

Read this book and almost magically it is the Second World War again. For those who were there, I hope this book will be an aid to memory that will fuel your rocking chair years. Edward Curotte of Campbellton, New Brunswick, Canada, who served with the Royal Canadian Air Force, now recalls those days: 'Croydon . . . ah . . . Croydon, what sweet nostalgic memories. The beautiful English summer evenings, Purley and Purley way. The green facing the airport, unfortunately marred by huge cement pipes in expectation of invasion by gliders or paratroops.

'There was the Greyhound dance hall, my favourite pub, 'The Propeller', where one could get cold beer (or should one say ale when in England?), the still excellent teas available, as rationing was not yet in full effect, this being June 1940, the roses in front of the tranquil English homes, the hospitable owners who would invite one for a cup of tea, the stoic English digging bomb shelters in their lovely gardens . . . precursor to the stark tragedy of mass bombings yet to come, the friendly and convivial atmosphere of the English pub, where we were introduced to civilised drinking, the everlasting game of darts to which we soon became addicted. Yes, Croydon, many times I sit back in my easy chair and close my eyes to enjoy it all over again as one enjoys a love of long ago!'

The area covered by this book had an early introduction to flying. Many sites were just open fields and cannot be listed as airfields, but warrant a mention. At Waltham Marshes, on July 13 1909, Alliott Verdon Roe made the first successful powered flight in an all-British aircraft, the Avro Triplane. Colonel Cody had made a flight in a French-engined aircraft the previous year. Roe succeeded in flying about 100 ft. Practice flights continued for a few more weeks before flying came to an end at Waltham Marshes. Maplin Sands in Essex was used briefly in November 1909. Macfie had moved there with his machine

* *Military airfields of Lincolnshire and the East Midlands* (Patrick Stephens Ltd).
† *Military airfields of Yorkshire* (Patrick Stephens Ltd).

but was ordered off the sands by the War Office and his machine was deposited in the Kursaal at Southend.

Other places that have some claim to flying activity are Canvey Island, Ilford and Ingatestone, which were all temporary flying fields. South Ash was only a home defence landing ground in the First World War. Waltham St Lawrence (OS reference *175/SU823768*), situated north-east of Reading off the B3024 road, was a Relief Landing Ground for the Tiger Moths of No 13 Elementary Flying Training School at White Waltham during 1940. Elstree, Hertfordshire (OS reference *176/TQ160966*), situated west of Borehamwood between the A41 and A5 roads, opened in 1937 and is today a very busy airfield for light aircraft, but it never had a military presence. During the war the concrete runway was put down, together with the present hangars and the aerodrome was used for modifying Wellington bombers.

During the First World War there was a balloon acceptance station on Kingston Hill in Richmond Park. Temple Sutton, Essex, was used in the 1930s by Sir Alan Cobham for an air display. Today it is completely built over.

Together with a site at Dover, Canewdon, Essex, was the first of the chain of radar stations used by fighter control in the early days of the Second World War.

For the first few months of the First World War the Royal Flying Corps only had enough aircraft to equip its four Expeditionary Force squadrons in France. The Admiralty accepted the responsibility for the homeland on September 3 1914. The Admiralty was also to assume responsibility for the defence of London but for a short time it agreed to accept the assistance of a few RFC aircraft which were stationed at temporary landing grounds at Joyce Green and Hounslow.

On March 25 1916 a new wing, No 18, was placed under the command of Lieutenant-Colonel F.V. Holt. It took over control of all the Royal Flying Club stations around London, and all the RFC detachments. New squadrons were formed specifically intended for home defence alone. The first such squadron to be formed was No 39 on April 15 1916 with headquarters at Hounslow and detachments of two BE2s each at Sutton Farm and Hainault Farm. At the end of July 1916 a special Home Defence Wing was formed.

Night flying increased and in 1916 'Money' flares were introduced. These were buckets filled with paraffin with a spout something like a watering can. A wire cage filled with asbestos was placed in the can and a wick pulled through the spout. When in operation the 'Money' flare burned for 1¾ hours per gallon of paraffin, and was visible for about 8 miles.

Squadron offices and living quarters were tents initially, and temporary huts later on. Stores of small bombs, ammunition and canned petrol were kept in amounts relating to the number of aircraft to be serviced. Landing grounds were divided into three categories, 1, 2 and 3, determined by the number of flares and the facilities.

On July 2 1917, the Cabinet gave approval to a War Office recommendation that the Royal Flying Corps increase its service squadrons from 108 to 200. This meant new methods were needed for aircraft production, which was already stretched to the limit. To overcome this, new measures were announced in October of that year. The sum of £1,500,000 was to be spent on building three national aircraft factories. Sites chosen were Aintree (Liverpool), Waddon

(Croydon) and Richmond (London). The latter was never built; instead, a partly built factory at Heaton Chapel (Manchester) was taken over. This became a vast industry, employing 350,000 people and produced the incredible number of 30,000 aircraft in a year.

During the Second World War there was a mushrooming growth of fighter stations in this area and it was mainly in the skies above the Kent countryside that the Battle of Britain was fought. This was fighter country. Once the Battle of Britain had been fought and won, it was not the beginning of the end of the war, but the end of the beginning.

The US 3rd Air Division Headquarters was at South Ruislip. Also, the US 8th Air Force had certain headquarters units in the London area, Sunninghill, Ascot being one. This became USAF Station No 472 for about a year until it was transferred to the 9th Air Force in the autumn of 1943. The units attached to Sunninghill were: 8th AF Air Support Command; No 10 Bomb Disposal Squadron; No 1093 Quartermaster Company Service Group; No 26 Service Group, Detachment A; No 928 Signal Battalion, Detachment A; No 320 Signal Company; No 40 Mobile Communications Squadron, Detachment A; No 204 Station Gas Defence Detachment. When it was necessary to fly in any top brass the Americans used Ascot racecourse with Piper Cubs, etc.

London had many famous airfields which became household names, Biggin Hill, Kenley and Hornchurch being but three. They breathed life and freedom and there were many unsolved mysteries regarding accidents during both the First and Second World Wars. During the 1914-1918 war sabotage was rife and a most effective way of preventing an engine from firing was to place a piece of paper between the points. It took many hours to locate the reason for the engine not firing and this was maybe sufficient to keep the aircraft grounded during a raid. Sabotage, faulty maintenance, call it what you will, but it does make one wonder.

On May 24 1979, Earl Louis Mountbatten formally opened Leisure Sports' Thorpe Park. Set in 400 acres midway between Chertsey and Staines the site lies on exhausted gravel pits. A lot of work has been put into the First World War airfield scene and the German and RFC hangars have a very realistic atmosphere.

From their wartime days Heathrow and Gatwick went on to become the two main civil airports to serve London. Flying has come a long way since those early days. In terms of height and length, the Wright brothers' first flight—12 seconds in 1903—could have taken place *inside* the fuselage of a Boeing 747 Jumbo Jet.

With the rapid deterioration, and, in many cases, the complete destruction of these airfields, which are part of our heritage, would it not be possible for some of the money spent on the Royal Air Force Museum at Hendon to be used by a representative of that organisation to tour disused airfields with a view to acquiring any remaining important pieces of historical interest? For example, at the time of writing, the old barn at Tempsford, a typical wartime water tower which was a most familiar landmark, and wartime paintings spring to mind. The list is endless. Our wartime history was much more than just aeroplanes.

Sadly, no one has thought to preserve one of the airfields for future generations. Left to die, the bleak airfields have a haunting, empty feeling as the wind sighs across them. The skylark climbs into the summer sky. Any moment one expects the stillness to be ripped asunder with the roar of Merlins—but all is still. Alas, no more of these sounds are to be heard, they exist only in the mind of the beholder.

Bruce Barrymore Halpenny,
Malta,
September 1983

Acknowledgements

Many thanks to Air France; Alitalia for Heathrow photographs; Robert H. Ballard, Newent, Gloucestershire for his help with photographs of Gravesend, Hornchurch and North Weald and Bill Baguley, for his valued help with developing the many photographs, providing research material and doing photography work on the airfields, also for stepping in to help during my illness. He is a true friend who spent many hours with me sorting out the material and photographs. My sincere thanks also go to the Rt Hon Lord Balfour of Inchrye PC, MC Kensington, London for the two wartime poems and material; Dave Benfield for his help with research material; Ken Border for ready assistance with research material and present-day photographs; British Aerospace, Aircraft Group, Kingston-Brough Division, Kingston-upon-Thames; British Aerospace Dynamics Group, Hatfield Division, Hatfield for their help and excellent photographs; British Airports Authority, Heathrow Airport; M.V. Brown, Deputy PR Manager British Aerospace, Aircraft Group, Hatfield-Chester Division, Hatfield for a selection of excellent photographs; P.T. Capon for the airship photograph at Hanworth; the Central Library, Dartford, Kent; Charles Lloyd Carbert, Port Colborne, Ontario, Canada; Command Public Relations Officer, HQ Strike Command, RAF High Wycombe; Harry Coulby, a true friend who was always ready to help; *Cross & Cockade Journal*; Edward H. Curotte, ARW, (ex-6106 RCAF) Campbellton, New Brunswick, Canada for his most interesting weekly letters and endless supply of wartime data and photographs; Department of the Air Force, Arlington, Virginia for the US Air Force photographs; the late Hon Walter Dinsdale, MP (Brandon) House of Commons, Ottawa, Canada for his wartime memories and photographs; Mr W.C.J. Easterbrook, Airport Director, Luton International Airport; Editor—*The Legion*, Dominion Command, Royal Canadian Legion, Ottawa, Canada; John Elliott, Manager, Press and Public Relations Swissair for his help with information and photographs; Neville Franklin for his valued help with aircraft identification and for many of the photographs; Peter Green, Irby, Grimsby; Mr E. Hine, Imperial War Museum, for Northolt, Heston and Uxbridge photographs; KLM Royal Dutch Airlines; Squadron Leader D. Logan, RAF Biggin Hill, Kent; Lufthansa German Airlines; Major G.E. MacManus, Commanding Officer, Canadian Forces Photographic Unit, Ottawa, Canada and the Canadian Government Photo Centre for the excellent wartime photographs; R.J. Millichap, Regional PR Manager, British Caledonian Airways Ltd; Bill Miles, North Weald Restoration Flight; Robert E. Morrow QC, Montreal, Canada (ex-402 Squadron RCAF fighter pilot) for the excellent wartime photographs; National Defence Headquarters, Ottawa, Canada; Officer Commanding RAF Northolt for material; Keith Palmer for his help with material and Gatwick and Heathrow photographs; Officer Commanding Royal Air Force Stanmore Park, for information about RAF Bentley Priory and RAF Stanmore Park; Mr L.P. Patch, Airport Director, Southend Airport, for information and photograph; Arthur Pearcy Jr, AMRAeS, for some of the Bovingdon photographs; Air Commodore H.A. Probert, MBE, MA, RAF (Rt'd), Head of the Air Historical Branch (RAF), London; R.C. Shelley, for Eastchurch and Brooklands photographs; R. Simpson, Department of Aviation Records, The Royal Air Force Museum, Hendon, London; Singapore Airlines for photographs of Heathrow Airport; Doctor Charles Spalding for his understanding and making it possible for me to survive this cold English climate and complete this book: without his help it would not have been possible; The *Daily Telegraph* for the 18th Century Prophecy poem; Mr Peter Tory of the *Daily Mirror* for his help and the photograph of his Chipmunk at Denham; USAF, Department of Defense, Texas; Wing Commander R.A. Wiles BSc, MBIM, RAF, Royal Air Force Uxbridge, Middlesex; and Cyril Woodward for taking me to and from Heathrow Airport.

Once again my very dear thanks to my valued friend and assistant, Margaret Morris of Lincoln, for all her work and effort with typing and retyping. Thanks also to my wife Marion for the hours of proof reading and a big thank you to my son Baron who tried to help in his special way.

My very special thanks for all those who gave help during my illness and for those who loaned me material and photographs, with apologies to any that I have forgotten to mention.

I would be interested to receive any new facts, photographs or other material for incorporation in further publications.

Glossary

AA Anti-Aircraft.
AAP Aircraft Acceptance Park.
AC Army Co-operation.
A/Cdre Air Commodore.
AOC Air Officer Commanding.
AOC-in-C Air Officer Commanding-in-Chief.
ASR Air Sea Rescue.
ATA Air Transport Auxiliary.
AVM Air Vice-Marshal.
BAT Flight Beam/Blind Approach Training Flight.
BEA British European Airways.
Bf Bayerische Flugzeugwerke (Messerschmitt).
CAG Civil Air Guard.
CFI Chief Flying Instructor.
CGM Conspicuous Gallantry Medal.
Channel Stop Operations British air operations to prevent German shipping passing through the Straits of Dover by day.
Circus Operations by bombers or fighter bombers, escorted by fighters and designed primarily to bring enemy fighters into action.
C&M Care and maintenance.
CO Commanding Officer.
D-Day June 6 1944—Allied armies began landing in Normandy with support from both Tactical and Strategic Air Forces (Operation *Overlord*).
DFC Distinguished Flying Cross.
DFM Distinguished Flying Medal.
Do 217 Dornier 217.
DSO Distinguished Service Order.
Drem Lighting System of outer circle lights leading into flare-path installed at many wartime airfields.
EFTS Elementary Flying Training School.
E & RFTS Elementary & Reserve Flying Training School.

F, Ftr Fighter.
FIS Flying Instructors' School.
F/Lt Flight Lieutenant.
F/O Flying Officer.
FPP Ferry Pilots Pool.
FTS Flying Training School.
Fuller Counter-measures against the escape of the *Scharnhorst* and *Gneisenau* from Brest.
Fw Focke-Wulf Flugzeugbau.
GCA Ground Control Approach.
GS Gliding School.
HE High Explosive.
HP Handley Page.
HQ Headquarters.
Intruder operations Offensive night patrols over enemy territory intended to destroy enemy aircraft and disrupt flying.
LAC Leading Aircraftsman.
MAP Ministry of Aircraft Production.
Me Messerschmitt AG.
MT Motor Transport.
MU Maintenance Unit.
NAAFI Navy, Army and Air Force Institutes.
NCO Non-commissioned officer.
PDC Personnel Despatch Centre.
P/O Pilot Officer.
PoW Prisoner of War.
PR Photographic Reconnaissance.
PT Physical Training.
RAAF Royal Australian Air Force.
R AuxAF Royal Auxiliary Air Force.
RAFVR Royal Air Force Volunteer Reserve.
Ramrod An operation similar to *Circus* except that its principle objective was the destruction of a specific target in daylight.
RAT Flight Radio Aids Training Flight.
RCAF Royal Canadian Air Force.
Recce Reconnaissance.
RFC Royal Flying Corps.

Rhubarb Low-level strike operation mounted in cloudy conditions against enemy fringe targets in occupied countries by pairs of aircraft against road and rail traffic.

RLG Relief Landing Ground.

RN Royal Navy.

RNAS Royal Navy Air Service.

RNZAF Royal New Zealand Air Force.

RS Reserve Squadron.

R/T Radio Telephone.

SABENA Société Anonyme Belge d'Exploitation de la Navigation Aérienne.

SAC Senior Aircraftsman.

SBC Small Bomb Container.

S/Ldr Squadron Leader.

SNETA Syndicat National Pour l'Etude des Transports Aériens.

TAF Tactical Air Force.

TDS Training Depot Station.

TS Training Squadron.

USAAF United States Army Air Force.

VC Victoria Cross.

V/STOL Vertical/short take-off and landing.

W/Cdr Wing Commander.

Window Metallised strips dropped from aircraft to simulate aircraft echoes to disrupt enemy radar systems.

W/T Wireless Telegraphy/Wireless Telegraphist.

Airfield Camouflage

RAF static camouflage 1938-1944

The important requirement of concealment of military installations and dispositions in and behind a battle front was, of course, fully appreciated by the Royal Air Force prior to the expansion years of 1935-1939, but camouflage was viewed largely from the experience of the European War of 1914-18, concerned primarily with battle area reconnaissance and deception and mutual concealment from the eyes of opposing armies.

The development of aircraft and air warfare technique, however, made it clear that in a future war the long-range offensive power of the aeroplane would constitute a major factor in general strategy and that deception, and conceal-ment of military installations, industries and communications against heavy air attack at home would impose a revised conception of the camouflage problem.

The first exponent of defensive static camouflage at home under modern war conditions was the then Air Ministry Director of Works. In 1935 he emphasised to the Air Staff the absence of any policy for concealment and camouflage of RAF establishments and stations at home. No thought had been given to civil policy or action on concealment of industrial undertakings and communica-tions. It was, of course, natural that one or other of the fighting services should be the first to realise the potentialities of camouflage defence and that the civil ministries responsible for industry should await some initial lead and direction from the departments primarily concerned with war and its consequences. It was even more natural that the Air Ministry was expected to guide and advise on a defensive policy against the air offensive weapon they were preparing.

Although in 1935 the Director of Works realised the necessity for camouflage defence, and, in fact, carried out some elementary and preliminary experiments in the camouflaging of new RAF stations, it was not until 1937 that the Air Staff, stimulated by the Director of Works, gave some preliminary consideration to camouflage requirements and policy. In this year a sub-committee of the Committee of Imperial Defence was set up to consider the problem of camouflage of industrial undertakings.

The Munich crisis of 1938 accelerated the national awareness of camouflage requirements and it was in that year that the three service departments began to organise the camouflage of undertakings and factories engaged in production of their war requirements. In this year the Air Ministry also set up an establishment under their PAD organisation to consider the problem of the aircraft and allied industries. By this time the Director of Works had formed a camouflage section within his department to concentrate solely on RAF requirements.

By 1939 and 1940 all three Service departments had formed camouflage branches and were responsible for their own camouflage requirements—both their planning and execution. On the civil establishment side the Ministry of Home Security catered for all civil undertakings except those few of the Ministry of Supply which were handled by the War Office, ie, Royal Ordnance Factories and Experimental Establishments. Co-ordination, pooling of experience and experiments, and problems of supply were dealt with by an Inter-Service Camouflage Committee set up by the Ministry of Home Security in 1939.

From the beginning the Department was potentially well equipped to design, experiment with and execute camouflage. Among the members of its design staff were trained architects of particular artistic bent who had the necessary flair and capacity for colour and form appreciation. On the more practical side the whole engineering staff, with experienced trained civil engineers, was available for execution and control. Therefore, as far as the directorate was concerned, camouflage was merely one more architectural and engineering task to plan and execute.

Prior to 1939, when the department was ploughing a lonely furrow with little encouragement or interest from the RAF, the work was limited to self-inspired schemes and experiments, with a very small design staff, to test out important general conceptions, to get the broad principles established, and to achieve some basis on which the first and most important job of camouflage of operational stations could be tackled.

Early in 1939 a separate camouflage section of W(War) was formed. This branch W(War)b was responsible for the formulation and interpretation of policy, initiation of design, co-ordination and control of material, and for the issue of executive instructions to works areas. It was responsible for controlling the inspection of camouflage works by area camouflage officers. At this time it was also considered necessary to secure the services of an artist of repute who could act as general adviser to the Director of Works and who could carry out inspections of schemes and direct and advise on alterations and the adoption of new ideas. Mr Norman Wilkinson, OBE, PRI, a well-known artist, was appointed to this post and in order to facilitate co-operation with the RAF and general Services liaison he was granted the honorary rank of Air Commodore. Mr Wilkinson held this appointment until early 1942, when, after the formation in September 1941 of the camouflage section of Colonel Turner's Department, the responsibility for general direction and advice previously given to Mr Wilkinson was transferred to Colonel Turner's Department.

The Air Ministry Camouflage Section in May 1938 consisted of one officer working directly under the Director of Works. By September 1939, it had increased to 19 men including the head of the section. By the end of 1942 the whole organisation had an Air Ministry headquarters, decentralised areas and supervisory staff totalling some 330.

Camouflage policy

The problem as visualised in 1938 was to be able to treat, in a practical and economical manner, distinctive features of an RAF station—buildings, landing grounds, boundaries, etc—so that at effective heights and distances in varying weather, in daylight and darkness, the pilot of an enemy aircraft would be deceived or confused. It was assumed that the main purpose of airfield camouflage would be achieved if recognition of a target could be delayed—so preventing the attack, or at least causing it to be inaccurate. Basic definitions of critical distances and heights were made as follows—in fine weather 10,000 ft height at a distance of 6 miles, in cloudy weather 5,000 ft at 3½ miles and at 300 ft 2⅓ miles in fine weather. This general camouflage policy was developed in 1938 and remained the basis on which all camouflage was carried out during the ensuing war years until final discontinuation in 1944.

In the experimental work, both in design and practical application, the main objects or principle aimed at was to ensure that the target blended with, and was lost in, its surroundings when observed from the prescribed heights and distances. Militating factors against achieving this, and therefore the deception of the pilot, were: *1* Regularity. Nature is irregular—man introduces regularity. Permanent stations were designed to be regular in layout. Buildings were large, conspicuous and unlike other types to be found in normal civil areas. *2* Reflection of light. Reflection varies considerably, depending on the orientation and angle of observance. Natural objects such as trees and grass reflect little light. The natural object shows innumerable little shadows from leaves or grass stems, etc. Such surfaces or objects are said to have 'texture' or 'contained shadow' and appear dark when viewed from a distance. Surfaces of buildings, glass roofs and concrete areas have little texture, and in addition they are frequently covered with glossy paint or bitumen. *3* Conspicuous colour. Certain colours, eg, white, yellow and certain reds are most conspicuous and attract the eye at once. *4* Roads and railways, buildings and water, all attract attention because of their shadows, reflections and characteristics of regularity.

These then were the main factors to be contended with when devising systems or schemes of camouflage for RAF stations. How the problem was met, and with what success, is described in the following narrative.

Technique and execution

I do not propose to detail all the trials and schemes attempted in the process of arriving at some practical policy and basis for large-scale camouflage of RAF installations and stations. Many mistakes were made and many ideas and processes had necessarily to be tried out, which for reasons of inadequacy, ineffectiveness or cost were quickly abandoned. Other processes were abandoned due to their operational interference with the use of the station and others to material supply difficulties. The following account is given, as far as possible, in chronological sequence and can be regarded as a brief history of camouflage development and application from 1938-1944.

Development 1938-1939

Early experimental work in 1938-39 was conducted at Cranfield and other stations with two main objectives: firstly, to break up the regularity and conspicuousness of the buildings and to prevent reflection from roads and aprons and secondly to 'break up' the airfield into a pattern more closely resembling the surrounding countryside. The first objective was attempted by 'disruptive patterning', ie, by painting different coloured irregular patches on the roofs, by painting bold division lines on roofs of large buildings such as hangars, and by the continuation of these measures to the surrounding ground with paint or coloured dust. The prime objective was the breaking up of the roof outline and the division of large buildings into smaller sections more clearly akin to other objects or buildings in the district.

In addition, in 1939, 'scrimmed' netting was used as slanting draping on the sides of hangars in order to hide the conspicuous sheer vertical walls. Landing ground disruption—there were virtually no concrete or hard surface runways in 1939—was attempted by painting hedge lines over the open grass area in an effort to simulate the continuation of the surrounding natural hedge pattern. Field colouration was also attempted with the use of powders or ochres—black, yellow and brown—to imitate different tones of fields devoted to agriculture.

The reduction of reflected light from roofs was effected by various treatments with matt paints, paint and brick dust, varnish and sprayed dust and so on. Some suffered from the drawback of expense, some from a short life and others from mere ineffectiveness.

Roads and aprons were a special problem owing to wear and tear of traffic. Special forms of silicate paint, bitumen and ashes and coloured cements were tried with fair success. Principal defects at the time were the flaking of oil paints, blowing off of sand and grit by propeller blast and alkaline disintegration of cement paints. Bitumen paints and bitumen tended to 'bleed' through, resulting in black and shiny patches. The problem of adequate treatment of concrete and tarmac surfaces was of course enormously amplified subsequently, during the war, when runways, tracks and paved dispersal areas were introduced.

At this stage some special mention should be made of the problem of materials as it existed and was appreciated in 1938-39. The problem was to find materials which were available or could be made available in large quantities, which were cheap, and which were simple to use. Paint—the obvious material— was the object of intensive trial and research. The Paint Research Station at Teddington carried out a considerable amount of work for the Air Ministry in 1938 and 1939 and published a paper in April 1939 on camouflage paints.

Many types of paint were considered at this time, with a view to the fulfilment of the main characteristics required, which were colour maintenance, durability and price. It was decided that the types most adequately meeting requirements were. *1* Bituminous emulsions, which consisted of a bitumen base in suitable solvents emulsified with water and coloured either with dyestuffs or pigments. They were intended for application to surfaces such as tarmac, felted roofs etc. Their main disadvantage was that in the early stages the colouring power was limited and not very permanent. Black bitumen emulsion paint was used for 'hedge' painting and was most effective. *2* Silicate paints, which consisted essentially of solutions of potassium or sodium silicate with inorganic pigments added. These were used particularly for cement and concrete surfaces. *3* Oil bound distempers, which consisted of water-oil emulsion and barytes and lithophone as the basic pigment with colouring extenders to suit requirements. These distempers were used on buildings and roofs—they withstood weathering but not mechanical wear and tear.

In co-operation with the Royal Aircraft Establishment, Farnborough, specifications were drawn up for these paints. Specifications were based on performance requirements rather than on actual composition. At the same time the Paint Research Station standardised special tests to check durability, water resistance, colour, chalking and general reflective properties. Dusting powders, consisting usually of chalk or gypsum, pigment and adhesive finely ground together were intended for simulation of field patterns on airfields.

Another important material investigated at this time was a substance to arrest grass growth. The necessity for this became apparent as a result of the method of painting hedge lines on landing grounds. Prior to painting, the grass was cut short and the paint then applied by spray. It was realised that in the spring or early summer the hedge line soon faded due to rapid grass growth. It was considered that if retardation of growth could be achieved by the application of an arrestor in the form of a dilute weed killer a considerable economy in the painting of hedge lines would be achieved. Sodium chlorate was found to be effective and later a proprietary mixture of sodium chlorate and chloride—'Atlacite' by name—was used with success. A solution (1 lb/5 gall) was found to check but not destroy the grass. Subsequently, however, it was found that serious damage was being caused to turf and grass through uncontrolled use and the practice was discontinued early in 1940.

Experimental and development work was carried out with hemp netting garnished with coloured Jute Scrim. These nets were used in the camouflage of certain types of hangars ('C' and 'D' Types) by draping the nets over the sloping sides. They were intended also for covering small vulnerable targets such as

---

Organisation for camouflage control, design and execution

Colonel Turner's Department   W(War)b

Special concealment and decoy   Administration and control of all RAF camou-
      branch   flage. Initiation of design and contracts.
                                                       Control of materials. Executive directions to
                                                       works areas
                                                  Staff:
                                                  1 Superintending engineer
                                                  1 Technical officer (chemist)
                                                  1 Assistant surveyor
                                                  3 Camouflage officers
                                                  1 Architectural and engineering assistant

Works areas (Nos 1-20)   W8
Administration of work in accordance with   Design and model experimental
    instructions received from W(War)b on   work
    all sites within the works areas   Staff:
Average staff in each works area: 1 Architectural and engineering
1 Camouflage officer   assistant Grade 1
1 Assistant camouflage officer   15 Camouflage officers and
2 Draughtsmen   designers
1 Clerk

Supervision of all work on site in each of the
works areas
Average staff in each works area:
1 Camouflage inspector
6 Foremen of trades

bomb stores and defence posts. Wire nets were also considered to replace hemp, but they were ruled out on several counts at this stage—principally high cost. Actually, shortly after the outbreak of war, in 1940, this high cost had to be accepted because of a threatened shortage of jute and hemp. Wire nets, basically chicken netting garnished with steel wool, were found to be effective as a simulation of textured ground.

In this period, special consideration was also given to the types and use of plant for rapid application of camouflage materials. This was principally required for spraying hedge lines and concrete areas and for treating large surfaces such as roofs and walls of buildings.

After considerable testing two petrol-engine-driven pressure sprayers—one manufactured by Messrs Henry Miller & Co Ltd and the other by Messrs Air Industrial Development Ltd—were adopted as satisfactory types. A drill was worked out in detail and selected stations were camouflaged in order to gain practice. The teams required to man the plant and ancillary lorries consisted of 10 to 15 men and a foreman. An average rate of application of 16 sq yds per gallon of paint was aimed at, but in practice the coverage obtained was more usually 10 to 12 yds per gallon. The output approximated to 5,000 sq yds per hour. The position therefore at the outbreak of war was that considerable planning had been completed, an organisation was in being, and immediate action could be taken to carry out camouflage measures in conformity with accepted policy.

Execution and further development 1939-1944

On the outbreak of war, camouflage schemes were put into operation as planned. Contracts were let for materials' supply and application, and direct labour forces engaged to maintain landing ground schemes to required standards. The rapid increase in the number of RAF stations and installations and the later complication of almost universal provision of runways and dispersal areas on operational stations (which necessitated a completely revised conception of the requirements for airfield camouflage) led to a vast increase in the scope of the problem and a considerable increase in the organisation to meet it.

Availability of materials quickly determined camouflage processes. Where originally it had been customary to think in terms of thousands of gallons of paint it now became necessary to plan in terms of millions of gallons. The problem of both the supply and application of the materials soon reached such dimensions that some form of centralised control became necessary in order to secure allocation of available supplies, plant and labour between competing works areas. Term contracts were placed by the Air Ministry for the supply of the various kinds of materials required and for their application. Firms were allotted one or more works area each and work in accordance with standard requirements was ordered direct by the superintending engineer who was responsible for the effective camouflage of his station.

The control of design and execution was administered through a section of Air Ministry branch W(War). This section co-ordinated and interpreted policy, design (by W8) and instructions on execution through the decentralised works area organisation. The accompanying table illustrates the complete camouflage organisation as it existed during the peak period of 1942. It shows the chain of administration and executive control and includes the link with

Oblique aerial view of Northolt, July 1 1941. Note that some kind of camouflage can be discerned on the hangars and on the runways, over which was painted a winding stream with a pond. This was so effective that it was reported that two swans crash-landed on the 'water' one early morning. Even Northolt-based pilots failed to locate the airfield at times.

Colonel Turner's Department on direction of policy. An account of the responsibilities and duties of Colonel Turner's Department and the camouflage officers of his organisation is contained in the War Book of that department— Chapter V, *RAF Camouflage Policy and Organisation.*

Previous to September 1941, the Air Staff had not directed the policy of camouflage. In that month Colonel Turner's Department was made responsible for obtaining direction from the Air Staff and for laying down the detailed policy to be followed. Service criticisms or requirements for camouflage which could not be resolved locally by the superintending engineer were referred to Colonel Turner's Department for discussion and decision making with W(War)b.

The preparation and design of schemes was carried out by a special section of W8 and issued to areas for execution. This W8 section was also responsible for training camouflage assistants prior to posting to works areas. The peak strength of the section in 1942 rose to 15 assistants with an architectural and engineering assistant, grade 1, in control.

While the main technique and policy of camouflage during the war remained virtually as envisaged in 1939 there was one fundamental development in the construction of air stations which created new problems and completely altered the relative importance of the various items constituting the station. On pre-war stations, buildings were probably more conspicuous than the airfield but on the large-scale introduction of runways, perimeter tracks and dispersal points the balance was immediately reversed. This was particularly so as the introduction of runways coincided with widespread dispersal of buildings and building sites.

Paint by itself was of little value in reducing the conspicuousness of large areas of hard surfacing. From a height of over 5,000 ft, in weather of average visibility, it was difficult to differentiate between two concrete runways, one of which was painted and one untreated. This is not to say that toning down or painting of glaring areas of new concrete or light excavation was unnecessary or unimportant but that as an effective or more permanent camouflage some form of texture was essential.

During the winter of 1939 the particular problem of 'shine' of concrete and tarmac surfaces was experimented with at Stradishall and Gosport. At the former station, paved areas were treated with fine pre-coloured slag chippings, and at Gosport with coarse pre-coloured stone chippings. At both these stations the specifications were suggested by specialist firms of contractors and were essentially based on non-shine hard tennis court practice. It was apparent from these experiments that the texturing of surfaces could be considerably improved by such forms of treatment and it was decided that all existing runways, particularly on fighter stations, should be treated in a similar manner.

At this time also the general camouflage treatment of aircraft storage units was considered an urgent problem. Apart from the concealment and texturing of large structures, sheds, etc, the question of numerous access roads and tracks on these stations presented a special difficulty. Some time before the war, a number of tracks and roads on these stations had been constructed with a grassed surface on a hardcore base. These proved ineffective, and it was at Hullavington that considerable trials on an open-textured bituminous surfacing were carried out in an attempt to produce a shine-free road surfacing. These experiments were very successful and brought about an improvement on the original Gosport and Stradishall systems. The construction was reasonably cheap, and could be produced by existing plant using normal technique. It was decided to adopt it for all ASU dispersal tracks and standings.

By the spring of 1940, it had been decided to use the 'Stradishall' system of texturing runways and paved areas, which was essentially the use of fine pre-coloured slag chippings on a bituminous adhesive. All Commands agreed to this policy except Fighter Command, which was unable to accept the abrasive nature of a 'chipped' surface owing to excessive tyre wear on fighter aircraft. For fighter stations, therefore, it was decided to use the 'Hullavington' specification, and work was put in hand to treat all fighter runways and hardstandings with a coat of what came to be known as 'pervious asphalt'. This pervious asphalt on fighter stations was successful in its objective, and for two years effectively produced an acceptable, if expensive, non-shine surfacing to fighter runways. It suffered from the disadvantage that to achieve the open texturing required it had, of necessity, to be somewhat pervious in its nature. Unfortunately, this was the very antithesis of what a final sealing coat on a runway should be.

In the meantime, work had been proceeding on bomber runways on modifications of the 'Stradishall' technique. The original specification involved a considerable amount of $\frac{3}{16}$ in pre-coloured slag, and, although the 'Stradishall' experiment had been all green, it was required that bomber runways should be patterned with several different kinds of precoloured chippings.

It soon became obvious that a number of stations requiring treatment could not be given the precise specification of 'Stradishall' and a modification to suit local availability of stone had to be accepted. The chips were laid uncoloured and painted *in situ*. Naturally, there were many individual cases which proved unsatisfactory, more often than not due to the wrong type or grade of adhesive, or, as the demand for chippings exceeded the supply, due to the difficulty in obtaining the correct grading. On some sites sharp laminated material was accepted, and this together with a percentage of over-size hard stone particles caused excessive tyre damage. In spite of the generally satisfactory results on the majority of stations, the few isolated bad cases gradually condemned the system as a whole and a reaction developed against this form of texture for bomber runways.

Concurrently with the experiments on pervious asphalt and chipped surfaces for runways on fighter and bomber stations, a considerable amount of experimental work was carried out in an attempt to find some material which would produce a textured effect but which would be softer than stone chippings, yet be capable of firm adhesion. It was necessary for it to be in generous supply. Sawdust, shavings and grass had all been tried but had proved unsuccessful. Their greatest disadvantage was that they 'ironed out' under traffic, and, even when freshly laid, had not a great amount of texture effect. Other ideas were seaweeds, heather, soft types of slag and rounded pebbles, etc. None of these was very successful under traffic although most of them worked tolerably well on roofs.

One material which showed promise in its experimental stages is worthy of particular mention. It was found that there were large quantities of tan bark available in waste heaps at tanneries. This had the property that, when sprayed with an iron salt, a more or less intense black could be produced. Several experiments with this material were carried out at the Royal Aircraft Establishment and a full-scale trial was tried at Stanton Harcourt. There were some initial experimental difficulties, but eventually an excellent camouflage effect and soft cushion were obtained. Unfortunately, the material became soft and slushy after prolonged wet weather and lost its inherent strength. The surfaces of the runways so treated were eventually reduced to a mushy slime and caused the danger of aircraft skidding.

A further stage in this work was achieved when, after considerable experiment, it was found that a remarkably good texture effect could be produced by the use of granulated rubber scrap. After initial difficulties with the grade of chippings and the type of adhesive, a system and specification were produced which proved very successful. Granulated rubber became the standard texturing material for all fighter runways and extensive arrangements were made to have the necessary material produced by the trade on an adequate scale. About 7,000 tons of this shredded rubber scrap were produced and used successfully until the fall of Malaya, when the use of rubber for this purpose was banned and all unused stocks on airfields had to be returned for regeneration.

The search for a good surface-texturing material inevitably came back to wood as the one material that was strong, soft, and in adequate supply. The particular difficulty with this material was the practical one of producing the right sized, clean pieces in bulk. The question was referred to the Forest Products Research Laboratory by the Royal Aircraft Establishment and various samples of 'hammer mill' chips were produced. These 'hammer mills' were designed to pulverise various hard materials and were originally installed in woodworking shops for producing wood flour and pulverised fuel. By adjustments to the machine the right size and shape of piece was produced and after some experiments on a full scale at Pershore, it was decided to standardise this method for all runways.

Immediate steps were taken to speed up the supply and the Ministry of Supply undertook the organisation of production. Every 'hammer mill' in the country which was not on essential production for war purposes was set to work. The transport and bagging involved was considerable as the wood chips had so little density. Additionally it was very difficult to control the numerous small contractors to ensure the standard of product required. One manufacturer utilised 'blitzed' timber against specific instructions and ultimately produced in the bag a material which contained nails, screws, pieces of glass, brass hinges and even one rimlock.

On the whole, the wood chipping process was a considerable success. It lasted well where properly applied. It possessed very nearly the same optical properties as grass and in addition the method was cheap and fairly easily produced from scrap material. The process became the standard texture treatment for runways until the discontinuance of camouflage.

Although texture obtained by one of the methods described above was essential for maximum inconspicuousness it was soon realised that during construction, considerable 'give-aways' were unavoidable if light-coloured excavations and new untreated concrete were not at least temporarily toned down. It was therefore specified that concrete surfacing should be suitably sprayed or coated with black bituminous dressings to reduce conspicuousness to a minimum. The importance was constantly reiterated to supervising officers and contractors of this camouflage obligation and of the necessity to plan constructional operations with due regard to the minimum disturbance to ground and natural features at any one time. It was a strict instruction that new work should be toned down immediately on completion.

It became obvious by 1941 that the camouflage of landing grounds by the painting of hedge lines, and the 'break up' of field areas with coloured ochres, painting and treatments such as sulphuric acid spraying entailed not only considerable expense both in labour and materials, but, owing to the extremely short life of the treatments, involved repeated renewals which resulted in airfield work on camouflage being virtually continuous.

Increased operational use of the airfields made it necessary to achieve some more lasting method of aerodrome 'break up'. It was because of this that a longer-term scheme of agricultural treatment was introduced. Field effects were obtained by differential mowing of grass in adjacent areas, by seeding down areas of different grass mixtures, and by the chemical fertilising of selected field areas. Hedge lines were retained in some cases but the costly and slow process of hand spraying as originally developed was replaced by a rougher but considerably quicker and cheaper method using a drag net pulled behind a wheel tractor. The bitumen emulsion paint was gravity-sprayed from a simple tank immediately in front of the drag net. This machine, although simple and inexpensive in design, reduced the cost of hedge painting by over 75 per cent. It produced a yardage output of 50 sq yds per gallon of paint compared with the conventional spraying machine's coverage of 16 sq yds per gallon. It operated at a speed of 15 mph compared with the walking pace speed of the older method.

By 1942, building camouflage had become restricted or simplified to painting in greens, browns or blacks. In some cases texturing of roofs was effected by the application of either stone or wood chips on a binding medium.

By the middle of 1942, camouflage had reached its peak and the estimated expenditure for that year was £8,750,000. Paint requirement for the year was 22,000,000 gallons and some 8,000,000 sq yds of steel wool was in use. The output of wood chips for runway texturing rose to 55,000 tons for the year. Excluding the Air Ministry supervising staff of 330, some 1,000 men were continuously employed in camouflage execution.

Later in 1942 it was decided that the screening of bomb stores on stations should be abandoned since it was expensive and of doubtful utility. The screening of a station bomb store cost approximately £15,000 and it was rightly considered that expenditure of this amount on one feature—not by any means the most concentrated and conspicuous—was wholly unjustified.

One interesting link in the camouflage chain deserves particular mention. The design section in W8, besides carrying out the design of all schemes, had the sole responsibility for the initial exploration of new ideas, and the investigation of particular problems on special sites and their requirements as they arose. Expensive and full-scale trials of effects, layouts and colour schemes under various day and night conditions were impracticable, if only on account of the time factor. An experimental studio was therefore constructed and equipped with facilities for the investigation of camouflage problems, with models and colour drawings.

Additional assistance was obtained in 1942 by engaging women, some of whom were artists of repute, from the well-known art academies. Complicated and ingenious arrangements were designed and constructed to vary light conditions, simulate height and change the angle of viewing, etc. The special and important camouflage for AME stations was wholly developed in this experimental section. Models were used on an elaborate scale and proved invaluable in determining results before any site work commenced. A complete 1/2,500 model, with a vertical scale of 1/500 was constructed in considerable and precise detail. Based largely on an existing bomber station it included additional features of coastal AME stations, WT stations and dispersed bomb stores, etc.

In the spring of 1943 it was decided that the standard of camouflage could be relaxed in certain parts of the country, which was then divided, for camouflage purposes, into three priority regions.

In No 1 Priority Region, which comprised roughly the south and east coast of England up to the Humber for a depth of 70 miles, camouflage was continued to the standard required to be effective against observation from heights and distances substantially the same as laid down earlier. In No 2 Priority Region, comprising an approximately 30-mile east coast belt from the Humber to the north of Scotland, camouflage was restricted to night deception only. In the remainder of the country—No 3 Priority Region—the new requirements implied virtually the abandonment of camouflage in approximately 20 per cent of the total number of stations in the country.

Concurrently with this partial relaxation of camouflage, schemes and specifications were overhauled so that as much of the camouflage work as possible could be incorporated as a normal building or constructional item during initial construction or maintenance. Simplification of design, the natural camouflage

52316A

The Germans were also masters of the art of camouflage. This photograph shows the camouflaged aerodrome at Beaumont-le-Roger, France, under bombardment from Allied aircraft, June 29 1944. The aerodrome is in the bottom left-hand corner.

of aerodromes by agricultural methods and the merging of camouflage requirements into constructional processes which were in any case required, together with the reduction of camouflage on the priority regional plan, resulted in 1943 in the annual expenditure being reduced to approximately £1,500,000 compared with the previous year's figure of £8,750,000.

The second change in policy was introduced in April 1944. This effected a further reduction in camouflage standards in Priority 1 and Priority 2 areas. Only darkening down of buildings was permitted, either when newly constructed or when they became conspicuous due to the deterioration of old camouflage.

Selective seeding and mowing was permitted for field break-up but all hedge painting was stopped. Preservative painting and sealing of ground areas was accepted in dark colours.

In August 1944 camouflage was practically discontinued with the proviso that preservative painting would continue to be in dark tones or colours.

Conclusions

Like most other passive defence measures it is impossible quantitatively to assess the effectiveness of camouflage. Failure to bomb an objective may be due to one or more of many causes—weather, camouflage, active defence, bad navigation and so on. On the other hand a well-concealed station may be located and severely attacked due to causes for which camouflage has no remedy, eg, having lights on during operations at night.

There is little doubt, however, that where camouflage was carried out conscientiously a very severe handicap was placed on the attacking force. Of details available, for example, of over 800 attacks, or attempted attacks by day and night on RAF establishments during the war, it is established that in one concentrated part of the country where camouflage was efficiently carried out on some 30 airfields, only on one occasion was a successful attack carried out, and that one happened to be a lone intruder who was given permission to land at night!

In other parts of the country it has been proved that stations with conspicuous features such as new concrete, new excavation, etc, were attacked repeatedly to the exclusion of adjacent well-concealed stations. Decoy stations, deliberately conspicuous in an inconspicuous manner, have reminded us over and over again what the consequences of inadequate camouflage would have been. In any event it only requires the testimony of Bomber Command on the difficulties of attacking well-concealed enemy targets, to admit the necessity for the considerable and successful efforts made in camouflage of RAF establishments during the years 1939-44.

Undoubtedly in the past camouflage has suffered much from ignorance and prejudice—the latter arising chiefly from the former. There is nothing magic in camouflage, it is a thoroughly commonsense item of construction which is very much a normal architectural and engineering problem, capable of solution by the engineer in step with all other building processes. It has its place in the constructional sequence. Properly conceived and restricted it can be an inexpensive but valuable defence.

The Battle of Britain story

The Battle of Britain was one of the most crucial conflicts of the Second World War. It was fought in the skies over England and it lasted from July to October 1940. It was narrowly won by the Royal Air Force and others, and it saved the country from invasion.

The then Fighter Command lost 915 aircraft but inflicted fighter and bomber aircraft losses totalling 1,733 on the German Luftwaffe. Hitler had to cancel his planned invasion of England, when, in the Nazis' first major defeat, 2,790 German aeroplanes failed to smash Britain into submission during massive bombing attacks during the long summer of 1940.

On the face of it, the Luftwaffe should have won the battle. It possessed superiority in numbers and bases. It was the immortal 'Few' who stopped it. Those same languid young scholars and gentlemen who had resolved five years earlier in the Oxford Union, not to fight for King and Country, fought and flew with understated fury. By September, one in three of them was dead. It has become customary, since then, to wonder at the miracle that turned the Oxford pacifists of 1935 into the fighting few of 1940. Winston Churchill, wartime British Prime Minister, immortalised the allied pilots with his rich phrases in the House of Commons while the battle still raged: 'Never in the field of human conflict was so much owed by so many to so few.'

The German intention had been to destroy the RAF, as the air forces of Poland, France and the Low Countries had been destroyed in blitzkriegs across Europe from September 1939 to May 1940. If the RAF had been defeated, the Luftwaffe's bombing force would have been used to support a cross-Channel invasion of Southern England. All the efforts of the Army and Navy could hardly have averted defeat in the face of complete German air superiority. The German Army would then have made sure that England was put out of action as a base for operations against Germany.

The consequences of this, in terms of the Allied war effort, would have been incalculable. The British Government would have had to move, probably to Canada, there could have been no UK-based strategic air offensive against Germany and there would have been no base for the eventual Allied re-entry into Europe on D-Day, June 6 1944. The Americans would probably never have entered the European War. The undivided weight of the German war effort would then have fallen on Russia, with the United States completely isolated. It was a crucial time. The RAF was the only barrier between a triumphant Hitler and an invasion of the British Isles. As the defiant remaining beacon of

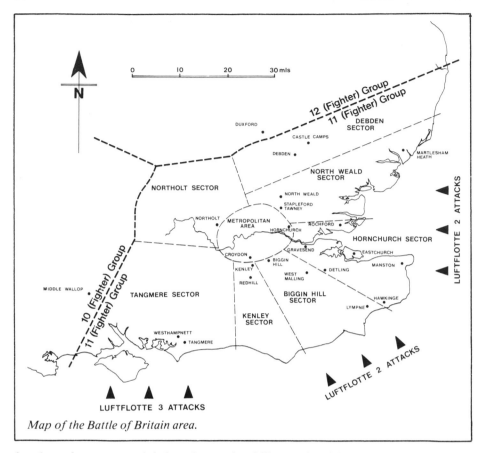

Map of the Battle of Britain area.

freedom, it was essential that the torch of liberty should not be snuffed out by the Nazi war machine.

When the Battle for Britain began, the Germans were undefeated, at the height of their military power in Europe. Their air forces in Northern France and the Low Countries (Luftflotten 2 and 3) had 2,600 aircraft—1,200 long-range bombers, 760 twin-engined fighters, 280 dive-bombers, 220 single-engined fighters and 140 reconnaissance aircraft. Against these RAF Fighter Command had 603 Hurricanes and Spitfires.

The battle was in five phases. The first phase was from July 10 to August 7 and began with probing attacks to test UK air defences with attacks on shipping in the Channel. The second phase, August 8 to 23, was more serious, with attacks on the radar chain. The bombing was intensified and fierce air fighting developed with heavy losses on both sides. Between August 8 and August 18, Fighter Command lost 94 pilots and 60 were wounded. Dowding was holding his forces in check and by husbanding his resources he was able to show a steady build-up in personnel and aircraft strength. On August 3 he had 708 fighters operational and 1,434 pilots.

The third phase, August 24 to September 6, was the most critical. During this period the Luftwaffe assaulted airfields in south-east England. On August 20, Goering had issued a new directive: to continue the fight against the enemy air force until further notice, with the aim of weakening the British fighter forces. The enemy was to be forced to use his fighters by means of ceaseless attacks. This phase was apparently to clear the air over Kent and Sussex preparatory to establishing an invasion bridgehead on the coast between Dover and the Isle of Wight. During this desperate period Fighter Command had 103 pilots killed or missing and 128 seriously wounded, 295 fighters were totally destroyed and 171 badly damaged.

Fresh squadrons moved in to replace battle tired units and very often lost more aircraft and pilots than the ones they replaced. For instance, No 253 Squadron at Kenley lost 13 Hurricanes and nine pilots in the seven days it was in battle, from August 30, before it was moved out of the front line and posted to Yorkshire. Also at Kenley was No 616 Squadron which lost 12 aircraft and five pilots between August 25 and September 2 and had to be retired to Coltishall in No 12 Group. Experienced pilots were like gold dust and each one lost was replaced by an untried man who would be an easy target for some time until he acquired battle know-how.

The fourth phase, September 7 to 30, saw the fatal error of the Nazis. On August 25 a number of bombs had accidentally fallen on Central London, due to bad navigation. This triggered a retaliatory RAF bombing mission over Berlin. Little damage was actually caused, but the effect on both Hitler and Goering was decisive. Luftflotten 2 and 3 were told to prepare for a daylight reprisal raid on London. Great, huge, sprawling, lusty, courageous London now became the target for the Luftwaffe's onslaught and the recipe for Nazi defeat. Now the RAF knew exactly where the enemy was heading. Now the men, the machines and the fuel could be more carefully husbanded and directed than ever before. By September 27 the worst was over, September 15 being recognised as the day of climax when the Germans threw everything they had against the capital. This day is now celebrated annually as Battle of Britain Day.

The Luftwaffe's attempt to eliminate the RAF, which had been planned to take four weeks, failed, and the scheduled fifth phase, October 1 to 31, the daylight offensive which was to have been a prelude to invasion, was called off. By November the Battle of Britain was over. It petered out as the Luftwaffe withdrew from the daylight assault during which Goering had resorted to the use of fighter-bombers operating at high altitude to avoid further bomber losses. But for all the German effort there was little to set against the loss of 1,653 aircraft. The Nazi war machine was no longer invincible. Conquered peoples now had room for hope. Operation *Sea Lion*, the intended invasion, was postponed, never to be remounted. The Battle of Britain was a triumph for British technology and the invention of radar. It was the 'magic eye' which gave British Hurricanes and Spitfires early warning of enemy attack.

The AOC-in-C Fighter Command, Air Chief Marshal Sir Hugh Dowding, had done an excellent job, yet just after the battle he was unceremoniously retired from the RAF and was not accorded the heroic status normally associated with victorious commanders. It was not until long after the war that Dowding received any official recognition for the decisive role he played in bringing about victory in the Battle of Britain. Churchill in his memoirs did not give Dowding due credit.

Dowding was not a yes-man and was apt to be misunderstood by many of his colleagues. He had no time for petty politics and got little support from Churchill, perhaps because he had been courageous enough to stand up to

Above *Some of the pilots who took part in the Battle of Britain. Left to right: Pilot Officer Crowley-Milling, Flying Officer Tamblyn, Flight Lieutenant Turner, Sergeant Saville, Pilot Officer Campbell, Pilot Officer McKnight, Squadron Leader Bader, Flight Lieutenant Ball, Pilot Officer Homer and Flying Officer Brown; Hurricane in background.*

Below *Typical dispersal scene, late summer, 1940. The wartime censor has almost obliterated the code letters.*

No 1 (RCAF) Squadron, 1940: Squadron Leader E.A. McNab and some of his pilots. Left to right: Flying Officer W.P. Sprenger, Flying Officer O.J. Peterson, Flight Lieutenant W.R. Polloch (adjutant), Flying Officer P.B. Pitcher, Squadron Leader McNab, Flying Officer P.W. Lochnan, Flight Lieutenant E.M. Reyno, Flying Officer Beardmore, Flying Officer S.T. Blaihloch (Intelligence Officer) and Flying Officer R.W. Norris.

him. Dowding foresaw that the fighters would soon be needed to protect British soil and he requested permission to present his case to the Cabinet. He was given a chance to speak, but not to the Cabinet. He made his plea to Churchill, Sir Archibald Sinclair (Air Minister), Beaverbrook (Minister for Aircraft Production) and Sir Cyril Newall (Chief of Staff).

Dowding explained that his 52 squadrons for home defence had been depleted to 36 and at the rate that Hurricanes were being shot down in France there would be none left after a fortnight. His pleas fell on deaf ears, so, on his return to his HQ, he sent a letter to the Under Secretary of State for Air to put on record the warning he had given to Churchill and the others, which also meant that if the Battle of Britain should end in defeat the politicians could not point the finger at Dowding.

Dowding's strategy and tactics during the battle were formulated to cause maximum disruption and confusion among the enemy formations for minimum possible RAF losses. Thus he put up small numbers of fighters to meet the raids and at the same time conserved his limited numbers of aircraft.

Dowding's theories were shared by Air Vice-Marshal Sir Keith Park, AOC No 11 Group. Like Dowding he knew the 'Big Wing' concept would only bring disaster. There was insufficient time to assemble large formations to strike a

Canadian fighter pilot.

decisive blow against the enemy. The main critics of Dowding and Park were Archibald Sinclair and Leigh-Mallory, supported by Sholto Douglas. They decided that much greater losses could have been inflicted on the Luftwaffe if the 'Big Wing' theories had been adopted in No 11 Group.

The results of the battle proved Dowding and Park to be correct. But the matter did not rest there for their unforgiving critics. However, one of the best-kept secrets was the fact that the Allied commanders were provided with detailed advance knowledge of the enemy's plans through the fact that Britain had broken the German signals code. This was with the help of the complex Enigma machine which was smuggled into British possession from the German factory in Poland where the machines were being manufactured. The operation was code named 'Ultra' and a few copies of the Ultra messages have now been released for public information, along with many other wartime secrets declassified after the passage of time. So tight was the security surrounding Ultra that only the most senior commanders were in on Ultra in a strict 'need to know' basis. Dowding was a recipient of Ultra information and because of No 11 Group's geographical position and importance Air Vice-Marshal Sir Keith Park, its AOC, was on the circulation list. Air Vice-Marshal Sir Trafford Leigh-Mallory, AOC No 12 Group, was not.

Dowding immediately recognised the value of Ultra and it is certain that Dowding and through him his No 11 Group AOC Air Vice-Marshal Keith Park, operated their aircraft in the most suitable way in the light of the knowledge that they had in advance as to what the Luftwaffe was planning to do. It must have been a big problem for Dowding, not to give away to his own stations that he had advance warning of impending attacks.

On October 17 1940, with the battle virtually over, Dowding's 'Big Wing' critics came in for the kill. A meeting was called and Dowding and Park had to face a line-up of senior officers and listen to their tactics being pulled to pieces. The attack was led by Air Vice-Marshal Sholto Douglas, then Deputy Chief of the Air Staff. Leigh-Mallory was present and seized his opportunity to voice bitter criticism. To support him, Leigh-Mallory saw fit to bring along one of his much more junior officers. This was Squadron Leader Douglas Bader. It was a most unprecedented incident that such a junior officer should be in on such a meeting with so many senior personnel. Bader, and quite rightly so, was not in on the Ultra secret. It was shameful that both Dowding and Park should be subjected to such shabby treatment, particularly after they had just helped to win the Battle of Britain. The two had committed the crime of being right At the meeting Dowding refused to divulge in his defence his knowledge of Ultra. This would have shot down in flames his more junior critics but to his great credit he did not mention it.

The meeting had already made up its mind about the outcome. Dowding was given 24 hours' notice to quit his office and Sholto Douglas became Air Officer Commanding Fighter Command in his place. Park was posted to Flying Training Command, Leigh-Mallory took over No 11 Group.

In retrospect the theories and tactics of Dowding and Park were correct. The 'Big Wing' concept was shown to be of no value whatsoever in the defensive stance. In most cases the wings would have become unmanageable. If such tactics had been pursued in 1940 as Leigh-Mallory and Bader had wanted the whole sector airfield and control system would probably have been reduced to a shambles by the Luftwaffe. Thank goodness we had such men as Air Chief Marshal Sir Hugh Dowding and Air Vice-Marshal Sir Keith Park.

Airfields
1   Acton
2   All Hallows
3   Ashingdon
4   Barking Creek
5   Biggin Hill
6   Booker
7   Bovingdon
8   Brooklands
9   Broxbourne
10 Burnham on Crouch
11 Chigwell
12 Chingford
13 Cricklewood
14 Croydon
15 Dagenham
16 Denham
17 Detling
18 Eastchurch
19 Fairlop
20 Fairoaks
21 Fambridge
22 Farningham
23 Feltham
24 Fyfield
25 Gatwick
26 Gravesend
27 Hainault Farm
28 Hatfield
29 Heathrow
30 Hendon
31 Henley on Thames
32 Heston
33 Hornchurch
34 Horne
35 Hounslow
36 Hunsdon
37 Joyce Green
38 Kenley

39 Kings Hill
40 Langley
41 Leavesden
42 Leysdown
43 London Colney
44 Luton
45 Maylands
46 North Weald
47 Northolt
48 Orsett
49 Panshanger
50 Park Royal
51 Penshurst
52 Radlett
53 Redhill
54 Rochester
55 Rochford
56 Smiths Lawn
57 Southend
58 Staglane
59 Stapleford Tawney
60 Stow Maries
61 Suttons Farm
62 West Malling
63 White Waltham
64 Wimbledon
65 Winkfield
66 Wisley
67 Woodley
68 West Pole Farm

Others
69 Bentley Priory
70 Bushey Hall
71 Bushy Park
72 High Wycombe
73 Kingston
74 Stevenage
75 Uxbridge

LUTON

ST ALBA

7

SLOUGH

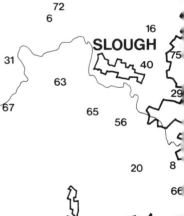

72
6
16
31
40
63
75
67
65
29
56
20
8
66

ALDERSHOT

GU

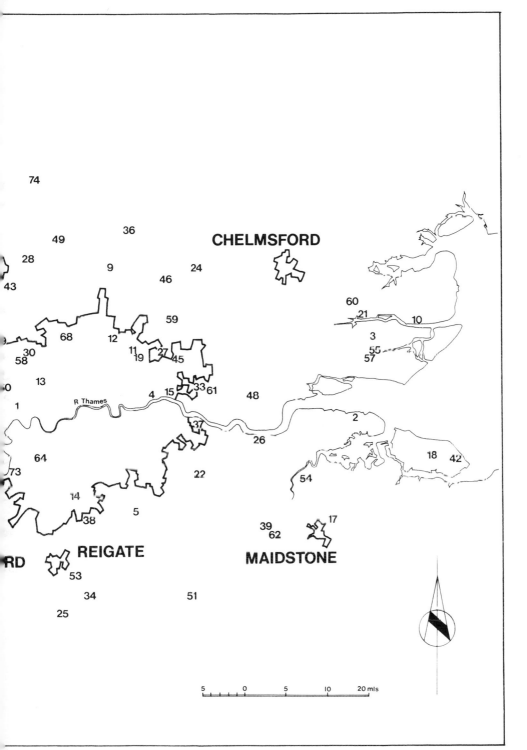

74

49   36

28   CHELMSFORD

43   9   24

46

60
21
59   10
68   12   3
11 27   55
19   45   57
30
58
13   48
R Thames
1   4 15 33 61   2
37
26   18 42
64
73   54
22
14
5   39   17
62
REIGATE   MAIDSTONE
RD   53

34   51

25

5   0   5   10   20 mls

The airfields

Acton, London

176/TQ195820. West of London between the A406 and A4000 on the south side of the A40

Acton Aerodrome opened during the latter part of 1910. The site was shaped like a triangle with Mason's Green Lane as the western boundary, the main railway line to the north and the Central Line of London Transport the third boundary. It was just south of Park Royal and access was very difficult.

The small triangle of land at Acton became known as the London Aviation Ground and was used by a variety of machines up until the outbreak of the First World War in 1914. The site was then taken over by the National Guard. During the latter part of 1915 and early 1916 a few aircraft were constructed at Acton.

In 1917 the Ruffy-Baumann Flying School took up residence. The school operated with about a dozen Caudron G2 tractor biplanes under unsatisfactory conditions. The Caudron was unique inasmuch as it had no throttle, no ailerons, no elevators, and no fuselage. The pupils who came to the school were Service personnel who were billeted in tents by the railway cutting and used a marquee as their mess. It was a very unsatisfactory arrangement. However, Service training continued until July 1918. Then, the Air Council gave notice that all operations must cease for the flying instruction was inadequate, the aircraft were obsolete and the instructors not up to standard. The temporary hangars were soon taken down. The other buildings were taken over by the newly formed Alliance Aeroplane Company. Pressures for more aircraft production caused Waring and Gillow, the furnishers and furniture

makers to form the new company and go into aircraft production. A large factory hangar was erected in the north-east corner of the site. This was ready by mid 1919 but the factory produced only a few de Havilland DH 9s, for the war was now over and there were widespread cancellations of war contracts.

To try to survive the post-war slump the Alliance Company decided to produce civil aircraft. They engaged the services of an experienced designer, J.A. Peters, who had worked for Robey of Lincoln. (There is a photograph of his aircraft on page 53 of *Action Stations 2*.)

Peters was set to design a long-distance aeroplane and the first machine, *K160/G-EAGL* was ready during the summer of 1919. This two-seater machine was powered by a 450 hp Napier 'Lion' engine.

On July 31 1919, *G-EAGL* set off from Acton Aerodrome to fly non-stop to Madrid. The aeroplane was piloted by Peters with Captain W.R. Curtis as navigator. The flight was successfully completed in 7½ hours. Encouraged by this flight, Peters prepared a second aircraft, *G-EAOX*, to fly to Australia. By November the aircraft was ready and he flew to Hounslow, his point of departure. On November 13 the aircraft took off for Australia but shortly afterwards crashed at Surbiton, killing its crew.

This brought to an end the Alliance Aeroplane Company and it closed in the early part of 1920. The factory remained the property of Waring and Gillow but the arifield was soon built over, with Western Avenue being constructed across the northern end between the main railway line and the Alliance hangar.

No further flying took place and between the wars the large hangar was used by various companies. In 1937 it was occupied by No 1 (MT) Storage Sub-Unit, Royal Air Force.

With the coming of the Second World War the hangar was pressed into service. It was requisitioned by the Ministry of Aircraft Production on September 30 1940 and taken over by the de Havilland Aircraft Company. A few Avro Anson fuselages were made here but its main use was the manufacture of wings and aileron flaps for the de Havilland Mosquito. On completion these were sent to the de Havilland factory at Leavesden. This remained the main role of the factory throughout the war years.

After the war the MAP relinquished the factory and Waring and Gillow sold it to W.H. Smith Ltd, on June 8 1945. They remained the owners until 1973 when they sold the factory to Techno Ltd. It was then used by various companies.

All Hallows, Kent

178/TQ832775. North-east of Chatham

Located on the Isle of Grain, All Hallows was a small site of only 32 acres, dimensions 530 yds × 150 yds in open and flat surroundings. It was listed as a 3rd class landing ground and was only used during the First World War by nearby Eastchurch and No 143 Squadron. The site was located 1½ miles from Stoke Holt railway station and the sea was ¾ of a mile to the north. It was all tented accommodation and the site saw very little use.

Ashingdon, Essex

178/TQ870930. A few miles north of Southend-on-Sea

At the end of 1931 the Southend Flying Club was established at Ashingdon by a keen group of enthusiasts with an Avro 504K. After only a few months the club disposed of the Avro and moved to a new site on the Ashingdon road. This was nothing more than the old Rochford pony track but from here they re-equipped with a Blackburn Bluebird III, two Moths and a new Avro 638 Club Cadet.

The flying club was now managed by Southend Flying Services Ltd and they also found that money could be made on the short air routes. During the summers of 1933 and 1934 they ran an hourly service to Rochester in pool with Short Bros.

In the early 1930s Southend Corporation decided to construct a municipal airport and bought the site of the former Rochford aerodrome just south of Rochford on the west side of the B1013 road. After

the new airport opened in September 1935 the club aircraft moved in and Ashingdon closed.

Barking Creek, Essex

177/TQ450830.

Barking was the home of the Handley Page works which was constructed in 1909 and had the first buildings in Britain to be erected exclusively for aircraft manufacture.

The first machine manufactured was a glider fitted with a pair of monoplane wings and this was tested from a small mound on Barking marshes. The first powered machine was completed by the autumn of 1909. This was known as the HP 1 and was a single-seat tractor monoplane, nicknamed 'Blue Bird' by virtue of the colour of its fabric. When the machine was tested on May 26 1910 it only managed a few short hops and was declared a failure.

Other machines followed, but at the beginning of 1910 a gale destroyed part of the works and damaged two machines. One was the HP 2B which had just completed a series of unsuccessful trials at Barking. However, it was rebuilt and taken to Freshfield Aerodrome, Liverpool, where it flew successfully.

Other machines built at Barking were the Baden-Powell 'Scout', the Mackensie-Hughes 'Triplane' and the Handley Page DHP 4 which crashed at Fairlop. None of these was successful and the first real aircraft was the Handley Page EHP 5 which emerged during 1911. This was a two-seat tractor monoplane powered by a 50 hp Gnome engine. During a flight from Fairlop to Barking the HP 5 crashed. It was then repaired and in 1912 it became the first aircraft to fly over London. It flew from Fairlop to Brooklands and completed the 30-mile journey in 55 minutes.

By 1912 Handley Page had expanded and was looking for a more suitable site. One was found at Cricklewood and the firm moved there that same year. The Barking Creek site had no further aviation connection and has now passed into history.

Biggin Hill, Kent

177/TQ415605. North of Biggin Hill and Westerham. On the east side of the A233

Despite the very severe winter weather, Biggin Hill was ready for business by

February 1917. Situated on a plateau on top of the North Downs, the site was of some 80 acres, approximately 1½ miles north of the village of Aperfield, or Biggin Hill as it became known. Biggin Hill was destined to become a household name.

Biggin Hill was officially opened on February 14 1917 as an RFC Radio Signals Unit and was used for early wireless experiments. Later that year the station was established as part of the inner patrol zone of the London Air Defence Area. No 141 Squadron was posted in on February 8 1918 with Bristol Fighters, each of which sported a bright red cockerel painted on the fuselage.

The Bristol Fighter was a two-man aeroplane in which the pilot and observer gunner sat back-to-back. One who served with 141 Squadron was Lieutenant Hardit Singh Malik who became known as the 'Flying Sikh of Biggin Hill'. A turbaned black-bearded officer was unique in the annals of the Royal Flying Club. While with 141 Squadron he ferried aircraft to St Omer in France. In the summer of 1918 Malik was posted to No 11 Squadron at Bapaume in France. No 141 Squadron was to remain for the duration of the war and was to claim at least one Gotha bomber which was shot down on Harrietsham aerodrome in Kent.

On May 1 1918, No 140 Squadron formed at Biggin Hill with a few Bristol Fighters. However, its life was very short

and it disbanded at Biggin Hill on July 4 1918. No 141 moved out on March 1 1919 and it was replaced 16 days later by No 37 Squadron. This unit disbanded at Biggin Hill on July 1 1919 and that same day No 39 Squadron re-formed. This was only a cadre unit and moved to Kenley on January 18 1922. That same year the Instrument Design Establishment, which had moved in after the war, moved to Farnborough. During May 1923, No 56 Squadron and the Night Flying Flight were posted in. On October 12 1927, No 56 Squadron, now with Siskins, moved to North Weald and two years later the Night Flying Flight, equipped with Vimys, also departed, leaving Biggin Hill empty except for a skeleton staff.

An extensive building programme began in 1929. A new technical site was constructed on the northern perimeter. Hangars, workshops, barrack blocks and administration offices were built to complete the station. The only building that did not need erecting was the officers' mess. This was a large house on the Bromley-Westerham road, opposite the main camp, and had been acquired by the RFC in the early days. After three years the new buildings and hangars were ready for occupation. Nos 23 and 32 Squadrons moved in from Kenley equipped with Demons and Bulldogs respectively. A new unit, the Anti-Aircraft Co-operation Flight, was formed at Biggin Hill to give training to the growing number of AA sites in the London area.

On December 21 1936, No 23 Squadron

Early hangars at Biggin Hill.

Fairey Seal, K.3483, *at Biggin Hill, March 1939.*

moved out to Northolt with its Hawker Demons, leaving 32 Squadron, now with Gauntlets, in sole occupation until No 79 Squadron re-formed from 'B' Flight of No 32 Squadron on March 22 1937. This unit was also equipped with Gauntlets.

Throughout the changes the familiar pattern of air displays continued and each Empire Air Day the station was thrown open to the public .

Further expansion took place in 1938 and 16 married quarters were among the new additions. At the time of the Munich crisis, No 601 (County of London) Auxiliary Squadron with Gauntlets joined Nos 32 and 79 Squadrons but fortunately the immediate crisis passed and the regular squadrons were able to re-equip with Hurricanes before the Second World War began.

After the Munich crisis the buildings were camouflaged and a number of trees planted to help disguise the aerodrome. Air-raid shelters were also dug around the airfield.

In the autumn of 1939 the main tarmac runway was constructed, measuring 4800 ft × 150 ft. Later two other runways were added, each 2370 ft × 150 ft.

On September 1 1939 the married quarters were evacuated, accommodation having been prearranged by the RAF six months earlier. The following day No 3 Squadron, which had been at the station since early May, moved to its war station at Croydon. It was replaced the same day by the Hurricanes of No 601 Squadron. On the outbreak of war the station HQ was under the command of Wing Commander R. Grice.

During the 'phoney' war, No 79 Squadron became the first to claim an enemy aircraft when it shot down a Dornier Do 17 on November 2 1939. The squadrons were kept busy with patrols and sorties to protect the Channel convoys. The days of Dunkirk kept the squadrons at full stretch, with constant patrols over the beaches by Nos 79, 213 and 242 flying Hurricanes. By the time the Battle of Britain was well under way the station was operating such Spitfire squadrons as Nos 72, 79 and 610.

Being one of the very early aerodromes, Biggin Hill had a decoy airfield at Lullingstone, a few miles to the north-east. This decoy site was equipped with dummy Hurricanes and was also equipped with dummy flarepath, 'Q'-site lighting. With the ending of the Battle of Britain and the subsequent night phase of attacks the need for decoys became less pressing and by 1942 all 'K'-sites except those at West

Wittering, Skipsea and Lullingstone (for Biggin Hill) had been taken out of service. It is difficult to understand why Lullingstone was retained, for between August 18 1940 and January 7 1941 Biggin Hill was attacked 12 times. The first attack took place at about 1.30 pm on August 18 and the raid lasted just over an hour, the main damage being the cratering of the landing ground. Fortunately most of the bombs fell on the adjacent golf course. Biggin Hill became a main target and clearing rubble became an everyday job.

In the second of two attacks on August 30, a small formation reduced Biggin Hill to a shambles. The first raid hit the aerodrome from high level at midday. Then, at 6.00 pm, nine Ju 88s swept in from the south, flying at less than 1,000 ft. No air-raid warning was given and the station was caught off guard. The raid lasted only half an hour but in that time a great deal of damage was done. The raiders dropped 16 HE bombs (estimated at 1,000-pounders) of which six scored direct hits on the technical site. Workshops, stores, barracks, WAAF quarters and a hangar were wrecked. Altogether casualties totalled 39 killed and 26 wounded. The following day

Biggin Hill was again hit twice, at 1.00 pm and 5.30 pm. The attacks did further extensive damage including a direct hit on the operations block.

At 1.30 pm the next day, September 1, the station was again under attack from high level. The defence teleprinter network was wrecked by a 500 lb bomb and for continuing to work the defence lines three WAAF teleprinter operators received the Military Medal for bravery. By now the aerodrome was wrecked and only capable of operating a single squadron. Practically no buildings remained in a habitable condition and because of the danger from collapsing buildings all equipment which was undamaged was salvaged. All services and communications were out of action and the operations room was temporarily moved to a shop in the Pantiles. Later, a permanent site, used for the remainder of the war, was found in the old requisitioned Victorian house 'Towerfield' beside the Keston crossroad some two miles from the airfield.

Five days later the Luftwaffe returned to finish the job but this time most of the bombs fell wide along the Westerham Road. By now Biggin Hill was a shambles

Left Hurricane of No 32 Squadron comes into land after a sortie, August 15 1940, Biggin Hill. Note airman with red flag to warn the pilot of bomb crater-filling parties at work on the landing area.

Above right No 92 Squadron at Biggin Hill, February 1941. Left to right: Pilot Officer Holland, Pilot Officer Wright, Flight Lieutenant Kingcombe, Squadron Leader Kent, Flying Officer Villa, Pilot Officer Saunders, Sergeant Bowen-Morris, Sergeant Kingaby, Pilot Officer Mottram and Sergeant Havercroft.

and Group Captain Grice was of the opinion that as long as the wrecked hangars remained the Germans would try to knock them down so he authorised their demolition by having them blown up. (Subsequently he was court-martialled for his action but was exonerated!)

The enemy was now turning to night attacks to supplement its dwindling daylight raids and No 141 Squadron was posted into Biggin Hill with Defiants but its stay was only five days, from September 13 to September 18 1940. During the Battle of Britain the official RAF Gang Show played at Biggin Hill during July/October 1940. The RAF Gang Shows were formed by Ralph Reader and they expanded to 24 units in Europe, six in the Middle East and six in India, plus six WAAF Gang Shows. They went to every theatre of war as serving airmen and airwomen entertaining millions of service personnel of the Allied Forces. Many famous people made their debut in these shows, including Dick Emery, Tony Hancock, David Lodge, Peter Sellers, Norrie Paramor, Cardew Robinson and Harry Worth. Among those taking part in the Biggin Hill show was one of the great wartime artistes, Anne Shelton. Over the winter months the station housed No 64 Squadron (October 13 to October 15), No 66 (November 11 to February 24 1941), No 74 (October 15 to February 20 1941) and No 92 (September 8 to January 9 1941).

When the spring came the following year, the enemy turned eastwards towards Russia instead of continuing the onslaught on the UK. Released from its defensive role, Fighter Command turned to the offensive. Over the next three years the air offensive grew in size. The spring of 1941 saw the arrival of the first Spitfire Vb with its two cannons and four machine-guns. 1941 saw the following squadrons housed at Biggin Hill: No 72 (July 26 to October 20), No 92 (February 2 to September 24), No 264 (January 11 to April 14) and No 609 (February to July and September 24 to November 21). These squadrons made sweeps over northern France and provided convoy escort. Later the role became purely offensive, with attacks on all types of strategic targets.

The two squadrons to see in the New Year were Nos 124, which had arrived from Castletown on November 11 with Spitfires, and 401 (RCAF), which had arrived from Digby on October 20, also with Spitfires. On January 25 1942, Squadron Leader A.G. Douglas (RAF) DFC took over command of the Canadian squadron. No 401 moved out on March 18 only to return again in August and September 1942. No 124 Squadron moved out during May of that year. No 72 Squadron made three visits during 1942, March to June, July and August. During 1942, No 133 'Eagle' Squadron paid the station two visits, the first was in May and the second from August 30 to September 23.

Additional American visitors in August were Nos 2 and 307 Spitfire Squadrons which came for a month's experience. August also saw a four-day visit from No 602 Squadron.

In August 1942 the combined raid on Dieppe, code-named Operation *Jubilee* was mounted and the Biggin Wing claimed 15 enemy aircraft destroyed for a loss of only six pilots. That same month Biggin Hill received its first Spitfire IXs which were in answer to the German Fw 190s. The tide was now running in the RAF's favour and the Biggin Hill squadrons were taking part in every type of Fighter Command operation. By July 1942 the station's score of enemy aircraft destroyed reached 900, the 1,000th victim being downed the following year on May 15 1943, establish-

ing a sector record which remained unequalled to the end of the war.

On September 18 1942, No 609 Squadron returned for the third time, this time flying Typhoons, having rearmed with them four months earlier. With the Typhoons it became one of the most successful train-wrecking squadrons, with dozens of locomotives destroyed or damaged. September 23 saw the arrival of Nos 340 and 611 Squadrons, which replaced the outgoing 133 Squadron. The Biggin Hill squadrons continued to operate throughout the winter months. On November 2 1942, No 609 moved to Manston. Then, on January 20 1943, the Luftwaffe returned. They came in low and on reaching the aerodrome first flew around the perimeter, which gave the resident aircraft

Above left *Here a group of deadly scorers talk it over with their Squadron Leader, following a highly successful sweep by 401 Squadron over the English Channel and Northern France. They all made their mark at German expense, downing four, getting one probable and damaging four others. Left to right: Pilot Officer Ian Ormston, Montreal; Pilot Officer Don Blakeslee, Fairport Harbor, Ohio; Squadron Leader Norman R. Johnstone, Winnipeg; Sergeant Don Morrison, Toronto, and Sergeant Omer Levesque, Mont Joli, Quebec. Photographed at Biggin Hill, November 1941.* **Left** *All from Ontario are these Mustang pilots who flew with 400 (City of Toronto) Squadron from Biggin Hill. Left to right: Flying Officers Bill Jessiman of Fort William, Bill Kennedy of Toronto, 'Tip' Tummon of Foxboro and Ian McLeod of Toronto. Taken November 26 1943.* **Below left** *A typical scene in the flying control tower of Biggin Hill fighter base where 400 (City of Toronto) Squadron is operating its Mustangs against the Hun. Left to right: Flight Lieutenant Harold Day, Toronto, officer in charge; Corporal Joe Penner; LAC Dudd Boyle; Flying Officer Bert Aldridge, California; LAC Reynolds, London, England, and LAC Bill Culquhoon, Toronto. Taken November 26 1943.*

Below *Flight Lieutenant Ken Morham points to the 10 mph speed limit warning but Flying Officer Lurry Seath ignores him. 'Too slow for a Mustang pilot, particularly if he's from St Lambert', he says. Both Sneath and Morham hailed from St Lambert, Quebec, and flew with 400 (City of Toronto) Squadron led by Squadron Leader R.A. (Dick) Ellis, DFC, of Montreal West, Quebec, another suburb of Montreal. At the time this photograph was taken at Biggin Hill on November 26 1943, they had each a destroyed German aircraft to their credit.*

Pistol Packin' Momma *is the name which Flight Lieutenant Edward Carl 'Lucky' Likeness painted on his Spitfire, shown here at Biggin Hill on April 3 1944 with 412 Squadron.*

time to scramble. In the ensuing fight six German aircraft were shot down for no loss to the RAF. On February 9 1943 the Typhoons of No 1 Squadron arrived from Acklington. They remained five weeks and moved out to Lympne in March. That same month No 340 Squadron moved to Turnhouse and was replaced by 341 Squadron. During May the Spitfires of 41 Squadron put in an appearance for one week.

July 1943 saw the departure of No 611 Squadron and the arrival of No 485 Squadron (RNZAF) flying Spitfires. On September 19 1943 St George's Chapel of Remembrance was dedicated, Group Captain 'Sailor' Malan unveiling the altar during the service.

The Canadians, by way of Nos 401, 411 and 412 Squadrons, returned in October to replace No 485 Squadron, and they were to remain throughout the winter months. Late in 1943 the Canadians were joined by the Americans with their P-47 Thunderbolts and during a visit by a high-ranking American officer the Thunderbolts put on a low-level display. During the flypast one aircraft came in too low and struck a tree, crashing onto a bungalow in Jail Lane, killing the pilot.

During April 1944 the Canadians moved out, No 401 to Fairwood Common, South Wales on April 7 and Nos 411 and 412 to Tangmere, Sussex on April 15.

One week after D-Day the first V1 flying bombs made their début over England.

A fighter mission over France completed, Flight Sergeant L.W. Larry Love steps from the cockpit of his Spitfire. His Canadian squadron was No 412, based at Biggin Hill when this photograph was taken on March 6 1944.

Above *Gloster Meteor F 8 WF760 'K' of No 615 Squadron, Biggin Hill, 1952.* **Below** *Douglas DC-3, G-ALXK at Biggin Hill on May 5 1963.* **Bottom** *A Stinson Reliant, G-AFVT, at Biggin Hill, May 1968.*

Above *Lancaster* G-ASXX (NX611) *which had recently arrived from the South Pacific, seen here at Biggin Hill on July 13 1965 surrounded by a dozen Garden Horizons led by Sferma Maquis* F-BKOP.

Below *Back view of Control Tower at Biggin Hill on July 28 1981.*

The close proximity of Biggin Hill to London brought it within the defensive balloon barrage belt and at the end of June the station was taken over by Balloon Command. The airfield lay right in the middle of 'Bomb Alley' and no less than six V1s crashed inside the airfield boundary.

In September 1944 Balloon Command moved out, station headquarters returned from Redhill and the squadrons returned. During October, Nos 91 and 345 Squadrons arrived. They resumed the offensive fighter role, escorting RAF Lancaster and Halifax bombers in daylight raids into Germany. By November, Nos 154 and 322 Squadrons had taken over from 91 and 345 and they remained for the rest of the year. No 322 moved to Holland on January 3 1945, leaving only 154 Squadron, which soldiered on until March 1 1945. During this period the fighters had been joined by aircraft of Transport Command and Biggin Hill was a terminal for services to the various parts of Europe which had been liberated. The first unit to fly from Biggin Hill on transport duties was a detached flight of No 168 Squadron RCAF which operated seven Dakotas.

In June 1945 Biggin Hill was transferred completely from the famous No 11 Group Fighter Command to No 46 Group, Transport Command. No 168 Squadron RCAF and No 314 Squadron, USAAF operated from the airfield with Dakotas. The station now became even busier. In December 1945, No 168 Squadron returned to Canada, being replaced at Biggin Hill by the Dakotas of another Canadian squadron, No 436. Services were flown to such places as Schipol (Amsterdam), Evere (Brussels), Munster and their home base at Down Ampney in Gloucestershire. No 436 Squadron returned to Canada in June 1946.

On May 10 1946, two Royal Auxiliary squadrons, Nos 600 (City of London) and 615 (County of Surrey) re-formed at Biggin Hill. In August 1946 the station was handed to Reserve Command, under whose control it remained until November 1949, when it again switched back to Fighter Command. In 1950 the two auxiliary squadrons exchanged their Spitfires for Meteors. They were joined on March 29 1951 by a regular squadron, No 41, which arrived from Church Fenton. No 41 Squadron converted to Hunters and in 1957 the main runway was extended for the safer operation of the faster jets coming into service, but the writing was

on the wall for Biggin Hill as a fighter station. On March 10 1957, both Nos 600 and 615 Squadrons were disbanded in common with all the other auxiliary squadrons up and down the country.

Then, with the rundown of Fighter Command and with the increasingly crowded airspace around Biggin Hill, No 41 Squadron disbanded on January 31 1958 and gave its number-plate to No 141 Squadron at Coltishall. Attending the ceremony at Biggin Hill was Group Captain Jamie Rankin who had flown from Biggin Hill in 1940. The station took on a new role and No 1 Air Experience Flight was formed at Biggin Hill in September 1958 for the purpose of supplying cadets of the Air Training Corps with flying experience. No 1 AEF served the City and County of London, Kent, Middlesex, Surrey and West Essex units of the ATC. The unit operated ten Chipmunks and pilots were ex-RAuxAF and RAFVR who gave their services on a voluntary basis. About 140 cadets were flown each weekend. The RAF ceased flying operations from the station on February 7 1959 and No 1 Air Experience Flight moved to White Waltham. However, the RAF still retained the north camp to house the officers' selection centre which opened in April that year followed by the aircrew selection centre three years later.

The south camp was leased to Surrey Aviation for private flying, and with the closing of Croydon many other operators chose Biggin Hill as their base, by so doing giving it a new lease of life. Since then a busy civil airport has grown up there.

The London Borough of Bromley bought the actual airfield, so now the RAF station itself is confined to the north camp where the permanent buildings are good examples of the architecture of a fighter station.

Up until the mid-1970s the RAF staged an annual 'At Home' day there to mark Battle of Britain Day.

Late in 1979, the Government confirmed its earlier decision to close the RAF camp at Biggin Hill and its intention of demolishing all the buildings except the officers' mess (which was to house the RAF Chaplains' School) and the chapel. Today the only unit at RAF Biggin Hill is the officers' and aircrew selection centre, which assesses the suitability for training of all candidates for commissions and aircrew service and this role is unlikely to change within the next five years.

Booker (Wycombe Air Park), Buckinghamshire

175/SU828910. South-west of High Wycombe on the B482

This small aerodrome about three miles south-west of High Wycombe was originally built as Marlow Airport but it was requisitioned by the Air Ministry (from its owner, subsequently Wing Commander W.H. Wetton, a wartime flier) on the outbreak of war in 1939 shortly after it had opened.

A technical site was constructed on the eastern boundary of the landing area and this contained four Bellman hangars, the northern pair being the taller with a clear height of 25 ft while the other pair had clearance of only 17 ft. Some of the hutted accommodation was built adjacent to the technical site and the remainder was located on the opposite side of the minor road which formed the eastern boundary.

The area is undulating, with many woods, and it was June 1941 before Booker opened as a military airfield, occupied by Airwork Ltd which operated No 21 Elementary Flying Training School within 50 Group, Flying Training Command, RAF.

The EFTS remained at Booker until the end of February 1950, when it disbanded, but that was not quite the end of its military life as it housed No 1 Basic Flying Training School while the Korean war lasted. This school used Chipmunk T.10s and was also operated by Airwork. Other units at Booker since the war have included the University of London Air Squadron with Chipmunks and Bomber Command Communication Flight flying Pembrokes and Ansons.

After being vacated by the RAF the airfield was developed as Wycombe Air Park, now with a single paved runway, and became a very busy light aviation centre. In 1975 the clock was turned back when Booker Airfield was used to film *Aces High*. This was a film about the fighter pilots of the First World War and the days of the Red Baron over the battlefields of France. At present, British Airways Flying Club is a major user and the four Bellmans remain in use.

Bovingdon, Herts

166/TL005045. West of Hemel Hempstead off the B4505

Bovingdon airfield lies on the edge of the Chiltern Hills on the Hertfordshire/Buckinghamshire border and is bordered on its southern boundary by the B4505 and the village of Bovingdon, after which it was named.

It was built by John Laing & Son Ltd in 1941/42 as a bomber airfield with the usual three runways, but it was never developed to Class A standard. The main 04/22 runway was 4,950 ft in length and the two intersecting runways were each 4,300 ft long. These were surrounded by the usual perimeter track off which were 27 dispersal pans extending into the

Below left One of the four Bellman hangars at Booker. On the left is a Robin aircraft and the other is a Stampe biplane. Photographed December 1981. **Below** *Control tower at Booker, also photographed December 1981.*

woods, locally known as the 'Strawberry Woods', at the north of the airfield. The technical site and four 'T2' hangars were in the south-east corner close to Bovingdon village.

On June 15 1942 the airfield was taken over by No 7 Group, Bomber Command, RAF, but they did not use it and in mid-August the United States Army Air Force arrived at the airfield. However, for some unknown reason Bovingdon was not officially handed over to the American Air Force until April 28 1943 when it then became US Air Station 112. The troopship *West Point*, formerly the SS *America*, had brought over the ground echelon of the 92nd Bomb Group to Liverpool where the group entrained for Bovingdon.

In the meantime the air echelon, having completed its training at Dow Field, then made its historic non-stop flight from Gander Lake, Newfoundland to Prestwick, Scotland. The first squadron to make the crossing was the 326th and Captain André Brousseau flew the lead ship. The 326th left Gander Lake at 2200 hours on August 15, arriving in Prestwick at 0900 hours on August 16. Two days later they flew to Bovingdon.

The next squadron to make the crossing was the 325th with Colonel James S. Sutton flying the lead ship. The third squadron to make the trip was the 327th and the lead ship was flown by Captain Francis E. Winget. Bad weather hit the 327th and it broke formation. Lt Haas force-landed in Northern Ireland but managed to rejoin the squadron in time to make the final leg of the journey to Bovingdon on August 20.

The last squadron to make this hazardous crossing was the 407th which left at 2200 hours on August 26 and arrived at Prestwick at 0930 hours the next morning.

As part of the US 8th Air Force the personnel quickly settled down with Colonel Sutton as their commanding officer, but the 92nd Group was far from satisfied with conditions at Bovingdon. The barracks were dirty and sanitary facilities were very poor. Also the food was very British and not to their liking.

However, the Americans soon settled in and the locals made them very welcome. The Special Service section was overwhelmed with requests for social visits. GI Joe made himself welcome and the English pub was a welcome retreat.

Bovingdon did have some good points, one being that it was close to London and although blacked-out it had its attractions

Just before departing from Bovingdon for the United States in 1943, Captain Clark Gable broadcast to America from England over the Blue Network. His speech was on the purchase of War Bonds in support of the 3rd War Loan Drive Programme.

for the 92nd Group. They could visit the high spots and the more exotic side of London.

The 92nd was the first heavy bombardment group successfully to make a non stop flight of such duration and Colonel Sutton received a personal letter of commendation from General Arnold. However, almost immediately upon their arrival the B-17Fs were transferred to one of the two Groups which had arrived a few months earlier. The 92nd Group received its battered B-17Es in return and it was in these that it flew its first combat mission on September 6.

The target was the Avions Potez aircraft factory at Meaulte, France and it was the largest mission to date for the 8th AF with 30 Fortresses over the target. Two Fortresses were lost, one of which was from 92nd Group and these were the first two to be lost over Europe. The Bovingdon bomber was piloted by 2nd Lieutenant Leigh E. Stewart of the 327th Bombardment Squadron. Captain Frank

Ward's aircraft was also attacked and Corporal John E. Bungard, the tail gunner, was the group's first battle casualty. The whole aircraft was raked from stem to stern and Corporal Hubert Crowell was mortally wounded, Sergeant Robert Smith severely wounded and First Lieutenant John Segrest, the navigator, was slightly wounded.

It was very soon appreciated that there was a need for an effective replacement system for combat crews over occupied Europe because of the high casualty rate which had been sustained already by the three groups then participating in missions. Therefore, it was decided that Bovingdon should serve as the major heavy bomber operational training base for B-17 crews which were arriving in large numbers from the USA. Nevertheless, during the four months spent at Bovingdon, the group flew four operational bombing missions, plus three diversion missions not classed as sorties.

One of the missions in which the group participated was in the raid on Lille on October 9, when for the first time over 100 aircraft were dispatched by the 8th AF. It also highlighted many of the problems, for out of the 15 aircraft dispatched by the 92nd Group, seven turned back because of mechanical failures. Only one aircraft, piloted by Lieutenant Earl A. Shaefer of the 407th Squadron, bombed the primary target with 4,000 lb of GP bombs. Six aircraft bombed the airfield at St Omer, the last resort target, and one aircraft piloted by Lieutenant Francis Chorak of the 327th Squadron was shot down five miles north of St Omer. Many other aircraft received battle damage, and on his own initiative, Corporal Archie Cothren, a waist gunner of Major Keck's aircraft, bailed out over Gravelines, one mile south-west of Dunkirk, after the aircraft was attacked and he was severely wounded in the face, his oxygen mask having been blown to pieces.

The 92nd Bomb Group was assigned the role of B-17 Combat Crew Replacement Unit and settled down to the task. Liberty runs were made into Chesham and Hemel Hempstead but these caused problems on the home front, for during the early days at Bovingdon there was a sharp increase in respiratory infections which gave rise to concern. Also on the increase was VD, and 'prophylactic stations', which were open from 1700 hours to 2400 hours each day, were established in Chesham and Hemel Hempstead. But the

Above *Lieutenant Colonel Elliott Roosevelt, who was stationed at Bovingdon, receives the Distinguished Flying Cross in Algiers for outstanding services performed by his group in the Africa campaign.*

Right *Douglas C-47 0-49409 of the US Air Force seen here at Bovingdon.*

Below right *Iraqui Air Force Bristol Freighters visited Bovingdon bringing ferry pilots for newly built Percival Provost trainers from nearby Luton. This photograph, taken on October 6 1955, shows a Freighter plus the nose of some of the Provosts.*

signs gave cause for concern and the Public Health authorities in these towns required them to read 'First Aid Station' and not 'Prophylactic Station', which advertised what they were there for.

Bovingdon was to be visited by many famous people and one of the first was Mrs Eleanor Roosevelt, who flew in and out one day in November. Her second son, Lieutenant-Colonel Elliott Roosevelt, had spent several weeks at Bovingdon with the student detachment of the 15th Photo Mapping Squadron which was housed here for a few months.

92 Group participated in the organisa-

tion and training of the 12th Air Force during the latter part of the year and as it drew to a close the British-based Americans were now getting the hang of what was to come. Bovingdon had an important role to play. The Americans, attacking in daylight, had counted on the many defensive gun positions of the B-17 to ward off the fighters, but the skilful Luftwaffe, who at this period of the war had many top aces, soon found the blind spots. Bovingdon became the key airfield for bringing new crews up to operational standard—a most vital task as the daylight raids increased and the casualty list grew longer and longer. The night bombing was left to the RAF, which had the right skills and equipment for night bombing.

The New Year brought changes, and on January 4 the 92nd, leaving behind some of its key personnel and one entire squadron, the 326th, began moving to Alconbury where it eventually re-formed as a combat group. Those who remained at Bovingdon formed the nucleus of the 11th

Combat Crew Replacement Centre under the leadership of Major John P. Dwyer, who was director of training. Most combat bomber crews arriving in Britain during the next two years received training at Bovingdon.

When General Eisenhower came to England for the setting-up of the forces for the eventual invasion, his personal B-17, piloted by Major Larry Henson, was housed in No 1 hangar. Bovingdon was the nearest USAAF airfield to the 8th Air Force and other command headquarters. Therefore, it housed several other units, including the 8th Air Force Headquarters Squadron and the Air Technical Squadron. The latter was responsible for the development of auxiliary drop tanks and these helped to extend the range of the fighters over the continent.

With Allied victory in Europe in sight, the Combat Crew Replacement Unit disbanded in September 1944. Shortly afterwards, the US Air Transport Command moved in and the airfield became

the base for the newly formed US Air Transport Service (Europe) with Douglas C-47s and C-53s. After VE-Day the base handled thousands of GIs through its air terminal, all were anxious to return home to the USA, and the airfield was very busy. Many famous film stars served at Bovingdon—Clark Gable, James Stewart and William Holden were all familiar faces. Also, Glenn Miller and his Band were frequent visitors—but now they were gone.

On April 15 1946, control of the airfield reverted to the RAF, but this was only for a short period until the newly formed Ministry of Civil Aviation took over the aerodrome for civilian airlines. BOAC used Bovingdon as a maintenance base and many other independent airlines were based there during the post-war period. British European Airways used it as a diversion airfield when Heathrow and Northolt were fog-bound. Because of Bovingdon's height, 535 ft above sea level, it was often clear. However, this was not always the case, for on May 20 1948, a Dakota III *G-AJBG* which was on a charter flight from Valence, France with a cargo of fruit, approached the airfield under a low cloud base and while in the circuit crashed into Bourne Grove Wood about half a mile from the airfield, killing the pilot, radio operator and flight engineer and seriously injuring the first officer.

The 1950s proved to be very busy for Bovingdon, for the Americans returned on May 25 1951 in the form of the 7531st Air Base Squadron which was flying Douglas C-47 transports. They occupied

Above *This aerial view from a Fighter Command Anson transport shows three of the four hangars, most of the runway area and quite a variety of aircraft parked on what was a very active airfield until its subsequent closure.*

Top right *Whilst the main runway at Blackbushe Aerodrome was being resurfaced, the US Navy used Bovingdon for its unique Martin P4M Mercator patrol bomber used by VQ-2 squadron at Port Lyautey, Morocco. Bu No 124373, PS/3 is seen parked at Bovingdon.* **Right** *Parked by the control tower is the personal Meteor F 8, WK943, of Air Vice Marshal V.S. Bowling. Note the control tower has a postwar addition to the roof. The Meteorological Office occupied the ground floor, Approach Control the second floor and Local Control was on the roof.* **Below right** *Boeing B-17G The Body seen here at Bovingdon during the filming of* The War Lover.

No 4 Hangar in front of which was built a new base operations building which looked out across the perimeter.

During this period there was a huge expansion programme under way for both the Third Air Force and Seventh Air Division (SAC) bases. On March 26 1954, a Bovingdon-based C-47, *43-48666*, took a number of VIPs to RAF Full Sutton, this being the nearest active airfield to Elvington which was earmarked for the Americans but was still under Care and Maintenance.

Mosquito B 35 HJ653, HT-F *that was used during the filming of* Mosquito Squadron *at Bovingdon, July 5 1968.*

Also based at Bovingdon were two RAF Communications units—one to support RAF Fighter Command HQ at Bentley Priory and the other for Coastal Command HQ at Northwood, Middlesex. Bovingdon was an obvious choice and its location also suited the Americans for Bovingdon was close to South Ruislip, the US 3rd Air Division HQ. Conferences at the Command HQs resulted in a huge volume of visiting aircraft and a varied selection was always to be seen at Bovingdon. For the Americans also, many different types of aircraft used the airfield and these included the B-26 Invader, B-29 Superfortress and B-50, to name but three. Only the runway length restricted some of the more advanced jets from paying a visit.

The 1960s revived the glamour and spirit of those wartime years when the clock was turned back with the production of three war films. In 1961 there was *The War Lover*: with Steve McQueen as the star it was aptly about the wartime B-17 squadrons. Then in 1964 came *633 Squadron* about a Mosquito squadron. It was a fictitious squadron number but with many wartime associations. This was followed by the sequel *Mosquito Squadron*, which was based on the legendary Amiens attack (see page 154) that was flown from Hunsdon.

In 1962 the Americans departed and that same year the RAF Communications

Flight was redesignated Southern Communications Squadron. Flying continued for the next few years, then in 1968 it was announced by the Ministry of Defence that Bovingdon was one of several airfields due for closure. It came as a surprise, for only recently the hangars had been renovated. The Southern Command Communications Squadron moved to Northolt on January 1 1969 and all Ministry of Defence property, except some married quarters, was disposed of by 1976. Through war and peace it had been a popular airfield being in beautiful countryside and with easy access to London for off-duty periods.

Today, the hangars have gone and the control tower stands forlorn among the cultivated fields. To many thousands of people, American and British, Bovingdon holds a special place, but soon it will be only memories for Amey Roadstone Corporation is ready to remove it from the map.

Brooklands (Weybridge), Surrey

176/TQ067620. South-west of Weybridge just north of the A245 at Byfleet

Brooklands motor track was built in 1906/7 by the Honourable Hugh Locke King on his own land. The circuit measured 4,730 yds in length and was 100 ft wide. It was completely concrete-covered and it took 1,500 labourers less than a year to construct it. It was officially opened on July 22 1907 by S.F. Edge, one of the leading motorists of the time.

Interest in flying goes back to 1907 when Lord Brabazon built his own aeroplane and endeavoured to fly it at Brooklands, but without success. The first flight at Brooklands was made in 1908 by A.V. Roe. This was in fact the first flight in England. However, Roe was not popular with the motor racing clan at Brooklands and after crashing his first tri-plane in the middle of the track in 1909 he was invited to remove himself and his equipment to pastures new! He sold his aeroplane shed for £15 and moved the rest of his equipment to Lea Marshes in East London where he continued his experiments. After a period at Lea Marshes, followed by a successful venture in Manchester, he was invited to return to Brooklands in 1910. More pioneers took up residence and Short Bros put up a shed next to A.V. Roe's and started building aeroplanes. In 1910 Martin and Handasyde were building the Martinsyde monoplane, which proved successful.

The *Daily Mail* round-Britain Air Race started at Brooklands on July 22 1911. In 1912 Vickers opened a flying school at Brooklands which became a focal point of aviation before the outbreak of the First World War. Such distinguished pupils as Sir Sefton Brancker, Marshal of the Royal Air Force, Viscount Trenchard and Air Chief Marshal Lord Dowding, were trained in the famous Vickers School at Brooklands Aerodrome.

The aerodrome was in the centre of the Brooklands motor track and on three sides were high tension cables. Also, on the east side were two 95-ft-high chimneys and about a mile distant was a wooded hill 200 ft high. The small town of Byfleet nestled in the south-west corner, Wey-bridge was to the north and it was close to the railway station.

During the First World War the site was taken over by the Royal Flying Club and Brooklands became a training station for *ab initio* pilots. The main aircraft used for instruction were Maurice Farman Short-horns and Avro 504s. No 1 Squadron arrived from Farnborough in August 1914 but had moved out to Netheravon before the end of the year. On January 1 1915, No 8 Squadron re-formed at Brooklands as a general duties squadron with an establishment of BE 2c aircraft. Two weeks later, No 10 Squadron arrived from Farnborough. The following April, Nos 8

and 10 Squadrons moved out. No 9 Squadron re-formed on April 1 under the command of Major H.C.T. Dowding, later to become Air Chief Marshal Sir Hugh Dowding, AOC-in-C, Fighter Command, during the Battle of Britain. No 9 Squadron was equipped with Avro 504s and it moved to Dover on July 28 1915. The following month the 'Wireless Testing Park' moved to Joyce Green. This research unit had been set up by the RFC earlier in the year under the command of Captain (later Major) C.E. Prince.

By 1915 Sopwith had begun to build aeroplanes at Brooklands and the Sopwith test pilot, Harry Hawker, used to fly the 'Pup' under the Byfleet bridge. That same year Vickers established an aircraft factory on the site of the Itala motor works and went on to produce the Vickers Gunbus, its first venture into military aeroplane production. The factory later turned out more than 1,650 SE 5s, the famous single-seat fighter of 1917-18. The total number of aircraft produced at Brooklands air-craft factories was over 4,600. During this period Brooklands became No 10 Aircraft Acceptance Park for SE 5s from Bleriot, Martinsyde and Vickers. Snipe from Sopwith also passed through Brooklands. Accommodation for storage was one 190 ft × 70 ft hangar and seven 170 ft × 80 ft hangars. On January 31 1917, No 2 RS, which had been at Brooklands during this early period, moved to Northolt.

Despite its obvious drawbacks the air-field continued to be used after the First World War. A period of recession, which continued until the mid-1920s, took place in the aircraft industry after the Armistice. By this time many of the famous wartime firms had been liquidated and new names replaced the old. Hawkers took over the Sopwith concern at Kingston-on-Thames and built a huge new hangar at Brook-lands. To weather the storm Vickers Ltd began production of civil aircraft and in 1919 the famous Transatlantic crossing was made by the Vickers Vimy. Powered by two 350 hp Rolls-Royce Eagle VIII engines, the Vimy covered the 1,890 miles from Newfoundland to Ireland in 15 hours, 57 minutes, which represented an average speed of 120 mph. Vickers rode out the depression and expanded its works at Weybridge by the addition of a hangar similar to that of Hawkers. It had worked up to the full scale production of Vimys by 1924.

Light aeroplane clubs sprang up all over the country in the late 1920s and Brook-

lands quickly moved to the forefront of the new hobby. The first post-war flying school was started in 1927 by the Henderson School of Flying, in Avro 504Ks. The school was owned by Colonel G.L.P. Henderson who designed and built several aircraft, one of which, the Gadfly, broke the world's height record for light aircraft in May 1929.

In 1927 Duncan Davis became Chief Flying Instructor. The following year he took over the Henderson School of Flying, renaming it the Brooklands School of Flying. Davis had very little money but with the help of several wealthy pupils he managed to buy three Avros. The school proved very successful in its fight for survival. It usually sent two red Avro 548s to work an area between Canvey and the Wash. They moved from place to place with ladders and tents strapped on to their machines. By April 1929 the school was operating eight aeroplanes and during 1929 more than 40 pupils gained their 'A' licences. That same year 'Mutt' Summers became Chief Test Pilot to Vickers and George Bulman took the same role for Hawker Aircraft.

The aerodrome continued to expand and the Brooklands Aero Club was formed in the spring of 1930 with one aeroplane, a Gipsy Moth. The club charged £2 per hour and the cost of training a pupil, at this time, to 'A' licence standard worked out at £42-10s. By the summer of 1931 the club had introduced both advanced flying and blind flying courses. It was also possible to take courses in aeroengineering. In October 1931 the College of Aeronautical Engineering became established at Brooklands and the following years it formed its own flying club, using the school aeroplanes. During this period a new building for the Brooklands School of Flying was completed. The old Cirrus Moths were replaced by Gipsy Moths.

A modern clubhouse, complete with control tower, admin offices, club-rooms, restaurant and other facilities was built in 1932. It still stands, having been scheduled by the Department of the Environment as a building of historical and architectural interest. A preservation order protects it. Vickers rebuilt its works in 1932 and turned its efforts to the development and production of new types for the Air Ministry. The circuit was very busy and in the autumn of that year a large electric 'R' was put up on the Vickers factory as a

Top left *Brooklands sheds in 1927.* Left *Vickers B 19/27 New Type twin-engined night bomber seen here at Brooklands, May 1932.* Below left *Aerial view of Brooklands, 1934. In the picture is K1996, which was completed as a Hart trainer.*

Below *Circa 1936. Brooklands racetrack can be seen in the background.*

reminder that a right-hand circuit was in force at the aerodrome. When a left hand circuit was in force the sign was switched off.

During the early 1930s R.O. Shuttleworth started his collection of antique aeroplanes. The Shuttleworth Collection is now kept at Old Warden Aerodrome and is well worth a visit. Many people kept their aircraft at Brooklands, one aircraft being *Rouge et Noir*, the celebrated Gipsy Moth owned by John Grierson.

By 1934 the club had five Gipsy Moths and was kept very busy. Duncan Davis was still instructing. The new Hawker sheds were in use and it was here at Brooklands that they assembled Hart Hind and Fury biplanes. The Hawker team of test pilots consisted of Summers, Lucas, Bulman and Johnny Hindmarsh.

In October 1935 the prototype Hawker Hurricane *K5083* arrived at Brooklands from the Kingston factory and on November 6, Bulman test flew the small silver monoplane. On June 15 1936, the prototype Vickers Wellington, *K4049* piloted by 'Mutt' Summers made its first flight from Brooklands. The Wellington was designed by Barnes Wallis, inventor of the Dambusters' 'bouncing bomb', and in August a contract was received from the Air Ministry for production. No 9 Squadron of the Royal Air Force was the first to receive the new bombers in 1939 and by this time they had attained a top speed of 243 mph and a maximum range of 3,200 miles at 180 mph. When war broke out, six squadrons of Wellingtons were on active service. A total of 2,514 Wellingtons was built at Weybridge. 1936 saw the Vickers Wellesley in full production. This was a large single-engined monoplane powered by a Bristol radial engine.

On September 4 1940, about 25 Me 110s attacked the aerodrome and inflicted severe damage on the Vickers workshops. Eighty-three aircraft workers were killed and 419 injured. The principal damage was to the main repair hangar, machine

Top left *Breda 15, G-AAVL, at Brooklands circa 1936.*

Left *The prototype Wellington B9/32, K4049, being wheeled over the River Wey from the works to Brooklands aerodrome in May 1936.*

Above *Wellington fuselage erecting shop at the Vickers-Armstrongs factory, Weybridge, July 6 1939. The fuselages shown provide a fascinating glimpse of the British 'geodetic' system that was used in the Wellington bomber.*

shop and electrical wiring department. Several other bombs fell on the aerodrome and adjoining buildings. Hawker's erecting shops escaped without damage. There were no more air raids for the rest of the war. Hawker vacated Brooklands early in the war and concentrated production at Langley and Kingston.

Even before the outbreak of war, the technical staff at Weybridge had been considering the design of an aircraft to succeed the Wellington, but so good had the Wellington proved that its larger successor closely resembled it. It was called the Warwick and first came into production at Weybridge at the end of 1942. The Warwick never had the major role of bomber, as by the time it appeared, Bomber Command was already re-equipping with the bigger, four-engined bombers, such as the Halifax and Lancaster. Nevertheless, it performed many useful functions, the more important being those of air-sea rescue and submar-ine destruction.

The Warwick should have been followed by the Windsor, a big four-engined bomber, also of geodetic construction, designed to surpass the Lancaster in bomb-carrying capacity, in range and in general performance and intended to be used in the war against Japan. However, changes in the requirements of the Air Staff delayed the production of the prototype and by the time production was to begin the end of the war was in sight, and it was decided that a sufficient number could not be built in time to play an effective part. The Windsor had several novel and interesting features, one being the use of four separate under-carriages.

In January 1948, Brooklands was sold to Vickers Armstrong for £330,000. That same year a concrete runway was laid. There were also extensions to the Vickers plant and new test facilities were built.

Viscounts followed the Viking on Brooklands' production line in 1951. The

Left *Luftwaffe target map of Brooklands, August 1940.*

Below *A British European Airways Vickers Viking 1a makes a low pass over Brooklands.*

Bottom *Viscount 700 prototype during its first flight on August 28 1950 at Brooklands.*

Right *Map of Brooklands.*

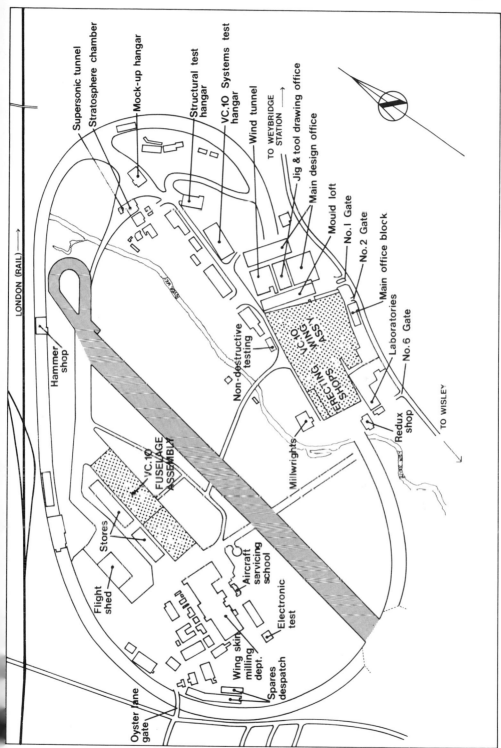

Supersonic tunnel
Stratosphere chamber
Mock-up hangar
Structural test hangar
VC.10 Systems test hangar
Wind tunnel
TO WEYBRIDGE STATION →
Jig & tool drawing office
Main design office
Mould loft
No.1 Gate
No.2 Gate
Main office block
Laboratories
No.6 Gate
TO WISLEY
Redux shop
Millwrights
Non-destructive testing
VC.10 ERECTING WING ASSY. SHOPS
VC.10 FUSELAGE ASSEMBLY
Stores
Flight shed
Aircraft servicing school
Electronic test
Wing skin milling dept.
Spares despatch
Oyster Lane gate
Hammer shop
LONDON (RAIL) →

TSR2 joint venture between Vickers-Armstrong and English Electric was assembled at Brooklands and was road transported to Boscombe Down for test flying. It first flew on September 27 1964. Despite its successful performance the Labour Government of the day saw fit to cancel the whole project. The uncompleted aircraft were cut to pieces outside the Vickers erection sheds at Brooklands. BAC 1-11s were then erected at Brooklands. VC10s were the last aircraft to be designed and constructed at Brooklands. They were first test-flown here on June 29 1962. Fifty-four VC10s and Super VC10s were built, the last one taking off from Brooklands in February 1970. The event heralded the closure of the runway and the end of Brooklands as an airfield, although helicopters of the British Aerospace headquarters still fly in and out.

There are plans for a Brooklands Museum of Aviation in the not-too-distant future. Over the years more than 8,000 completed aircraft have left the factories at Brooklands. These factories also contributed the largest share of the components for Concorde, larger than any other manufacturer, ie, forward fuselage, flight deck, nose section, tail fin, rear fuselage and electrical harness.

A Brooklands memorial was erected and unveiled in July 1957 by Lord Brabazon of Tara. It consists of a bronze plaque with a relief maple, the circuit and a brief history of the site.

Broxbourne, Hertfordshire

166/TL378065. North of Waltham Cross near Nazeing

Some agricultural land south-east of the Hertfordshire town of Broxbourne was developed into a small aerodrome and on November 13 1930, it was licensed to the newly formed Herts and Essex Aero Club, so named because the county boundary ran across the new aerodrome. The two founder members were well-known speedway riders—'Buster' and Roger Frogley—and at first they had a single DH 60 Moth *G-EBVK*.

By the spring of 1931 a club house and hangar had been erected and flying was being carried out in earnest under the Chief Flying Instructor, W.R. Bannister (later killed when a Dragon Rapide crashed in the English Channel in 1935). On Sunday June 14 1931, comedian Will Hay and Jim and Amy Mollison performed the official opening ceremony. Other flying clubs and organisations made use of the aerodrome, which soon had to be expanded, and by 1936 the clubhouse had been enlarged to include sleeping accommodation. Additional hangars and workshops had been built and the flying field had been enlarged.

The fame of the club spread abroad and foreign students enrolled, for Broxbourne was indeed one of the finest privately owned aerodromes of that period. In 1938 a unit of the Civil Air Guard was established here. The club also gained a contract to operate an RAF Elementary and Reserve Flying Training School at Waltham Aerodrome, Grimsby, Lincolnshire. By the end of 1938 there were 202 CAG members at Broxbourne undergoing instruction. At this period the Herts and Essex Club had 24 aircraft, 13 instructors and 50 ground staff.

At the outbreak of war in September 1939 civil flying ceased and all private and club aircraft were impressed by the Government. Many of the aircraft were considered unsuitable for military use and left to rot. Broxbourne became a repair and maintenance base for light aircraft

Moths, Desoutters, etc, in line-up at Broxbourne.

Westland 'Wessex' with engines running seen here at Broxbourne.

and in 1942 a new hangar and dope shop were built enabling the repair facility to be organised on a production line basis. As well as repair and rebuilding, most of it being Percival products, a contract was awarded to modify Canadian-built Harvards to RAF standard. Broxbourne remained in this role throughout the war and a number of operational aircraft landed at the tiny airfield. These included Battles, Spitfires, Hurricanes, Oxfords, Ansons and even Wellingtons.

After the war the Herts and Essex Aero Club (1946) Ltd was established and club flying recommenced. It flourished for several years after an early set-back in 1947 when fire destroyed two large hangars and eleven aircraft. However, the site was very limited and in 1953 Buster and Roger Frogley decided to sell their aerodrome at Broxbourne so that valuable gravel on which it lay could be extracted. The Herts and Essex Aero Club moved to Stapleford Tawney. Broxbourne then closed and the site was sold for gravel working.

Burnham-on-Crouch, Essex

168/TQ958958. East of Burnham-on-Crouch

This was not a very good choice for a landing ground for the area was low-lying and marshy. However, it was found suitable and it was listed as a 1st class landing ground with an area of 102 acres, the dimensions being 750 yds × 600 yds.

The site was located on the north bank of the River Crouch just ¾ mile from the local railway station. It came under 50 Wing and throughout the First World War it was used by No 37 Squadron. It was quickly abandoned after the war and there is no trace of it today.

Chalk (Gravesend), Kent

See Gravesend

Crazies Farm (Henley-on-Thames), Berkshire

See Henley-on-Thames

Chigwell, Essex

177/TQ440935. North-west of Romford off the A113

RAF Chigwell became the recruiting centre for No 909 Balloon Unit on the opening of the unit on May 16 1938. On August 4 1938, No 4 Balloon Centre was established there and No 30 Barrage Balloon Group was based at Chigwell in 1940, but Chigwell is best remembered as the station housing the Central Test Board assessing airmen for ground trades.

Chigwell continued after the war and on April 1 1952 the HQ of No 253 Signals Unit was formed. A ground radar calibration unit was formed on August 15 1952. A special training flight, the Aerial Erectors School Unit was there from early 1956 to August of that year. Chigwell lost its status as an RAF station on December 1 1958. On October 16 1961, the Ground Radio Servicing Unit moved to Upwood and on the same date the station was placed on a Care and Maintenance basis. The holding party disbanded on March 5 1962 and with effect from the same date Chigwell was reduced to an inactive status for parenting by North Weald.

Chingford, Essex

177/TQ380950. Just north of London. Between Enfield and Chingford off the A110

Another of the south-east area sites, it was located just north of London and ½ mile from Ponders End railway station. It opened in 1915 and was listed as a 2nd class landing ground with an area of 150

acres, the dimensions being 1,500 yds × 400 yds. It was a clay soil, which gave problems in wet weather, and being in enclosed surroundings the approach was difficult except from the south. The Chingford reservoir was on the northern edge of the airfield and was a good landmark for the student pilots.

Chingford came under 49 Wing and was used by 44 Squadron while on home defence duties. The site was also a depot and the main training station for pilots of the Royal Naval Air Service. One of the many pupils to pass through Chingford in 1916 was Sidney Cotton. After a few short hops in a Farman Longhorn trainer he was ready for his first solo flight. It was a case of make 'em or break 'em and just three days after his first solo flight at Chingford, Cotton was posted to the Central Flying School at Upavon on Salisbury Plain. Such was the pace for training pilots in those early days.

Chingford became No 207 Training Depot Station with Hainault Farm as a sub-station and it remained in the training role throughout the First World War. It closed in 1919, and today the site has been engulfed by the sprawling suburbs of London.

Chiswick (Hatfield), Hertfordshire
See Hatfield

Cricklewood, London
176/TQ230857. Just south of Hendon off the main A5

In September 1912, Handley Page Ltd moved from Barking to some converted riding stables at Cricklewood Lane in north London. The aircraft built there included three BE 2As, the Type G biplane and the first HP O/100. All aircraft were moved by road to nearby Hendon for flying, but it was not a very successful arrangement, for the journey necessitated removing telegraph wires and other obstructions along the 1½-mile route. By the time the 0/400 was ready it was obvious that larger premises were needed with an airfield close by for test flying. Therefore, Handley Page acquired an 160-acre site at nearby Clitter-House Farm, large erecting shops were built and an airfield laid out adjacent to the factory.

By 1917 the factory was at peak production and over 1,000 people were employed. On May 22 1918, the V/1500 bomber made its maiden flight from

Above left *Airco DH 9A at Chingford 1918/19.* **Left** *Bristol F 2B Fighter F4579 seen here at Chingford in 1918.* **Below left** *Sopwith TF 2 Salamander E5430 seen at Chingford. Only six were built as experimental aircraft by Sopwith Aviation, which flew from April 27 1918 onwards.*

Below *Sergeant Collin Smith, fourth from left, who was an observer at Chingford. Note motley collection of uniforms, belts and hats.*

Cricklewood only to crash on Golders Green on June 8. After the Armistice in November there were widespread cancellations of orders and only 35 V/1500s were built.

After the war Handley Page quickly converted surplus RAF 0/400 aircraft into airliners and in February 1919 Handley Page Transport was formed. The company was soon in business and on September 2 1919 operated its first London-Paris service with HP 0/400 *G-EAAE*. The fare was 18 guineas return and 10 guineas single. On September 23, the airline began its London-Brussels service. However, the venture was not a success, mainly because of mechanical troubles and bad weather. Also, it was a very poor site for a major aerodrome for it was a bumpy surface flanked on three sides by the ever-increasing sea of houses whilst on the fourth side were the factory and railway line. There was little room for take-off from this little grass field situated between the Broadway and Golders Green. However, despite its obvious faults, the aerodrome was granted Customs facilities in February 1920 and at that time was the only London aerodrome with Customs. It was not to last and Cricklewood was destined not to be an international airport. On December 14 1920, *G-EAMA* hit a tree on take-off and crashed into a garden at Golders Green. The 20-year-old pilot and three others were killed, the accident being the first involving a British scheduled service to prove fatal.

Aerial view of the Handley Page works at Cricklewood.

The last service was flown out of Cricklewood on May 21 1921, and on that date the Customs facilities ceased. Handley Page Transport moved to Croydon, but the company continued to build and fly aircraft at Cricklewood until 1929, by which time the complaints about noise and low flying had forced Handley Page to stop flying. It was, however, clear that the site was no longer suitable for the larger aircraft, and in June 1929, Handley Page purchased a suitable site at Radlett. The aerodrome was quickly run down. In February 1930 Cricklewood closed to all flying and the aerodrome land was sold for over £100,000.

Today the Laing Estate occupies the site, but the factory continued in use right up through production of the Victor, which was test-flown at Radlett.

Croydon (Waddon), Surrey

177/TQ306635. South-west of Croydon between the B271 and B272

The German Zeppelin air raids on England in 1915 stirred the authorities to establish a number of landing grounds around major cities to be used by home defence aeroplanes. One of these was on agricultural land at New Barn Farm, Beddington, where an area to the west of Plough Lane was obtained on December 13 1915, ostensibly as a training aerodrome, and was equipped with Bessonneaux hangars and tented accommodation. At first it was known as Beddington Aerodrome and in January 1916 two Royal Flying Corps BE 2cs arrived. Six mechanics came with the two aeroplanes and also a party of Royal Engineers with a searchlight. In April all the air defence detachments in the London area formed into a new Wing—the 18th—and the detachment at Beddington formed part of No 39 Home Defence Squadron. Further changes took place in May when it was decided to concentrate these new units on the east of London.

Throughout 1916 and 1917 No 17 Reserve (Training) Squadron was housed here and there was a steady build-up of men and buildings. Three brick hangars on the RFC 1917 pattern were constructed together with hutted accommodation. Many airmen and soldiers were compulsorily billeted in the surrounding area. Among the men working at the airfield were some volunteers from Canada, distinguished by their dark blue uniforms and the maple leaf emblems on their hats.

During 1917 No 40 Training Squadron, Royal Flying Corps, replaced No 17 and this unit remained until early the following year when it then moved to Tangmere. For the early part of 1918 No 141 Squadron from Biggin Hill had used the airfield as a landing ground. No 29 Training Squadron moved in to replace the outgoing unit and among the pilots who came to do their flying training with this squadron was Prince Albert, later King George VI, who won his wings here in 1919. He was joined by his elder brother, the Prince of Wales, later Edward VIII (after his abdication, the Duke of Windsor).

In the summer of 1919 Winston Churchill crashed at Beddington after taking off for an evening flight. Luckily he was not hurt but one cannot help but wonder what course the Second World War would have taken had he died that summer evening.

Churchill's was not the only accident, for inevitably, since it was a training station, there were many crashes. Beddington also saw the return and disbandment of many squadrons from France. One returning airman described Croydon as 'more of a club house than anything else'.

In July 1919 the aerodrome was used by an Air Council Inspection Squadron as No 1 Group Headquarters. October saw the arrival of three squadrons, Nos 207, 32 and 41. None of the squadrons had any aircraft. Nos 32 and 41 had formed in 1916 and were now surplus to requirements. They both disbanded at the end of 1919. No 207 moved out on January 16 1920. The RAF left in February 1920 and the airfield returned to civil flying. At this period there were still two separate airfields, known as Beddington and Waddon Aerodromes, with Plough Lane running between them from Stafford Road through to Purley. Aircraft had to cross the road. This was not a very satisfactory arrangement and it was decided to concentrate the aerodrome chiefly on the eastern side of Plough Lane, near the factories, which by this time had been bought by Mr Frederick Handley Page for use by the Aircraft Disposal Company.

As part of the aircraft build-up, a factory, known as National Aircraft Factory No 1, was built on the other side of Plough Lane less than a mile from Beddington Aerodrome. This site occupied 240 acres south of Stafford Road and west of Coldharbour Lane (now Purley Way). The land between Plough Lane and the factory was a test-flying ground and this site came to be known as Waddon Aerodrome. The factory opened in January 1918 but with the Armistice in November 1918 the aircraft industry at Waddon came to an abrupt end— National Aircraft Factory No 1 was simply no longer needed.

There were now thousands of surplus aeroplanes and Waddon became the National Aircraft Depot. Smashed aeroplanes arrived in trainloads from France and there were huge stocks of engines, propellers and all other parts. When the Salvage Depot first opened, items were sold off cheaply just to make room. People flocked to the Depot and propellers were sold for hat stands and clock cases. Steel tubes were turned into bedsteads, and aeroplane wings, which sold for sixpence (2½p), made good roofs for chicken runs. Unfortunately the chickens ate the dope from the wings and it killed them.

In April 1920 the National Aircraft Depot at Waddon was sold to Handley Page's Aircraft Disposal Company along with all Government surplus aircraft and parts. By this time Beddington Aerodrome and the flying field at Waddon had become Croydon Aerodrome and with the war at an end swift developments took place. Croydon, as it was now officially called, became the Customs airport for

London on March 29, and several small commercial airlines moved in. The main firms were Air Transport and Travel, Instone Air Lines and Handley Page. During 1920, KLM, Sneta (later Sabena) and Wm. Beardmore started using the aerodrome. KLM made the first Amsterdam-Croydon flight. The two main French airlines, Compagnie des Messageries Aériennes (CMA) and the Compagnie des Grands Express Aériens (CGEA), which later in 1923 were merged into Air Union, forerunner of Air France, were making Paris-Croydon scheduled flights using Spad S.33s and Farman Goliaths. The latter was a development of a First World War bomber prototype and was a very familiar sight at Croydon Aerodrome.

The aerodrome continued to develop and during April 1921 the *R33* was moored at Croydon for a short time, a special 140 ft mooring mast having been erected for the purpose. The mooring experiment was successful but the airship never came back and the mast was dismantled that same year.

To keep pace with the expansion, subsidies were found necessary to enable services to keep running. Handley Page Transport obtained a dual subsidy from the British and Swiss Governments to run a service from Croydon to Zurich via Paris. The first flight under this agreement was by a Handley Page 0/10 piloted by Wing Commander R.H. McIntosh, known as 'All-weather Mac' for his determination to fly in all weathers.

The aerodrome was growing every day and by now it was accepted as being 'The London Terminal—The Continental Airport'.

The 1923 recommendations by the Hambling Committee that there should be just one British commercial airline led to the formation of Imperial Airways on April 1, 1924. This was a merger of Instone Air Line Ltd, Daimler Airways Ltd, Handley Page Transport Ltd and the British Marine Air Navigation Co Ltd. This was the forerunner of British European Airways and this formation of all the airlines brought together all the people involved with British aviation from the very beginning. It also brought some problems and almost immediately the new company was hit with a strike by the pilots and staff. This, however, was settled on May 2 and Imperial Airways went on to be one of the main airlines.

1925 was also a year of expansion, with the opening of the Croydon/Amsterdam/

Hamburg/Copenhagen/Malmo service. From May 15, Imperial Airways operated the Croydon-Amsterdam section in de Havilland 34s with Swedish Air Lines completing the other half in Junkers-G23s.

November 16 was a very important date, for on that day Mr (later Sir) Alan Cobham began a survey flight for Imperial Airways to Cape Town and back in a de Havilland 50J powered by an Armstrong Siddeley Jaguar engine. The flight of 8,100 miles with 30 stopping places took five months. For this historic flight the Postmaster General sanctioned special stationery cards. They bore a violet cachet 'By Special Air Mail/16-11-25/London/Cape Town'. Throughout this period many of the postcards that were issued showed the interiors of aeroplanes with the varied seating arrangements from wicker chairs to leather benches.

To accommodate the rapid build-up of traffic, all the old buildings on the Wallington side of the airport were replaced with a new complex, including a control tower and a private hotel on the eastern side of the landing field. The original airfield used by the Royal Flying Corps had been only on the west side of Plough Lane. Under the major alterations Plough Lane would be sealed off and the whole aerodrome site would become one. The plans for the world's first purpose-built international aerodrome were set in motion in 1925 when the Croydon Airport Act passed through Parliament. Work started on the new buildings in 1926.

That same year Lufthansa started a Croydon to Amsterdam service by Dornier and Fokker. Sabena started the Croydon to Brussels service and in mid-July the first of the three-engined Argossy-Armstrong Whitworths was used by Imperial Airways from Croydon to Paris. December 1926 saw survey flights being carried out from Croydon to Delhi taking 62 hours and the first of the many de Havilland 66s was delivered to Cairo to start the India service.

By January 1927 the Cairo to Basra service was well established and to cope with the extra leg some five de Havilland 66s were flown from Croydon to Cairo by the end of February.

Imperial Airways obtained quite a bit of publicity in May by running a Silver Wing lunchtime service to Paris with all the aeroplanes painted silver. This service proved very popular.

One remarkable event of 1927 was on May 29 when Charles Lindbergh flew into

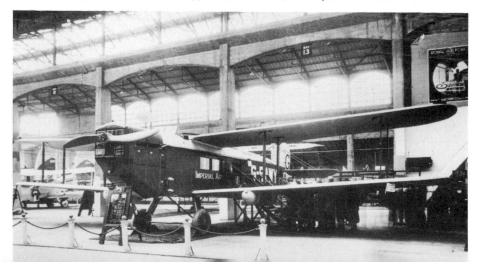

Top *Aerial view of Croydon in 1921. Plough Lane runs from the top right-hand corner across to the left.* Above *Aerial view of Croydon in 1928. The new airport is in the foreground. In the centre can be seen the half-demolished old aerodrome with Plough Lane running through it.* Below *Bristol Type 62, G-EAWY, at Croydon in 1922.*

Above left *Armstrong Whitworth Argosy of Imperial Airways at Croydon.* **Left** *Vickers Vulcan, G-EBLB, at Croydon 1925-1928. The Vulcan could carry six to eight passengers.* **Bottom left** *Vickers Vanguard, G-EBCP, at Croydon in 1928. The Vanguard could carry 20 passengers and was used on the London-Paris and London-Brussels-Cologne routes.*

Above *Croydon at night—an Imperial Airways HP 42 in front of the control tower in the 1930s.*

Croydon with his *Spirit of St Louis.* To welcome him a crowd of 120,000 people had gathered at Croydon and without any doubt it was the aerodrome's most historic day. The worldwide sensation created by Lindbergh's flight was greater than anything that had gone before and is still remembered to this day. He was the first man to have flown the Atlantic solo. At 22.22 hours, local time, Lindbergh landed at Le Bourget Airport, France, having covered 3,610 miles in 33 hours 30½ minutes. He then flew on in his 230 hp Ryan monoplane via Brussels to Croydon. Lindbergh was followed by two of his countrymen on August 28 when Schlee and Brock landed at Croydon during their round-the-world flight.

January 1928 saw the buildings completed and the new airport buildings (later officially opened by Lady Hoare on May 2) come into use. The design of the buildings attained worldwide acclaim. Many cities, notably Moscow, copied the control tower. By the end of April, all the old buildings, including the control tower, had been demolished.

On September 18 1928, Croydon witnessed a new form of flight when Señor Don Juan de la Cierva flew his autogiro from the airport to Paris. Tragically, he was killed in an airliner crash at Croydon on December 9 1936.

One interesting event that took place was the Swedish experiment of the travelling post office between Stockholm and Croydon which ended after some five or six flights.

By 1929 Croydon was the busiest airport in Europe. Not only the largest companies were making money but also many of the small firms. Surrey Flying Services did very well offering 10/- flights around the Croydon area. It also worked from its base at Croydon a blue Avro on Shoebury Common. At Croydon itself, Imperial Airways started 'tea flights' over London at £2-02s and these went on for three years.

The 20th anniversary of the first-ever cross-Channel flight was celebrated on July 27 1929 by M. Louis Blériot who flew from France to Dover and was subsequently brought to Croydon where he was received by the Air Minister, Lord Thomson of Cardington and other officials. Three days later a three-engined ANT-9 monoplane, piloted by M. Grommoff and with ten passengers flew into Croydon. This must have claim as being the first Russian aircraft at Croydon. It was making a tour of the capitals of Europe.

To bring 1929 to a close, Francis Chichester flew out from Croydon to Australia in his Gipsy Moth, a name that was to become famous years later.

Inside view of Croydon control tower in the mid-1930s.

Throughout the 1930s Croydon became the place where many famous fliers left on record-breaking and pioneering flights. History was made at Croydon by many people. The flier who captured the imagination of everyone was the Yorkshire-born Amy Johnson who took off from Croydon on her famous flight to Darwin, Australia in 1930. Amy was the first woman to fly solo from Britain to Australia. She had flown 9,960 miles since leaving Croydon 19½ days earlier in her de Havilland DH 60 Gipsy Moth *G-AAAH*. Other famous names linked with Croydon are Jim Mollison, Charles Kingsford-Smith, Bert Hinkler and Jean Batten.

The 1930s were the golden years for

Croydon and the airport continued to grow over the next few years with passengers and goods arriving from all over the world. Records were being broken almost every year and in November 1937, A.E. Clouston (later Wing Commander Clouston) broke the London to Cape Town record which had previously been held by Amy Johnson. Towards the latter part of 1937 Air Dispatch received a Government contract for Army flying and by the following year was operating 23 aircraft. These were used mostly on night flying.

On May 11 1937, the day before the Coronation of King George VI, Hermann Goering arrived uninvited at Croydon Airport in a Junkers Ju 52. He was even then a much-hated figure and there was a

An aircraft renowned for its safety and economy, the tri-engine Junkers Ju 52, nicknamed 'Aunt Ju', was put into Lufthansa service in 1933. This photograph shows a Ju 52 standing in front of the control tower at Croydon just before the outbreak of war.

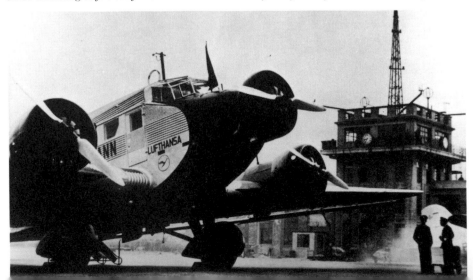

public outcry against him attending the coronation. The Foreign Office warned him off and after spending the night at the German Embassy with the Ambassador, Herr Von Ribbentrop, he was driven back to Croydon. His visit lasted just 12 hours.

There was no doubt that Hitler was building his air power under the guise of civil aviation and towards the end of the 1930s the mechanical and administrative staffs of Lufthansa quadrupled. The Germans also flew with extra crews and would land and take off from the airport in total darkness. This was obviously done to perfect their night flying. Even in bad weather they could find their way to Croydon.

What was happening to Lufthansa meant only one thing—preparation for war. It was observed during 1938 that whenever the weather conditions gave an excuse, the German airliners would fly over the RAF airfields of Biggin Hill and Kenley.

During the Munich crisis of 1938 the sole defence of Croydon consisted of one gunner subaltern, one gun and six men. A few trenches were dug between the main building and the hotel but for what purpose, no one knew. It must have given the Germans great confidence to go back and report on the pathetic defences.

After the Munich crisis the Lufthansa staff felt free to continue as before. The

Below *Fokker FXII, G-ADZK, of Crilly Airways at Croydon in 1936.* **Bottom** *Prewar Croydon.*

Germans did not have a hangar at Croydon—they left their aircraft outside and used workshops in other hangars. The atmosphere was friendly right up to the departure of the last Lufthansa flight which was a Ju 52, *D-AXOS* on August 31, 1939. Just before war was declared the Imperial Airways fleet was dispersed to Whitchurch and Exeter.

There was great activity as Croydon prepared for war and made the change-over from a civilian to a military aerodrome. All the aircraft had been flown out of Croydon on Friday September 1 and the following morning No 615 (County of Surrey) Auxiliary Squadron flew in with its Gloster Gladiators under the command of Squadron Leader A.V. Harvey. The dispersal point was near the waste ground north of Roundshaw Recreation Ground and the aircraft were all neatly lined up facing due north. That same morning they were joined by the Hurricanes of No 3 Squadron from Biggin Hill who took over the two southern hangars previously used by Sabena, Air France and KLM. No 17 Squadron with its Hurricanes, coded *YB*, also arrived before the end of the day and the air around Croydon seemed filled with fighters.

No 3 Squadron, under the command of Squadron Leader H.H. Chapman, flew its first operational scramble of the war the day after war was declared. Before the end of the month, No 17 Squadron had moved to Debden. On October 10, No 145 re-formed at Croydon as a day and night fighter squadron. This unit, under the command of Squadron Leader J.D. Miller, was equipped with Bristol Blenheim 1fs, coded SO.

Next on the scene came No 607 (County of Durham) Squadron. This was under the command of Squadron Leader L.E. Smith and equipped with Gladiator I aircraft, coded *AF*. Two days later they departed with No 615 for Merville, France as part of the air component of the British Expeditionary Force.

December 1939 saw No 3 Squadron move to Hawkinge, near Folkestone and it was replaced by the newly formed 92 Squadron from Tangmere. This unit was equipped with Bristol Blenheim 1F fighters but in March began to re-equip with Spitfire Mk Is. That same month 145 Squadron began to convert to Hurricane Mk Is and on becoming operational with them it moved to Filton, near Bristol, in May 1940. By May, 92 Squadron was also operational and it moved to Northolt. During its period at Croydon, No 92 provided a detachment at Gatwick. Following the squadron's withdrawal from France on May 18, No 501 re-assembled at Croydon on May 21. The following day the tattered remnants of 607 arrived following its evacuation from France three days earlier. The unit had lost most of its aircraft and after a few days at Croydon it moved to Usworth to remuster and re-equip with Hurricane Is. In early July 501 Squadron moved to Middle Wallop after replacing its aircraft and personnel.

The wheel had come full circle. The aerodrome which had been conceived in war and became the best known civil aerodrome was now reverting to its original role.

During June and July the Canadians of No 1 Royal Canadian Air Force Squadron began to arrive and they were duly allotted a hangar. It was at Croydon that they joined up with their Hurricanes which had been brought over from Canada. They were two-blade types and as soon as they arrived in England they were modified to three-bladers. The Canadians were housed next to No 111 Squadron which had arrived from North Weald just before them in June. This unit had been heavily engaged in patrols over France. It was at Croydon to recover its strength. After a few nights under field conditions the sleeping quarters were changed to buildings outside the airfield and many Canadians ate in Croydon tearooms from their own resources. Excellent teas were still available as rationing was not yet in full effect.

It was a beautiful summer evening at approximately seven pm on Thursday August 15 when a group of Canadians saw a number of twin-engined aircraft. In blissful ignorance they thought nothing of it until an erk from 111 Squadron shouted: 'They're bloody Jerries'. It still meant little to the Canadians, until the aircraft lost altitude and they saw the bombs fall away. Edward Currote dived for cover under a loaded gasoline tender that was parked outside the hangar. He recalls: 'In my stupidity after seeing the first bombs hit I felt for the safety of steel over my head. Belly crouched under the loaded tanker I watched the bombing and a number of direct hits on various buildings. It was soon over. It took several minutes and remarks from others to realise that even a bomb fragment could have blown us past the pearly gates . . . Fortunately or unfortunately the officers' mess had been hit and good liquor was lying about and could be had without 'chits'. After several swigs my courage came back. Even in war, Heaven knows how to recompense a poor airman.'

That was the Canadians' baptism by bombing. The raid had lasted between five and ten minutes. Up to this point of the war, Croydon had experienced little to suggest that it was within the battle-ground. The attack came from Erprobungsgruppe 210, a special unit formed for attacks on the British Isles and was led by their Swiss-born Commander, Hauptmann Walter Rubensdörffer. At 6.30 pm No 111 Squadron scrambled nine Hurricanes with orders to orbit the base. Approximately 30 minutes later the Germans appeared on the scene and Rubensdörffer dropped the first bombs on the aerodrome. Before they had a chance to line up their targets the Hurricanes were amongst them in an attempt to interrupt the enemy's bombing runs. The enemy was taken off balance and many of the bombs fell wide around the aerodrome, causing casualties among the civilian population.

The attackers broke away and as Rubensdörffer's Bf 110 sped south-east he was followed by RAF fighters and shot down in flames near Bletchinglye Farm, Rothersfield, Sussex. Rubensdörffer and his gunner, Obergefreiter Kretzer were both killed. Seven German aircraft of Gruppe 210 were shot down that day, six Bf 110s and one Bf 109. It was a high price to pay for a mistake for the target should have been Kenley.

In the space of ten minutes Croydon had received considerable damage. The armoury had taken a direct hit and the airfield resembled a lunar landscape with large potholes. 'C' hangar used by Rollason Aircraft Services was hit by incendiary bombs and all the training aircraft stored inside were destroyed. Rollason factory and workshop were badly hit and this caused many civilian casualties. 'D' hangar received blast damage and was raked by cannon fire. 'A' hangar escaped with only a few broken windows. The officers' mess was reduced to a heap of rubble from the blast which was strong enough to damage a concrete block-house nearby. Six airmen died in the attack, five from 111 Squadron and one from Station Headquarters. Sixty-two civilians were killed. Four 111 Squadron

airmen, one officer from No 1 (RCAF) Squadron, two civilian telephone operators and 185 civilians were injured.

Following the attack, No 111 Squadron was diverted to Hawkinge while repairs to the airfield were carried out. Within two days the craters had been filled in and Croydon was again operational. On Sunday August 18 the airfield was again under attack. High-level raiders had entered the area and 111 Squadron was scrambled with orders to orbit Kenley at 3,000 ft. Croydon lay undefended and was an easy target for the high-flying Dorniers. Within the space of five minutes, 11 high explosive and 8 delayed-action bombs fell onto the airfield and around the boundary. There were no service casualties arising from the raid.

The dust had only just settled when on Monday, August 19, 18 Hurricanes of No 85 Squadron arrived from Debden, led by their CO, Squadron Leader Peter Townsend. This unit came to replace 111 Squadron, which then moved to Debden. His Royal Highness the Duke of Kent visited Croydon on August 25. No 85 Squadron had been scrambled and on its return the members of the squadron were introduced to the Duke of Kent by Peter Townsend.

New recruits were posted in almost daily and life continued at a very hectic pace. No 1 (RCAF) Squadron was now considered fully operational and in mid-August moved to Northolt. At the end of August, Croydon was again attacked with bombs and strafing by machine-guns but the only injury reported was to a soldier of the Royal Artillery employed on aerodrome defence.

On September 2 1940, No 85 Squadron was transferred to Debden. Of the 18 pilots who had arrived with the squadron 13 days earlier, 14 had been shot down, three had been killed and five wounded. No 111 Squadron returned to Croydon to replace 85 Squadron, and it was still well below strength. No 111 Squadron had sustained further losses whilst at Debden and Martlesham Heath. During the early part of September, No 72 Squadron arrived and it operated alongside 111 Squadron. Battle scarred and weary, 111 Squadron moved its seven remaining Hurricanes to Drem in Scotland on September 7 in exchange with No 605 'County of Warwick' Squadron. Led by Squadron Leader W.M. Churchill the squadron was soon in a battle which reached its peak on September 15. Throughout the month

Above *Percival Proctor III G-AHMV (ex-RAF LZ789), photographed at Croydon on July 20 1950.*

Left *Croydon control tower as at July 1981.*

every available aircraft remained airborne. The station was again bombed twice. It also had a visit from a lone German raider on October 15 and again on October 19 and 23.

During November, No 605 began to re-equip with Hurricane Mk IIAs. The unit commenced working-up exercises with the new machines. By February 1941 they were operational and that same month moved to Martlesham Heath. They were replaced by the Hurricane IIAs of No 17 Squadron. Their stay was again brief and in March they too flew north to Martlesham Heath. The following month the Hurricanes of No 1 Squadron arrived. Like its predecessors, the squadron was actively engaged on *Rhubarb* and *Circus* operations.

Changes were now in the wind as the RAF prepared for a fighter offensive which would bring terror and destruction to returning German bomber crews. Because of these changes airfields nearer the Channel were needed and Croydon began to drop out of the limelight as a front line station. No 1 Squadron moved to Redhill in May 1941 and the station fell into the backwaters, being used only as a resting base for squadrons engaged on offensive sweeps.

On August 13 1941, No 414 (RCAF) formed as an Army co-operation unit at Croydon. This was the RCAF's 12th squadron formed overseas. Unit code letters were *RU* and it was equipped with Westland Lysander Mk IIIs and Curtiss Tomahawk Mk Is and IIs. In June 1942 the unit re-equipped with North American Mustang Mk Is and their first mission was flown on June 30 1942 when three Mustangs were on defensive patrol over the south coast. The first victory came on August 19 1942 while on a tactical reconnaissance during a Dieppe raid. Flying Officer H.H. Hills in *AG470 RU-M*, was attacked by three Fw 190s and during the ensuing battle destroyed one of them. From the mission two aircraft were lost but both pilots were saved.

During this period the station had housed two Polish squadrons, No 302 'Poznan' and No 317 'Wilno'. Both units had arrived in June 1942 and were equipped with Spitfire VBs. They carried out many offensive operations. July saw the departure of the Poles, No 302 moved to Heston and No 31 / to Northolt.

The status of the station at June 6 1944 was No 287 Squadron which had arrived in mid-November 1941 with Oxfords and Hurricanes, No 116 Squadron with a few Oxfords and Ansons and No 1 Aircraft Delivery Flight which had arrived in 1942 with Dominies. During the first week of July 1944, Nos 116 and 287 Squadrons moved out. No 1 Aircraft Delivery Flight remained for a few more months.

On September 5 1944, No 147 Squadron re-formed at Croydon with an establishment of Dakotas and later that year RAF Transport Command started scheduled services with a fleet of Dakotas to liberate Allied-occupied Europe, on November 13 1944. The first civil air service to operate since the war was inaugurated by Railway Air Services between London and Belfast via Liverpool. At the end of the war other companies, which included Scottish Airways, Jersey Airways and Morton Air Services, moved into Croydon.

By September 23 1945, No 110 Wing had carried its 100,000th passenger and this unit continued throughout the winter months. During early February 1946 responsibility for certain air services was transferred from No 110 Wing to British European Airways, which was operating out of Northolt. By the end of the month the wing had disbanded.

During this period a detachment of No 271 Squadron had arrived on April 2 1945, with a few Dakotas, but after only five days they moved out. On October 9 1945 the Dakotas of No 147 Squadron were joined by a detachment of ten Dakotas of No 435 (RCAF) Squadron from Down Ampney. The Canadians remained until March 16 1946. No 147 Squadron disbanded at Croydon six months later. The airport then began to get back into civil flying but its days as a major international airport were now numbered. The new breed of aircraft rendered the runways too short and there was no room for expansion. Consequently, Heathrow was officially designated London Airport on March 25 1946. The following year British European Airways departed for Gatwick and Croydon was left with independent companies operating scheduled charter services, and some flying clubs. A Government report in the mid-1950s sealed its fate and Croydon closed to flying. Most of the companies moved to Gatwick and the clubs to Biggin Hill.

Today, the club house and playing fields are used by the John Fisher School. The site of Croydon Aerodrome, where air transport began, is now the Roundshaw Estate. To retain the last link some of the roads have been given suitable aviation names. The terminal building and control tower remain, having been converted into offices. These buildings seem sure of continued survival as they have been added to the Department of the Environment's list of buildings of architectural or historic interest. The Aerodrome Hotel survives and is still in use as a hotel. The former National Aircraft Factory burned down in the 1960s. The flight shed has also gone.

On December 7 1978, a public meeting was held in the Aerodrome Hotel to discuss the formation of the Croydon Airport Society. It was duly formed and regular newsletters are sent out to members. The aim of the society is to keep alive memories of the old airfield and to see the setting up of a permanent civil aviation museum on the site.

Dagenham, Essex

177/TQ495825. Just south of Dagenham between the River Thames and the A13

A piece of ground on the north bank of the River Thames, east of Dagenham Dock, was chosen in 1909 as a landing ground. It was enclosed on all four sides by water but the surrounding land was flat and a private road afforded good access to the site. Situated near Dagenham Railway Station, this small site was opened on February 5 1909 by the Aeronautical Society of Great Britain (later to become the Royal Aeronautical Society). Four sheds and a club house were erected on this half-mile-square plot which became known as the Dagenham Experimental Ground.

During the summer of 1909 many aeroplanes were housed at Dagenham, these included the Baden-Powell Quadruplane which was fitted with a 50 hp Antoinette engine and a 1-gallon capacity fuel tank. A far cry from the 44,260 Imperial gallons of the Jumbo Jet of today. Others that were at Dagenham were the Saul Quadruplane No 1, which was tested by Frederick Handley Page, and a large Voisin biplane, which was owned by Mr C.A. Moreing, who also owned an 105 ft long dirigible balloon.

However, despite plenty of enthusiasm, the site closed down in early 1910 and no further flying took place. The members departed for pastures new. Some went to Brooklands, others to the Royal Aero Club ground at Shellbeach. The sheds were sold to Handley Page at a bargain price and they were dismantled and taken to the Barking works.

Today, the site forms part of the Ford Motor Company's plant. The firm has occupied the site since 1925.

Denham, Buckinghamshire

176/TQ030886. South-west of Rickmansworth

Situated between the A412 and A413 roads, this small site was first used during the latter part of the First World War. From September 1917 to January 1918 it housed Nos 5 and 6 Schools of Military Aeronautics. The schools gave two months' ground instruction for pilots and observers before going on to flying training. Some of the subjects taught were aero engines, rigging, armament, photography and map reading. The pupils passed out as 2nd Lieutenants and were then passed to a Training Depot Station. The airfield, which was surrounded by woods, was never developed and was abandoned after the departure of the schools. In August 1929 James Martin came to Denham with a mission to build aeroplanes. Its facilities were meagre in the extreme; no water, no main roads and the building consisted of a solitary shed of breeze and wooden construction, accompanied by three rather disreputable Army-type wooden huts. The company became Martin-Baker and from the modest beginning grew a factory plant of over 130,000 sq ft of floor area. Flight testing and research were done from Chalgrove, Oxfordshire.

After the start of the Second World War the airfield was re-activated and two Bellman and three Blister hangars were erected. The runways remained grass and were north–south 3,150 ft, north-east–south-west 2,580 ft, east–west 4,150 ft and north-west–south-east 2,400 ft. From November 18 1941 to July 9 1945 Denham was used as a Relief Landing Ground for

Aircraft sheds at Denham.

Ex-RAF Chipmunk now owned by Peter Tory of the Daily Mirror *and housed at Denham.*

the Tiger Moths of No 21 Elementary Flying Training School at Booker.

After the war the airfield continued to be used by light aircraft. In 1952 Air Schools Limited began to operate at Denham and Elstree. The fleet consisted of nine Chipmunks and four Auster Alphas. Denham is still in use today for light civil aircraft.

Detling, Kent

178/TQ812595. South-east of Maidstone off the A249

Detling, high on the North Downs began life in 1915 when selected as a flying field for home defence. It was used by an RNAS flight of three Curtiss aircraft until the flight developed into No 3 Aeroplane Wing and moved to Manston in May 1916. London defence duties were then taken over by the Royal Flying Club and the airfield was transferred to RFC control. The newly formed No 50 Squadron then detached a flight of its BE 2cs to Detling and these aircraft stayed there until February 8 1918, when they moved to Bekesbourne to rejoin the parent unit, which eventually disbanded there in June 1919. Their place was taken by No 143 Squadron which arrived in March 1918 and stayed until disbanding at Detling on October 31 1919. The station was then reduced to Care and Maintenance, eventually reverting to agriculture.

As the RAF began its expansion programmes in the 1930s, Detling was surveyed and found suitable to be included in the scheme, and rebuilding work began. No 500 (County of Kent) Auxiliary Squadron moved in from Manston on September 28 1938. The station had been reopened and its headquarters formed in No 16 Group, Coastal Command, a few weeks previously. No 500 Squadron was equipped with Hawker Hinds and on November 7 1938 became a general-reconnaissance unit equipped with Avro Ansons. The last of the peacetime Empire Air Days took place at Detling on May 20 1939.

At the outbreak of war in 1939 the station was ready and within a few hours of the start of hostilities 500 Squadron was flying anti-submarine patrols and surprised an enemy submarine lying on the surface in the Channel.

The lumbering Ansons of 500 Squadron were not without teeth. On several occasions they shot down attacking fighters. On January 1 1940, for instance, three Ansons were jumped by nine Me 109s over the Channel. 500 Squadron shot down two of them without loss.

On May 22 the Lysanders of No 4 Squadron arrived from France but after only two days they moved to Hawkinge. The station was not without dramatic incident. On May 30 1940 an Anson of 500 Squadron returned to Detling having developed engine trouble on its way to an attack on the enemy coast. On reaching the airfield the pilot attempted a wheels-up landing with the crippled engine now blazing furiously. A heavy landing was effected but the machine caught fire, and an explosion from the full bomb load was imminent. However, Corporal Daphne Pearson of the WAAF, who worked as an orderly in the medical section, fought her way to the edge of the blaze and dragged the injured pilot clear, she then shielded him with her body as the wreckage blew up. For her gallantry she was commissioned in June 1940 and awarded the Empire Gallantry Medal the following August. (The medal was exchanged for the new George Cross in November 1941.)

During this period 235 Squadron from Bircham Newton took part in many

engagements over the Channel and from May 26 to June 24 1940 used Detling as an advance base.

By the start of the Battle of Britain the station was occupied by 500 Squadron with Ansons, 53 Squadron with Blenheims and 801 Squadron, Fleet Air Arm, with Skuas and Rocs.

The first air raid on Detling took place at 1600 hours on August 13 1940 when the Stukas of Luftflotte 2 attacked the station. The flying field was extensively damaged by the ensuing attack, all the hangars were set on fire, more than 20 aircraft were destroyed and living accommodation and administrative buildings severely damaged. The Station Commander, Group Captain Davis, was killed when the operations room, in which he was assisting, received a direct hit.

The second air attack on the station was on August 31 1940, when a mixed force of Me 109s and 110s strafed the field with cannon and machine-gun fire. Again the damage was considerable, petrol and oil stores being set alight and the electricity supply destroyed.

Two days later the Luftwaffe was back and in a high-level attack by Do 17s showered the airfield with more than a hundred HE bombs, causing more devastation. This was the last major attack suffered by Detling. Repairs and renovations were put in hand and rebuilding work was still in progress well into 1941.

No 500 Squadron re-equipped with Blenheims during the early part of April 1941 only to exchange them a few weeks later for Hudsons. The squadron moved to Bircham Newton on May 30 1941.

Sole surviving Bellman hangar at Detling (August 1979).

No 2368 Squadron RAF Regiment was stationed at Detling. The members of the squadron did guard duty at Buckingham Palace for two weeks in April 1942.

Detling was transferred to Fighter Command in mid-1942 and was then used for brief periods by Fighter Squadrons of 11 Group. No 26 Squadron visited three times during 1943, Nos 132, 184 and the Polish 318, 567 and 602 Squadrons all arrived in 1943. The Detling Spitfire Wing was formed on May 19 1944, comprising Nos 80, 229 and 274 Squadrons. The Spitfires of the Detling Wing flew on *Rhubarbs* over occupied France and also escorted bomber missions. The wing also gave valuable support to the Allied invasion of Normandy. The wing stayed until June 22 1944, when Nos 80 and 274 Squadrons moved to Merston and 229 to Tangmere.

In 1944 the airfield had one Bellman, one Bessoneau and 14 Blister hangars. The three runways had remained grass, the north–south was 2,700 ft, the east–west 2,700 ft and the north-east–south-west 4,200 ft.

No 504 Squadron arrived on July 11 1944 for the purpose of supporting the Arnhem Parachute Brigade landings. They moved to Manston on August 13 1944. Other squadrons to use Detling were Nos 1, 118, 124, 132, 165 and 602 Squadrons. The last to leave were the Spitfires of No 165 Squadron which moved to Bentwaters on December 16,

1944. The station was then reduced to a Care and Maintenance status by January 1, 1945.

For the remainder of the war the station did not receive any more flying units and after the war 615 Gliding School moved in and supplied instruction to ATC cadet squadrons. The school was then transferred to Kenley. Civil gliders of the Kent Gliding Club set up a temporary base at Detling until moved to Challock.

The airfield then closed and Detling was eventually sold back to its original landowners from whom several hundred acres were purchased by Kent County Council. Part of the old aerodrome is now used as a permanent showground for the Kent County Agricultural Show—a major event in the county calendar. A few of the old buildings still remain. Some of the perimeter track is still visible and some defence pillboxes and air raid shelters remain. The rest have passed into history.

Eastchurch, Kent

178/TQ985695. On the Isle of Sheppey just south of the A250 at Eastchurch

Towards the end of 1909, Frank McClean purchased a large tract of land on the south side of Stanford Hill near Eastchurch and leased it to the Aero Club at Leysdown for a shilling per annum. The marshy landing ground at Leysdown was proving to be unpopular and both the Aero Club and the firm of Short Brothers began moving to the new flying ground at Eastchurch.

The first machine to land at Eastchurch was a Short (Wright), piloted by the Hon C.S. Rolls, on November 20 1909. On the same day a similar machine (Short No 1), belonging to Mr McClean, was brought there by road from Leysdown, where it had unfortunately crashed a fortnight before. By the end of the year, Messrs Rolls and McClean were making full use of Eastchurch, while Captain Dunne and Professor A.K. Huntington were beginning experiments with machines designed to be inherently stable.

In February 1910, the Aero Club of the United Kingdom became 'Royal'. On March 1 Moore-Brabazon flew 18¾ miles, and during the same month Cecil Grace and Mr Rolls flew from Shellness to Eastchurch, over Queenborough, returning to Eastchurch without landing. They then circled over Shellness, finally landing at Eastchurch. On Good Friday Rolls also made a lengthy flight under bad conditions.

By the end of April 1910, the move to Eastchurch was practically complete, and the Short brothers had much improved their accommodation and the facilities for the manufacture and repair of machines.

The summer of 1910 was noted for the increased interest taken in aviation all over the country. At Eastchurch by September there were 18 sheds occupied by members, including Messrs McClean, C. Grace, Howard Wright, Alec Ogilvie, Batchelor, Colmore, Jezzi, George, Moore-Brabazon and W.L. Travers and the Hon Maurice Egerton and Professor A.K. Huntington. McClean and Grace were most prominent during October and November, and it was generally thought that one or the other would win the de Forest prize. The Hon C.S. Rolls had unfortunately been killed while flying at Bournemouth in July. He had previously flown from Dover to Calais and back on a Wright biplane in June.

About this time, Mr T.O.M. Sopwith, who had come to the front during the summer, arrived at Eastchurch, and on December 18 1910, on a Howard Wright biplane (ENV engine), he flew in 3½ hours to Thirlemont, in Belgium —a distance of 177½ miles—thus winning Baron de Forest's prize of £4,000 for the longest flight from England into the Continent of Europe.

During 1910 the Admiralty watched these experiments with increasing interest, and when in February 1911, McClean offered the loan of aeroplanes for the purpose of instructing naval officers in aviation, it accepted the public spirited offer.

The Admiralty then asked for volunteers from officers of the Fleet to undergo a course of flying instruction at Eastchurch. This resulted in over 200 being submitted, which shows the extent to which aviation interested naval officers even at this early period. Four officers were selected to undergo the first course, which began on March 2 1911. Their names and ranks held at the time were Lieutenant G.R. Samson, R. Gregory and A.M. Longmore, RN, and Captain E.L. Gerrard RNLI.

Another member of the Aero Club, Mr G.B. Cockburn, gave up his time for a year entirely free of cost to the Admiralty, to instruct these officers in the art of flying. The flying instructor was to have been Cecil Grace, but unfortunately in December 1910, he lost his life in the

English Channel whilst returning from France to make another attempt for the de Forest prize. Cockburn thereupon undertook the actual flying training of the first four officers himself. The initial course was successfully carried out in six weeks with only two crashes, neither of them very serious.

In addition to flying instructions, these officers underwent a course of technical training at Messrs Short Brothers' works at Eastchurch, and also visited the principal French aeroplane factories and the French Military aeroplane trials of 1911 held at Reims with a view to studying foreign developments.

The senior naval officer at Sheerness, Captain Godfrey Paine, took great interest in the flying instruction, and Eastchurch soon afterwards became the recognised centre for the flying training of naval officers.

To Cockburn, to whom is due the credit of carrying out the training arrangements with the Admiralty, a few words must be given. He was the only British aviator at the first flying meeting in the world, that at Reims in 1909. After completing the first course of instruction at Eastchurch, at the end of April 1911, he went to Larkhill, on Salisbury Plain, to continue his flying experiments, and there he co-operated quite unofficially with No 2 Company, Air Battalion, RE, which had been formed on April 1 of that year, under the command of Captain Fulton, RFA, who later organised the Aeronautical Inspection Department, RFC. Cockburn

was afterwards continuously at work on Salisbury Plain for about four years and later, as a civilian, during the 1914-18 war, he gave his help first in the AID and afterwards in the investigation of accidents for the Royal Flying Corps and Royal Air Force.

The original agreement between McClean and the Admiralty was that two machines should be lent on which the naval pilots should be taught. One of these two machines, however, was being flown by Cecil Grace when he disappeared in the Channel, so another was built in its place and an old one known as 'The Dud' was added. The first three machines therefore were: Short No 26 (McC No 3) Farman type with a 50 hp Gnome, familiarly known as 'The Dud'; Short No 28 (McC No 5) Farman type, first fitted with a 60 hp Green, and later with a 50 hp Gnome; Short No 34 (McC No 6) Farman type with a 50 hp Gnome. The latter two were afterwards purchased by the Admiralty and were known as RN No 28 and RN No 34 respectively.

In addition to the above, the following four machines belonging to McClean were flown by naval pilots during 1911 and early 1912: *1* Bleriot monoplane (McC No 9) with a 50 hp Gnome, known as 'The Birdling', it was wrecked; *2* Short No 39 (McC No 10) fitted with two 50 hp Gnomes, known as 'The Triple Twin',

Short S 27 pilot—Frank McClean at Eastchurch, October 29 1911.

SHORT TANDEM TWIN BIPLANE, 1911

and afterwards purchased by the Admiralty. This was the first twin-engined machine that ever flew. It was a biplane with pilot and passenger in a nacelle on the lower plane. In front was a 50 hp Gnome, driving by chains, two tractor screws. Behind was a separate unit consisting of another Gnome and airscrew rotating inside with four-boom tail, which carried a triple rudder with elevator and stabilising plane above. In front was a second elevator coupled to the rear one. The aircraft first flew in September 1911; *3* Short No 27 (McC No 11) fitted with two 50 hp Gnomes, called the 'Tandem Twin', it was wrecked. This was converted from a single-engine pusher by simply adding a second power unit in front, placing the pilot and passenger side by side between the planes and adding wing extensions. She was essentially unstable in every direction and incapable of flying a level course. The rear airscrew was 10 in behind the pilot's head, and his feet were in close proximity to the front engine carburettor. She was familiarly called the 'Vacuum Cleaner'; *4* Short No 36 (McC No 12), 70 hp Gnome, which was eventually returned to McClean.

Among the early naval machines of 1911 was a monoplane on Bleriot lines, a tractor with two engines in tandem under a bonnet 16 ft long, known as 'The Field Kitchen', and a twin-engine monoplane called the 'Double Dirty', after which the Admiralty went in for several tractors similar to Short No 36.

During this year the Short brothers also produced a machine which was partly amphibian, in that it could get off or alight on land, and alight on water, but could not get off water. The machine was an ordinary standard biplane of that day with pusher airscrew, front elevator and tailplane on outriggers. The flotation gear consisted of three rubber fabric bags (as used for balloon construction) in which were embodied a wooden keel-piece. One float was attached to each main skid and one float supported the tail on the water. The bags were merely inflated with air and weighed about 8 lb each. This test proved the strength of such bags, and led to the adoption of air bags as flotation gear for ship aeroplanes used during the 1914-18 war.

During the latter part of 1911, facilities were given at Eastchurch for the London Balloon Company, RE, to learn aviation, and two machines, Short pushers of Farman type with 70 hp Gnome engines were put at their disposal by Lieutenant Samson. Instruction in flying was chiefly given by Mr Travers, and in Care and Maintenance by Horace Short.

Unfortunately, this arrangement did not meet with the approval of the War Office, which, in a letter dated February 5 1912, stated that: 'It has been decided that the personnel of the London Balloon Company should not be trained in aeroplane work'. The following four officers, however, took advantage of this abortive effort: S.P. Cockerell, who had already obtained his Aero Club Certificate No 132; H.D. Cutler, No 189; V.A. Barrington-Kennet, No 190; and C.W. Meredith, No 193. They all qualified at Eastchurch on March 5, 1912.

Mr Claude Grahame-White (Great Britain) having won the Gordon-Bennet Aviation Cup at New York the previous year, the third annual contest for the cup took place at Eastchurch on July 1 1911, under the control of the Royal Aero Club. There were originally 12 entries, three each from Great Britain, France, USA and Austria, but all the Austrians and two of the Americans withdrew. The competitors on the day of the race were: Great Britain—Mr Alec Ogilvie on a 'Baby' Wright, Mr D. Graham Gilmour on a Bristol, Mr Gustave Hamel on a Bleriot; France—M A. Leblanc on a Bleriot, and M Chevalier and M de Nieuport on Nieuports; USA—Mr C.T. Weyman on a Nieuport.

Unfortunately, just before the contest, Mr Hamel, while giving an exhibition flight, crashed, and his entry was therefore deleted. The result was: 1st, Weyman (25 laps or 94 miles), 71 mins 36.1 secs, 78.77 mph; 2nd Leblanc, 73 mins 40 secs, 76.86 mph; 3rd Nieuport, 74 mins 37.2 secs, 75.62 mph. Mr Ogilvie, who was the only other pilot to finish, took 109 mins 19.2 secs to complete the 25 laps, his speed being 51.88 mph.

During the year Mr H.E. Perrin, the Secretary of the Royal Aero Club, was tireless in his efforts to popularise East church as a flying centre in connection with club competition.

In October 1911, Lieutenant Samson, who remained at Eastchurch after his course, and was in fact its first Commanding Officer, persuaded the Admiralty to buy two training machines and send 12 naval ratings to Eastchurch as the basis of a naval flying school. This was agreed to by the Admiralty, with the result that on December 25 1911, an agreement was reached between the Royal Aero Club, the brothers Short and Mr F.K. McClean for the Admiralty to rent the aerodrome at £150 a year with a proviso that the Admiralty could, if it so desired, purchase the ground at the rate of £16 per acre as from December 25, 1918.

Actually the aerodrome was taken over under the Defence of the Realm Act early in the war and was purchased by the Air Ministry in December 1918. It is interesting to note that in the agreement it was stipulated that the maximum number of machines in use at any one time was not to exceed ten, without the sanction of the Royal Aero Club. Training in flying was thus an integral part of the Navy's work in 1911.

Towards the end of 1911, Messrs Short Bros built various experimental floats at Eastchurch for use on their aeroplanes. A 'pusher' biplane thus fitted was erected at Shellness, beyond the aerodrome at Leysdown, and from there Lieutenant A.M. Longmore, RN (later Air Commodore, RAF), flew on several occasions to Sheerness Harbour and alighted on the water, afterwards flying back to Shellness. On more than one occasion he moored his machine within a few yards of HMS *Actaeon*, went on board, and returned afterwards with his machine.

The first public announcement of anything to do with fleet operations was made on January 12 1912, when the newspapers announced that Lieutenant C.R. Samson had flown, during the preceding month, from Eastchurch to Sheerness. There he had had his machine conveyed to the deck of HMS *Africa*, whence he succeeded in flying from a staging erected over her bows while the ship was at anchor.

This was the first time an aeroplane had flown off a British ship, but a similar feat had already been performed by Eugene Ely on a Curtiss biplane from an American warship in San Francisco harbour.

The machine used by Lieutenant Samson on this occasion was a Short 'pusher' biplane, known as the S.38, fitted, in addition to wheels, with torpedo-shaped floats, one alongside each wheel skid and one under the tail. This was in order to insure against loss in the event of a forced descent over water, a system devised and tested previously at Eastchurch. The machine was able to start from land or from a launching platform and alight on the water, but it was not able to get off the water again afterwards.

During the naval manoeuvres in May 1912, Commander Samson (as he had then become) and Lieutenant L'Estrange Malone both flew the same machine off HMS *Hibernia* at Weymouth, when the ship was steaming at 10½ knots. As the ship was under way at the time, this was a marked advance in the naval experiments being carried out with amphibian aircraft. These were in fact the first flights ever made from a moving ship.

During this period, the Short brothers had also developed at Eastchurch a tractor biplane on floats which was known as the S.41. This machine was flown at Weymouth by Commander Samson and Lieutenant Longmore. Lieutenant Gregory also flew the S.38 off the deck of the *Hibernia*, and both the S.38 and S.41 were carried in this ship during her voyage from Sheerness to Weymouth and back.

These two machines, both produced at Eastchurch, represented the beginning of real naval aviation and it is worthy of note that the first form of naval aviation was a flotable machine launched from the deck of a ship and not a float machine intended to get off the water.

It should also be noted that by this period, Mr Glenn Curtiss, the American aircraft designer and pilot, had already flown from the shore at San Francisco and had alighted on the deck of an American warship. This feat was not accomplished by the British until some time after the outbreak of war.

McClean was not idle during this period, and he flew a seaplane from Harty Ferry, Isle of Sheppey, to Westminster, on August 10 1912, landing in front of the Houses of Parliament, after flying under Tower Bridge.

The development of seaplanes was continued throughout 1912 and a Short biplane (having a 80 hp Gnome engine) of tractor type, with pontoon floats under the fuselage and torpedo-shaped floats on the wing tips and under the tail was built at Eastchurch, and was shown at the Aero Show at Olympia in February, 1913.

In 1913 Ogilvie also developed a Wright seaplane, while during this year McClean entered a Short tractor seaplane with a Green engine for the round-Britain race organised by the *Daily Mail,* but there was a difference of opinion between the engine and machine as to the power required, and the total distance flown was only 35 miles. Later a Short pusher seaplane with an 160 hp Gnome engine was built for him, and he flew it from Alexandria to Khartoum. This machine was purchased by the Navy at the outbreak of war.

Thereafter, development was rapid and a number of seaplanes were used during the naval manoeuvres in the North Sea in July 1913. Right up to the outbreak of war, Eastchurch was the centre of the seaplane industry and of seaplane experimental work.

For these developments, most of the credit is due to Horace Short, one of the outstanding characters not only of British aviation but of international engineering. Mr Short was working at Newcastle with the Hon Charles Parsons on turbine experiments when flying began, but when he saw that it was a practical proposition Horace Short left, at the request of his brothers, and came to the Short Brothers balloon factory at Battersea which was run by his brothers, Eustace and Oswald. Thence he and Eustace removed to Leysdown where brother Oswald afterwards joined them.

Horace Short's extensive engineering knowledge was always at the disposal of the experimenters at Leysdown, and afterwards, he and the four officers detailed by the Admiralty for flying at Eastchurch thrashed out between them many of the problems of naval aviation.

Subsequent to the first four officers to qualify, the following qualified for Aviators' Certificates on the dates stated: Engineer-Lieutenant C.R.J. Randall, RN, February 1912; Lieutenant C.J. L'Estrange Malone, RN, March 1912; Captain Godfrey Paine, RN, May 1912; Private Edmonds, RNLI, July 1912; Engineer-Lieutenant E.F. Briggs, RN, July 1912; Lieutenant J.W. Seddon, RN, September 1912; Lieutenant C.L. Courtney, RN, October 1912; Paymaster E.R. Berne, RN, October 1912; Electrician Deakin, RN, October 1912; Boatswain H.C. Bobbett, RN, October 1912; Leading Seaman Russel, RN, November 1912; Shipwright R.W. Edwards, RN, December 1912; E.R.A. Susans, RN, December 1912. Also during 1912 several officers who had learned to fly privately joined Eastchurch, amongst others were Lieutenants W. Parke and S.D.A. Grey, and Sub-Lieutenant F.E.T. Hewlett, all RN, and Captain R. Gordon, RNLI.

In March 1912, Colonel J.E.B. Seely (Under-Secretary for War) announced in the House of Commons that 30 or 40 officers would be required forthwith for the Naval Flying Wing which was about to be formed.

The Royal Flying Corps was constituted by Royal Warrant on April 13, with effect from May 13 1912. It consisted of a Naval Wing and a Military Wing, and Eastchurch was the headquarters of the former. The Royal Naval Flying School was, as we have seen, already established during the previous year. For administrative purposes the school and wing were placed under the orders of the Captain of HMS *Actaeon*, of the Nore Command.

The idea was that all pilots should graduate at the Central Flying School at Upavon, which was charged jointly on the naval and military estimates and those destined for naval work were to be detailed to join the Naval Flying School at Eastchurch for further instruction. Actually the sub-title 'Naval Wing' shortly after dropped out of use, and its place was taken by the title 'Naval Air Service', which received official recognition in June 1914, as the 'Royal Naval Air Service'.

The original scheme was for the Naval Flying School to devote its time to furthering the interest of naval flying only, but for the first two months the energies of the school, pending the establishment of the Central Flying School on June 19 1912, were given to general elementary flying. After the Joint Central Flying School was opened for instruction in August 1912, Eastchurch (up to the outbreak of war) did not therefore carry out elementary flying training, but such were the demands on training establishments during the war that it trained naval flying officers from the beginning.

During the summer of 1912 the Admiralty took up the question of wireless in aircraft and in August appointed Lieutenant R. Fotzmaurice, RN, to carry out experiments at Eastchurch and subsequently to arrange for the installation of wireless apparatus in naval aircraft. Unfortunately, this officer was often away working on airship wireless experiments and was unable to give all his time to Eastchurch.

The Hon Maurice Egerton was the first to use wireless at Eastchurch. He fitted it at his own expense to his Short biplane, and had a receiver set in his aeroplane shed during this year.

In November of that year, M Rouzet brought over from France his first engine-driven wireless set, which was fitted in a triple-tractor biplane built by Messrs Short Brothers at Eastchurch, and transmitted signals up to 30 miles.

About the same time the design of efficient bomb-dropping gear, together with the study of the trajectory of bombs, also engaged the attention of the Admiralty. On the initiative of the Air Department, of which Captain Murray F. Sueter, RN, was the director, a very valuable series of experiments was carried out at Eastchurch, at first by Lieutenant Samson, and later by Lieutenant R.H. Clark-Hall, who was appointed in March 1913 for armament duties with the Naval Wing.

During 1913 Captain Dunne and Professor Huntington proved their slow but inherently stable machines and Mr Jezzi was flying a machine constructed entirely by himself, including the airscrew, but excluding the engine. With Captain Dunne at this time was Mr C.R. Fairey, who later became famous as Chief of the Fairey Aviation Co Ltd, and constructor of the Fairey III type biplanes, the Fairey Fox and other notable aircraft.

Experiments were carried out at Eastchurch during 1913 in connection with the destruction of enemy airships. The first of these consisted of towing an explosive grapnel, which, suspended from an aeroplane, made contact with the side of an airship. Although not properly tried out, this was subsequently abandoned in favour of dropping a sensitive fused bomb or firing Hale grenades at the target, and preliminary experiments were made on dummy targets nearby in October.

At the same time the wireless experiments continued and during the year more Rouzet sets were fitted in Maurice Farman and Caudron land machines and Sopwith seaplanes. Experiments in air reception were also made.

On December 30 1913, the administration of the Naval Wing underwent an important change as on that date the post of Inspecting Captain of Aircraft was created. This was a new appointment on the Staff of the Commander-in-Chief, Home Fleets, at the Nore, to deal with air matters. Hitherto the flying school had been responsible to the Commanding Officer of HMS *Actaeon*, and all officers and ratings attached to the school were borne on this ship's books. When, in May 1913, the Light Cruiser *Hermes* was fitted out and commissioned as a parent ship for seaplanes, the command of the wing and school passed to the Captain of that vessel and this state of affairs continued until the end of the year, when the discipline of all coastal stations was taken over by the Inspecting Captain of Aircraft,

Captain F.R. Scarlett, RN. This officer (ICA) was consequently responsible to the Commander-in-Chief for the administration and discipline of the Naval Unit, but on air technical matters received his orders from the Director of the Air Department at the Admiralty. The headquarters of the Naval Wing was in consequence transferred from Eastchurch, on December 30 1913, to the Central Air Office, Sheerness, which was formed as Captain Scarlett's headquarters.

Early in 1914, Lieutenant Clark-Hall, RN, experimented with the mounting of machine-guns in aircraft and carried out a series of tests at the Isle of Grain. He afterwards advised the Air Department that at least two machines on each station should be fitted with guns.

Mr Winston Churchill, who was First Lord of the Admiralty at the time, did much to further naval aviation by stimulating interest in flying in the Navy. To achieve this, demonstrations in naval districts were carried out by noted pilots, and one of the most successful was that of Mr Hamel, who, at Eastchurch on May 19 1914, gave a wonderful exhibition on his Bleriot machine.

During this month Lieutenant D.H. Hyde-Thomson, RN, who had already been responsible for the first torpedo-dropping experiments (on Southampton Water), was appointed W/T Officer at Eastchurch as a full-time job, and in September, Flight Sub-Lieutenant N.B. Tomlinson, RN, and Lieutenant B. Binyon, RNVR, joined him. In October, Lieutenant Binyon designed, constructed and tested a small light set of apparatus for single-seaters and designed and worked out the first rough model of a spark-coil transmitter which was afterwards made by the Sterling Telephone Company. This transmitter was first known as the 'Sterling type', but afterwards was called 'Type 52'.

A design was also produced for an aerial reel and receiver and late in October 1914, models were made and trials done by Flight Commander W.P. de Courcy Ireland, RN, and Flight Commander Hyde-Thomson, RN. These were eminently successful, signals being read at a distance of 16 miles. The apparatus was afterwards used at Dunkirk.

On June 23 1914, the Naval Wing of the RFC ceased to exist as such, its place being taken by the Royal Naval Air Service, and the Military Wing of the Royal Flying Corps now became simply the

Baby Wright aeroplane at the Gordon Bennett Aviation Race which was held at Eastchurch in July 1914.

Royal Flying Corps. It is worthy of note that henceforth, up to April 1 1918, the ranks Wing Captain, Wing Commander, Squadron Commander, Flight Commander, Flight Lieutenant, and Flight Sub-Lieutenant were substantive ranks in the Royal Navy.

The Naval Flying School was now placed under the joint administration of the Air Department of the Admiralty and the Sheerness Central Air Office.

For the Review of the Fleet by HM the King at Spithead from July 18 to 22 all the available naval aircraft from Eastchurch and other stations were concentrated. On July 20 a flight of 16 seaplanes flew over the assembled Fleet, and saluted the Royal Yacht in line ahead. These were followed later by two flights, each of three aeroplanes in Vee formation, led by Commander Samson. The formation flying had been practised at Eastchurch previously. At the conclusion of the review, the two flights of aeroplanes went to Rochester and then on to the Central Flying School, but the same day that they arrived at Upavon, they were ordered to return to Eastchurch, where they arrived on July 27.

On July 31 1914, two flights of No 4 Squadron of the Royal Flying Corps under the command of Major G.H. Raleigh were temporarily transferred to Eastchurch to assist the RNAS in the patrol of the coast during mobilisation. These flights remained at Eastchurch until

August 13 1914, when they flew direct to Amiens, in France, to join the Expeditionary Force. The transport proceeded via Southampton.

During the summer of 1914 it was realised that fighting in the air was only a matter of time, and mock fights were arranged at Eastchurch, usually two machines attacking and eight defending.

On August 25 1914, the armament equipment at the flying school consisted of ten hand grenades, 42 rifle grenades, 26 20 lb bombs and a Maxim gun fitted to a land machine. A few days later a number of 6 in shells were fitted with tail vanes and thus converted into bombs.

When war broke out all the aeroplanes at Eastchurch were ordered to remain, with the exception of three, one of which was sent to Yarmouth and the other two to Felixstowe. A number of officers were entered direct from civilian life and sent to the flying school to learn the rudiments of naval flying.

On August 5 1914, Mr (later Lieutenant-Colonel Sir) F.K. McClean, who was responsible for the training of the first naval pilots, joined the RNAS as a Flight Lieutenant, and offered his private house at Eastchurch Aerodrome for officers' accommodation. The station now became the generating centre of the RNAS units which afterwards achieved distinction in almost every theatre of war.

On August 8 the Navy was in possession of an organised aerial coast patrol, with a base, amongst others, at Eastchurch. A detachment of aeroplanes under Wing Commander Samson was on that day despatched to Skegness for the purpose of patrolling the East Coast in the vicinity of the Wash. On August 25, this unit was withdrawn to Eastchurch and two days later sent to Ostend racecourse to co-operate with the force of Marines landed there. This was the first RNAS unit to proceed overseas. The aeroplanes were flown over on August 27 and the stores were embarked at Sheerness in HMS *Empress* and SS *Rawcliffe* on the same day.

The machines consisted of three BE biplanes, two Sopwith biplanes, two Bleriot monoplanes, one Henri Farman biplane, one Bristol biplane and a converted Short seaplane. The personnel comprised ten flying officers, seven ground officers and 80 ratings. All machines with one exception arrived safely. They remained at Ostend for three days only, but during this time carried out reconnaissance flights over the area between Bruges, Ghent and Ypres.

On August 30 the detachment was ordered to return to England, and the same day flew to Dunkirk, but owing to one of the machines crashing there, the force was delayed three days. During this time the General commanding the French troops at Dunkirk made urgent representations to the British Foreign Office asking that the squadron should co-operate with the French.

On September 1, therefore, the Admiralty ordered this squadron to remain at Dunkirk to operate against Zeppelins and enemy aircraft and to carry out reconnaissances required by the French. It stayed there until February 1915.

In accordance with the decision taken by the Government on August 24 1914, as to the formation of the RNAS squadrons to be trained for military duties in the field, two squadrons were formed, one at Fort Grange, Gosport, and the other at Eastchurch, during the early part of October 1914. The Eastchurch unit, which was designated No 2 (Naval) Squadron, was formed on October 17, under the command of Squadron Commander E.L. Gerrard. Its machines were chiefly 80 hp Gnome-engined Bristols. That at Gosport, No 1 (Naval) Squadron, was placed under the command of Squadron Commander A.M. Longmore. At the end of February 1915, No 1 Squadron crossed to Dunkirk and relieved Wing Commander Samson's unit, which proceeded to the Dardanelles. No 2 Squadron continued training and experimental work at Eastchurch until

August 4 1915, when, as No 2 Wing, it crossed to Dunkirk to relieve No 1 Wing, which was ordered to reinforce the air units at the Dardanelles. These orders were, however, modified and No 1 Wing remained at Dunkirk. On August 13, No 2 Wing recrossed to Dover, and two days later embarked for the Dardanelles in lieu of No 1 Wing. On No 2 Wing vacating Eastchurch, its place was taken by No 4 Wing, which, as No 4 Squadron, had been formed at Dover in April 1915, under the command of Squadron Commander C.L. Courtney. No 4 Wing crossed to Petit Synthe, Dunkirk, a year later, in April 1916. Throughout this period the flying training school at Eastchurch continued as a unit apart from the active service squadrons. After the departure of Commander Samson's unit from Eastchurch in August 1914, the command of the naval flying school was taken over by Squadron Commander R. Gordon. He was succeeded in September by Flight Lieutenant E.T.R. Chambers, who in turn handed over to Flight Commander W.P. de Courcy Ireland. After a few weeks the command was taken over by Flight Lieutenant I.G. Vaughan Fowler, who remained until February 1915.

Flight Lieutenant F.K. McClean, who had been one of the instructing staff, commanded the school from February to March 1915, and was then posted away. Squadron Commander Alec Ogilvie, another instructor, now took over and remained for a year as Commanding Officer, when he left for Dunkirk.

In February 1915, the wireless experimental accommodation was enlarged and more naval W/T ratings were sent to Eastchurch. By March this was completed, and trials for a crystal receiver were carried out early in the year. Lieutenant Binyon during this year carried out the experimental and research work and the fitting and working of wireless apparatus in heavier-than-air craft. He and Lieutenant Tomlinson went to France in February 1916, to see what the French were doing and returned with much valuable information. Owing to the increasing needs of the RNAS the Eastchurch wireless experimental station moved to Cranwell in May 1916.

During 1915 Eastchurch was concerned with at least three enemy air raids on the east coast of England. The first occasion was on April 16, when just before noon a German Taube monoplane crossed the English coast at Kingstown and some

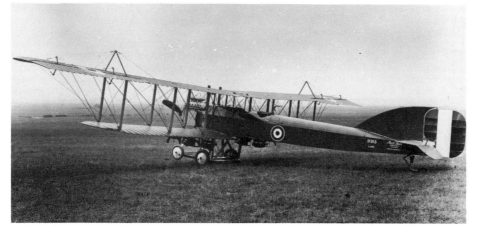

Short bomber, 9315, at Eastchurch in 1916. One of 35 built by Short Bros at Rochester.

dozen machines from Eastchurch, Manston and Dover went up, but they failed to find the Enemy.

On May 26, five naval aeroplanes ascended from Eastchurch and Grain to engage the German airship *LZ 38*, which was cruising in the Thames estuary, but they returned without having seen her, and two were damaged in landing.

The only occasion when bombs were actually dropped by the enemy on Sheppey occurred on August 9 1915, when the commander of the German airship *L 10*, in the belief that he had reached London, dropped a few on the island The only damage done was a few windows broken at Eastchurch.

During the following year on two occasions machines from Eastchurch aerodrome left to engage the enemy. The first was on March 5, when one machine ascended to intercept the German airship *L 13*, which was reported flying south from Lincolnshire. Owing to weather conditions nothing was seen of her. The other occasion was on September 23 when machines also went up from Eastchurch to attack raiding enemy airships. Two indecisive engagements took place off Yarmouth.

On March 29 1916, four Nieuport scouts with pilots were despatched from Eastchurch and arrived at Abeele, the headquarters of No 6 Squadron, RFC owing to the Fokker menace on the Western Front. This was the first naval detachment to co-operate with the RFC under military command. The machines were attached for 18 days and the co-operation was a success, the Nieuports afterwards proceeding to Dunkirk.

During the early part of this year, No 4 Wing fitted out at Eastchurch, and, as previously stated, at the end of April Wing Commander C.L. Courtney took them over to the Dunkirk Command. For station defence a flight of BE 2cs under Flight Lieutenant C. Draper remained.

At the end of March it was decided to enlarge Eastchurch and a station headquarters was formed under Wing Commander J.L. Forbes. The flying school ceased to operate for a few weeks while the sheds on the east side of the station were erected and reopened on May 1, with Flight Commander C.E. Mauds as Commanding Officer. This officer remained until February 1917. Wing Commander Forbes was succeeded as Station Commander by Wing Commander A.M. Longmore in September 1916. He remained until February 1917, when Captain J.M. Steel, RN, relieved him.

When the station headquarters was formed in 1916, the gunnery school came into being, its first Commanding Officer being Squadron Commander A.C. Barnby, who came from the Marines and remained at Eastchurch until February 1917.

In August 1916, Flight Lieutenant H.R. Busteed arrived from the Isle of Grain with what was then known as the Design Flight.

To complete the war history of the flying school the names of the following successive Commanding Officers must be mentioned: Flight Commander A.F.

Bettington, February to July 1917; Flight Lieutenant S.R. Watkins, July to September 1917; Flight Commander T.F.N. Gerrard, October 1917 to March 1918; and Acting Squadron Commander R.B. Munday, March 1918 to the end of the year. Major G. Draper was the last officer in command when training finished early in 1919.

To come back to the gunnery school, three officers took over in quick succession: Flight Lieutenant H. McClelland, February to March 1917; Flight Lieutenant W.B. Lawson, March to April and Flight Commander M.S. Marsden, April to August.

In September 1917, Flight Lieutenant E. McD. Wright took over the gunnery side and remained until the latter part of 1918, when Captain F.G. Brockman took over and finally closed the school down.

At the beginning of 1917 a marine observers' school was started at Eastchurch under Flight Commander K.S. Savory, who only remained a month, handing over to Flight Commander M.S. Marsden in February. This officer was succeeded by Flight Commander J.C.P. Wood, in April, and the latter by Flight Commander B.F. Fowler the following month. This officer remained until January 1918, when Squadron Observer F.H. Swan relieved him. The last officer to command the observers' school was Captain E.B.C. Betts.

Eastchurch was to participate in yet one more air raid, for on August 22 1917, ten Gothas attacked the Kent east coast, and three naval machines from Eastchurch were in the air awaiting the arrival of the hostile formation. They, together with 13 other machines from Manston, Walmer and Dover, attacked the Enemy with energy over Thanet, and afterwards pursued him down the coast to Dover. At no time was the Enemy free from contact and effective attack, and three aircraft were brought down before the engagement was broken off.

In April 1918, the gunnery school was split up, the ground section remained at Eastchurch and a school known as the 'Aerial Fighting and Gunnery School' was formed at Leysdown, under the command of Flight Commander J.H. Keene, who was released in July by Acting Squadron Commander A.M. Shook, who remained until the school ceased operations at the end of the year.

On the formation of the Royal Air Force on April 1 1918, No 58 Wing was formed at Eastchurch under the command of Captain J.M. Steel, RN, or, to give him his new title, Colonel RAF. During the year Lieutenant-Colonel E.T.R. Chambers relieved this officer, and in turn handed over to Lieutenant-Colonel A.E.E. Marsh.

The Short brothers sold their Eastchurch

Line-up of Gloster Grebe IIs and IIIs at Eastchurch.

works to the Government during the autumn of 1917 to enable the official aerodrome to be extended, and moved to Rochester, where they had previously started a branch in 1913-14. Horace Short died in April 1917.

In addition to the training schools already mentioned, namely flying, gunnery and observers, during the later part of the war officers of the American Expeditionary Force were put through an intensive course of flying instruction at Leysdown, and a boys' mechanic training school under Major G.B. Chainey was started during the summer of 1918. It continued at Eastchurch until it moved to Halton during the winter of 1919-20.

To revert to peacetime flying, it was from Eastchurch that during the afternoon of April 18 1919, a start was made to cross the Atlantic in a two-seater aeroplane especially built by Messrs Short Brothers, and called *The Shamrock*. Petrol sufficient for 40 hours was carried. The occupants were Major J.C.P. Wood (who commanded the observers' school at Eastchurch for a short period during the war) as pilot, and Captain C.C. Wylie as wireless operator and navigator. They intended to fly to the Curragh for the first stage of their journey, but unfortunately

Early means of transportation for aircraft. An RAF lorry and a Gloster Gamecock, J8088, at Eastchurch.

owing to last-minute alterations to the tank, the petrol feed system did not prove as efficient as was hoped and the Eagle VIII Rolls-Royce engine cut out after 3½ hours in the air. The machine was thus forced to come down in the sea about 12 miles from Holyhead. The occupants were eventually picked up unharmed by the British destroyer *Paisley*, another vessel towing the machine to Holyhead the following morning.

Wing Commander L.W.B. Rees, VC relieved Lieutenant-Colonel Marsh as station commander in 1919, and remained for about a year, during the Care and Maintenance period to which Eastchurch was reduced when hostilities ceased.

During 1920 an enormous amount of clearing up of material of disbanded units was done at Eastchurch by the few officers and airmen who remained, and several hundred colonial officers were repatriated from the station.

In May 1921, during the coal industry dispute, Eastchurch became a centre of activity for Reserve officers and airmen, who were mobilised for emergency duties.

Shortly after their dispersal, the station became a cadre for the armament and gunnery school, which was fully opened for instruction on April 1 1922. Training in connection with machine-guns and bombs thus became centralised and therefore systematic.

The first Commanding Officer of the post-war gunnery school was Wing Com-

Top *Armstrong Whitworth Siskin IIIA, J9378, at Eastchurch.* **Above** *A Westland Wapiti IIA, K1412 of 3 Flight, AA School, at Eastchurch in June 1930.*

mander A.W. Bigsworth, who arrived in June 1921, and left in March 1923, when Wing Commander J.R.W. Smyth-Pigott took over. In May 1924, No 100 Squadron arrived from Spitalgate in Lincolnshire, but its stay was short and in July it moved back to Spitalgate.

During the month of May 1925, Wing Commander Smyth-Pigott handed over the command of the armament and gunnery school to Wing Commander C.H.K. Edmonds. At that time, courses of instruction in armament were arranged for officers in three categories, as follows: an advanced course to qualify for the symbol 'A' to be posted for duty with groups, areas, schools and establishments; a technical course for flying officers to qualify as squadron armament officers; and a preliminary practical course for

young officers to enable them to carry out intelligently their air-bombing and gunnery training. Armament officers on the Royal Air Force Reserve were also attached annually for a fourth course for airmen. Instruction was given to airmen to enable them to become armourers and to service tradesmen in order that they might qualify for the air gunner's badge. Refresher courses were also periodically arranged for airmen on their return from overseas duty.

Practical work in the air and in the workshops as well as instruction in the theoretical side was carried out and every endeavour was made to include the latest developments of air armament in the various syllabuses.

On October 3 1923, No 207 (Bombing) Squadron, which was at one period No 7

(Naval) Squadron, arrived from San Stephano, Turkey, under Squadron Leader V. Gaskell-Blackburn, who was succeeded by Squadron Leader J.B. Graham. This officer took over the command of the squadron on January 20 1926.

Consequently, Eastchurch now included a Service squadron as well as being a school establishment. In September 1929 the Hawker Horsleys of No 33 Squadron arrived from Netheravon where the squadron had just re-formed. In November 1929, No 207 Squadron moved to Bircham Newton, Norfolk and a year later No 33 Squadron moved to Bicester, Oxford.

It was not until July 15 1938 that a Royal Air Force station headquarters was formed at Eastchurch, under the command of Group Captain C.B. Dalison, AFC. No 21 (Bomber) Squadron arrived from Lympne on 15 August 1938, and 46 (General Reconnaissance) Squadron on September 1 1938. Both units moved out during the spring of 1939. During that year training courses for the ground section of the RAF Volunteer Reserve were carried out but were then moved to Pembry and Cosford on the declaration of war in September 1939. Also during September the armament and gunnery school moved out. The armament group (later renamed No 25) had moved out the previous June.

In December 1939, the first detachment of Polish Air Force personnel for embodiment in the RAF arrived at the station and they were inspected the following month by the Secretary of State for Air. Training of Polish personnel continued in 1940, their numbers being increased as more and more members of the Polish Air Force found their way to England. After their training at Eastchurch, Polish airmen went to operational training units before passing to the newly-formed Polish squadrons of the RAF.

The station was transferred to No 16 Group, Coastal Command, on August 6 1940 and Nos 12, 19, 142 and 266 Squadrons subsequently arrived there. Shortly afterwards, on August 13, Eastchurch suffered a heavy raid by enemy aircraft which killed 14 and wounded 26, and caused considerable damage to station buildings. Similar attacks occurred throughout the Battle of Britain period of August and September, but none succeeded in putting the station out of action.

From the middle of August, offensive operations on a small scale were carried out from Eastchurch, commencing with a raid by ten aircraft on Boulogne on August 18 but the main effort of the station continued to be devoted to training.

A year later, in August 1941, the station was transferred to No 27 Group, Technical Training Command, and courses were started to train RAF personnel in the use of rocket weapons for ground defence. These courses ceased at the beginning of 1942 and were replaced by a new training programme organised by the RAF Artillery School which was formed at Eastchurch in February of that year.

On August 19 1942, Nos 65 and 165 Squadrons operated from the station in support of the Combined Operations raid on Dieppe. Both squadrons flew throughout the day and claimed between them four enemy aircraft destroyed and three damaged, without loss to themselves.

Later in the year, the station was transferred to No 72 Group, Army Co operation Command, and was used for a short period by Nos 303 and 316 (Polish) Squadrons which operated from there on offensive Spitfire patrols over France.

In April 1943, the RAF Artillery School was moved to Filey and Eastchurch was transferred to No 54 Group, Flying Training Command. A combined reselection centre was formed at the station to take over the duties previously performed by the reselection boards at Brighton, Blackpool and Uxbridge. The first intake for the centre arrived at Eastchurch in the June.

During the early part of 1944, an armament training camp was also formed at the station and amongst the units which spent periods there were Nos 174, 181, 184, 247, and 245 Squadrons.

That same year saw the completion of the Sanctuary chapel which had been restored with material salvaged from other buildings damaged in the enemy raids of 1940 and 1941 and the chapel was dedicated by the Archbishop of Canterbury on May 28.

The combined reselection centre remained at Eastchurch until it was disbanded in the middle of 1946. The station was then reduced to a Care and Maintenance basis and became part of No 21 Group, Flying Training Command, parented by RAF West Malling.

RAF Eastchurch became inactive in December 1948, and was transferred to the Prison Commissioners in June 1950. Eastchurch became an open prison and today continues to function as such.

Fairlop (Hainault Farm), Essex

177/TQ460905. To the west of Romford just north of the A12 trunk road

In 1915 land just to the west of Romford was taken over for a landing site and it was named Hainault Farm after the nearby farm of that name. The following year it housed one flight of No 39 (Home Defence) Squadron from April to August. One other flight was based at Sutton's Farm and one at North Weald Bassett. These gave cover for the east of London.

At the end of April 1917, another Zeppelin raid took place and again aircraft from Hainault Farm were hunting them. It was a successful night for the defending aircraft, with *L 32* shot down by Lieutenant Sowrey and *L 33* being hit by Lieutenant Brandon, flying a BE 2c. The airship was damaged and it crashed at Little Wigborough. The crew of *L 33* were taken prisoner and although the airship was partly burned its structure remained intact and was a great help to British designers. The British rigid airship *R 23* was based on the design of the *L 33*.

On July 24 1917, No 44 Squadron formed at Hainault Farm and was to remain there for the duration of the war. During the eight daylight raids made by the German Gothas on south-east England between May and August 1917 the Sopwith Camels of 44 Squadron at Hainault Farm had very little success. On January 25 1918, two pilots from 44 Squadron shared a kill when a Gotha was shot down at Wickford.

No 207 Training Depot Station at Chingford began to use Hainault Farm as a sub-station in May 1918. By August of that year it was transferred to 54 Training Depot Station but by February 1919 it had become surplus to the RAF's training requirements and all training ceased.

During this period No 151 Squadron had formed at Hainault Farm, on June 12 1918, and moved to France four days later. Another squadron, No 153, had also formed in November 1918. It remained at Hainault Farm until disbanding on June 13 1919. The following month No 44 Squadron disbanded and by the end of 1919 the airfield had closed and quickly went back to agriculture.

During the 1930s the site was purchased in order to make it the City of London's airport. However, the Corporation of London's proposed major airport at Fairlop, (renamed thus after the small village on the northern boundary), was shelved because of the gathering war clouds.

The site was then taken over by the Air Ministry, and on September 26 1940 was handed over to the contractors. By July 1941, three runways, living and technical sites were completed. Squadron Leader H. Ovendon was appointed officer in charge on August 18 1941 and he moved in immediately with personnel from Hornchurch to form an orderly room and organise squadron accommodation. On September 1, Group Captain H. Broadhurst flew in from Hornchurch and made trial landings on each runway. Two days later, electricity, telephones and water were all connected. By September 10 the airfield was fully operational. It officially opened as a satellite to Hornchurch on November 12 1941, when No 603 Squadron arrived from the parent station. By the end of the year its Spitfires had moved to Dyce. Next to arrive was No 411 Squadron, which stayed two weeks in February 1942. The airfield was then used by many fighter squadrons. No 313 arrived in mid-April and moved out again during early June. It was replaced by No 81 Squadron, from July to September 1942. Its Spitfires took part in numerous sweeps and shipping strikes, including the provision of air cover for the Dieppe landings of August 1942. It was succeeded by the Spitfires of No 64 Squadron which arrived on September 9 and remained until November 11 1942. During their stay they gave fighter cover to American Fortress bombers.

The Spitfires of No 122 Squadron operated from Fairlop in June and July 1942 and again in mid-November and early December, flying offensive sweeps over the continent, convoy patrols and as bomber escort. Also based here at that time was No 154, which put in two visits between July and September 1942.

By the summer of 1943, eight squadrons, Nos 19, 65, 182, 239, 245, 247, 350 and 602 had put in a brief appearance. On August 19 1943, No 302 Squadron arrived from Perranporth. Two days later it was joined by No 317 Squadron. Both were flying Spitfires and moved out after four weeks.

Next to arrive was No 164, which arrived from Manston on September 22 1943, equipped initially with Hurricanes and subsequently with Typhoon aircraft. In December it carried out an attack on the flying bomb launching sites in northern France but it was primarily engaged in training for its future role as a close support squadron.

A second Typhoon squadron, No 195, had arrived on September 23 and this disbanded at Fairlop on February 15 1944. Four days previously No 164 Squadron had moved out to Twinwood Farm. It was replaced by No 193 Squadron which arrived from Harrowbeer on February 20. Flying Typhoons, this unit moved to Thorney Island on March 15 1944 and brought to an end flying at Fairlop.

In September 1944, Fairlop became No 24 Balloon Centre and Nos 965, 967, 970 and 998 Balloon Squadrons were stationed there until September 1945, when the station became inactive. It closed on August 22 1946.

Fairoaks, Surrey

176/TQ005623. North of Woking, south of A319

Only four miles west of the First World War aerodrome of Brooklands, Fairoaks, which was also known as Dolley's Farm in the early days, became active as a result of the expansion scheme introduced in the mid 1930s by the Air Ministry for training pilots for the Royal Air Force. Hangars and offices were constructed in the north-western corner of the site near the A319 and on October 1 1937, No 18 Elementary and Reserve Flying Training School opened, operated by Universal Flying Services.

The main aircraft type was the Tiger Moth but these were supplemented by smaller numbers of Battles and versions of the Hawker Hart. On the outbreak of war

Airspeed Consul, G-AJLR, outside the hangar at Fairoaks.

the unit became Elementary Flying Training School, absorbing the former 19 E & RFTS that had been operated at Gatwick by Airports Limited.

During the war the hangars of the former civil airfield were reinforced by the erection of nine Blister hangars, and on the opposite side of the main road from the airfield several hangars were put up for the Ministry of Aircraft Production. The airfield surface remained grass and the main aircraft type used by the school throughout the war years was the Tiger Moth. It was a very busy station and to ease the congested circuit Winkfield and Smiths Lawn were used as relief landing grounds from the summer of 1941 to 1945.

After the war the name was changed to 18 Reserve Flying School on May 14 1947 and the Tiger Moths were slowly replaced by Chipmunks and a few Ansons. Then, as the RAF Reserve training programme was run down the RFS disbanded at the end of July 1953.

Relinquished by the Ministry of Defence in 1967, the field was purchased by Mr Douglas Arnold, who immediately started work on refurbishing both the flying area and the technical site. He renamed the 'drome Fairoaks Airport and installed his own organisation, The Fairoaks School of Flying, which offered private tuition, pleasure flights and charter flights.

The ex-BAC hangar was completely renovated and a building for use as a ground instruction centre erected. A further installation for club facilities was also built.

As well as equipping with Cessna F-172s for its own use, the organisation took on the distributorship for these aircraft in this country. Today Fairoaks is a busy light aircraft field.

Fambridge, Essex

168/TL850965. East of South Woodham Ferrers between the River Crouch and the main railway line

Fambridge caught the pioneer spirit when Noel Pemberton-Billing founded a flying school here in 1908, but he had very little success. He was later to achieve fame after he founded the company which became Vickers Supermarine, builders of the famous Spitfire.

The flying ground was situated on the bank of the River Crouch near the marshes at Fambridge. The main hangar, which had previously been a crane factory, was let off to various aircraft builders.

One of the first machines to appear at Fambridge was the Howard-Wright 1908 biplane. This achieved only a few short hops before being taken to Rye, Sussex for further trials.

Next on the scene was Jose Weiss with his No 1 tractor monoplane, but there is no record that this machine ever left the ground. Weiss was also unsuccessful when he returned in 1909 for powered trials with his glider.

With so many failures the interest in flying began to wane, and Fambridge was considered to be unsuitable. However, all was not lost, and on August 2 1909, Robert McFee began construction of his own machine in the Fambridge hangar. McFee was an American who was interested in flying and had come to England in 1909 to create his dreams.

In just six weeks, his machine, a single-seat tractor monoplane powered by an eight-cylinder, air-cooled, 35 hp JAP engine, was ready for trials. After four crashes and adjustments the machine was successful by mid-October. But McFee was not satisfied with the flying ground and on November 11 he moved to Maplin Sands, off Foulness Island. McFee was ordered off the sands by the War Office and on November 29 moved the aeroplane to the Kursaal at Southend and later, via London Docks, to France.

After McFee had moved out the site was run down and Fambridge was not used again until 1914 when a Talbot Waterplane, pusher hydro-biplane, powered by a water-cooled engine, re-activated interest in flying, but despite numerous attempts the machine was unable to rise from the water. The site was then abandoned and Fambridge faded into history.

Farningham, Kent

177/TQ555690. South of Dartford off the A225

In early 1915 Farningham was one of the ten aerodromes encircling London which were used by the home defence squadrons and it housed two BE 2cs for that purpose. It had very few facilities and could hardly be classed as an airfield.

Situated just south of Farningham Road Railway Station on the west side of the A225 this small site was never developed and it served throughout the First World War as an auxiliary landing ground for Joyce Green.

Feltham (Hanworth Park), Middlesex

176/TQ105716. South-west of London between Staines and Richmond

The aerodrome was situated between Feltham to the north and the village of Hanworth to the south-east with rows of houses lining the east and south sides along the A312 and A314 roads. It was known locally as Hanworth Park aerodrome but was also referred to as London Air Park or Feltham Aerodrome. It was built on a First World War site, for the parkland had been used during the First World War as an Aircraft Acceptance Park. Accommodation for aircraft storage consisted of

Hordern-Richmond Autoplane G-AEOG (Continental), seen here at Feltham in the 1930s.

A Weir W 2 at Feltham in August 1934.

21 storage sheds, 200 ft × 60 ft and 12 hangars, 150 ft × 60 ft. These were all dismantled immediately after the war. In 1929 National Flying Services Ltd started to build an aerodrome and brought flying back to the area. The old manor house, which had been part of the estate, had been converted into a hotel and housed the flying club. This was surrounded by many trees, 50 ft high, which formed an island in the middle of the aerodrome. The roadway to this island was set flush with the grass surface to enable aircraft to taxi over it without damage to the undercarriage.

During the building of the aerodrome a large stream that had flowed across the land from the Feltham end was channelled into a culvert which was later roofed over with hundreds of old railway sleepers laid flush with the surrounding grass surface.

The landing area was a grass-covered surface. From south-east–north-west it gave 1,000 yds and was just under 900 yds from north–south, north-east–south-west or east–west direction. Wind indicators were on the east and west sides and in the centre of the north area was a smoke wind indicator. These were produced by General Aircraft and consisted of a metal box about 2 ft square containing a tank of oil and a heating element. When the heating element was switched on, using either battery or mains, the oil dripped onto the mica surrounding the element causing the oil to vaporise into a dense white smoke which passed out of the box via a hole in the cover plate and thus gave the pilot an indication of wind direction and strength.

The box was designed to be sunk into the ground and was covered with a flush fitting lid.

Use was made of the island in the middle and hangars were built on three sides. The hangar on the south side housed the London Air Park Flying Club which operated with a few BA Swallows and three Aeronca C 3 aircraft with JAP engines. Flying Training Ltd (a subsidiary of Blackburn) occupied the hangar on the north side from where it operated No 5 Elementary & Reserve Flying School on behalf of the Air Ministry. No 5 E & RFS formed here on June 1 1935. The school had a variety of aircraft which included Blackburn B 2s, Hart Trainers, an Avro Anson and a Fairey Battle. The latter caused a lot of trouble by breaking through the old wooden railway sleepers which covered the culvert. The hangar on the eastern side was used by the Cierva School of Flying who used C 30as.

Other buildings were also sited on the north-west perimeter of the aerodrome and these were occupied by three firms, General Aircraft Ltd (who owned the aerodrome), the British Aircraft Manufacturing Co Ltd and Rollasons. The latter was a small company that carried out overhauls and repairs on privately owned light aircraft.

General Aircraft, originally founded at Croydon Aerodrome, was building ST 12 Monospars and had moved into more spacious premises owing to its success. The aircraft were twin-engined, all-metal, low-wing cabin monoplane types. After the ST 12 came the prototype ST 18 (later named Croydon), but this was lost on the return leg of a proving flight to Australia. Fortunately the crew was saved. Then

came the ST 25 and from this model the Chief Designer, Mr Crocombe, modified one for ambulance work.

This particular aircraft, *G-AEYF* was painted white with large red crosses on the wings and fuselage. A large upward-hinging cargo door was fitted into the port side of the fuselage so that a stretcher could be loaded and there was a small seat for the nurse. Other medical equipment was fitted into the cabin for use during flight. The British Red Cross eventually took delivery of *G-AEYF* and a further five were built. In addition to building their own aircraft General Aircraft also constructed a large number of Fury Mk IIs for Hawker's and Whitley sub-assemblies for Armstrong Whitworth.

British Aircraft Manufacturing Company, formerly British Klemm Aircraft Limited, which had originally produced the German-designed Klemm monoplanes under licence, also produced aircraft at Feltham. These included the Swallow, a low-wing two-seater wooden monoplane, the Eagle, a low-wing wooden cabin monoplane and the Double Eagle. This was a wooden high-wing cabin monoplane.

The aerodrome was very busy and there were many accidents. The crash services were one tender and one ambulance. Alarm bells were installed in all the hangars, which in turn were connected to manually operated switches which were situated around the aerodrome, the procedure being that any person seeing a crash or accident had to sound the alarm. The two service vehicles were then manned by the staff of Flying Training Ltd, who would drive around the aerodrome seeking the crash. It was a bit primitive against today's air traffic control systems.

Displays were plentiful and the aerodrome even had a visit from Clem Sohne, an American who was the forerunner of today's free fall sky divers. He wore a pair of flying overalls with additional material stitched between the arms and body and between the legs. He claimed this gave him extra flying surfaces and he would free fall down to rip-cord-pulling height. He had barnstormed around Europe, exciting the crowds, but shortly before the outbreak of war he was killed when his parachute failed to deploy properly.

After the build-up of the RAF in the mid-1930s most of the flying clubs joined the Government-sponsored Civil Air Guard scheme during 1938/39. This was designed to create a pool of pilots and the London Air Park Flying Club joined the scheme.

The Civil Air Guard pupils were fitted out with a flying overall in RAF blue with silver buttons embossed CAG. These pupils were charged 5/- per hour with the balance being paid by the Government and they turned up in great numbers at weekends.

During this period of build-up to the war a small amount of night flying was done at Feltham, mainly by the pilots of No 5 E & RFTS. This was always very difficult for there were no flare paths in those days and the means for night flying was to fix a floodlight with a shadow bar in the corner of the landing area. Also, the sheep which were used to keep the grass short had to be contained in one corner.

On the day war was declared, September 3 1939, No 5 EFTS formed from No 5 E & RFTS, and civil flying ceased. The school was now flying Magisters and by the end of the year it was using Heathrow as a relief landing ground. However, it was thought the school was too vulnerable to enemy action and on June 16 1940 it moved to Meir, near Stoke-on-Trent. From then until 1948 Feltwell was used by General Aircraft Ltd who repaired many light aircraft, including Hamilcar and Hotspur gliders.

Today, much of the aerodrome and buildings remain. The club house and hotel, Hanworth House, are now owned by the local authority and are used as a retirement home for 'senior citizens'. Considering that it is such a prime site it is miraculous that so much of the aerodrome still survives, and it is well worth a visit.

Fyfield, Essex

167/TL543038. Close to Chipping Ongar off the A122

This was a First World War site and the landing facilities comprised an area of 25 acres, the dimensions being 370 yds × 350 yds in open surroundings.

The landing ground was 1½ miles from Chipping Ongar railway station and close to the village of Chipping Ongar, after which it was named. It was a site in the

---

Opposite page, top *BA Double Eagle,* G-AEIN, *built at Feltham in 1936.* **Centre** *Graf Zeppelin seen here at Feltham in 1932.* **Bottom** *Airspeed AS 6 Envoy Mk 3,* G-AHAC *(ex-RAF P5626), at Feltham/Hanworth in 1946.*

south-east area, under 49 Wing, and was used by No 39 Squadron. It closed immediately after the First World War.

During the Second World War a site close to the old First World War landing ground became Chipping Ongar airfield and was used as a bomber station by the Americans.

Gatwick, Surrey

187/TQ270303. 28 miles south of London on the A23 with direct link to the M23 at Junction 9

Situated between Horley in the north and Crawley in the south the aerodrome was adjacent to the south end of Gatwick Race Course. The year 1931 saw many jockeys and racegoers arriving by air for meetings and it was a most convenient arrangement, yet it never became a success.

Gatwick, founded by Ronald Waters and John Mockford, was first licensed as an aerodrome on August 1 1930, but its owner, Home Counties Aircraft Services Ltd, was soon in financial difficulties and sold it to The Redwing Aircraft Company in May 1932. However, it also ran into problems and the following year Gatwick again changed hands and Airports Ltd became the new owner. It also experienced financial problems and it was only the defence situation that saved the day.

Throughout the changes the Surrey Aero Club, formed at Gatwick in 1930, had continued flying. The flying instruction was carried out by Ronald Waters. The redevelopment of Gatwick got under way and by 1936 the airport was ready. The terminal building, quite revolutionary in its day, was connected by an underground passageway to a new railway station. The

Below G-AEOT, *Fokker FXII ex-PH-AIH, had a life of less than a month. It crashed near Crawley, Sussex, on November 19 1936 with the loss of two lives, while approaching Gatwick at night.* **Bottom** *Fokker F VIII G-AEPT of British Airways Limited at Gatwick in 1936/38. This aircraft could carry 12 passengers.*

Lockheed Electra being unloaded at Gatwick.

night landing equipment consisted of three weather-protected floodlights, boundary lights and a neon beacon. Two hangars were built for the operators. That same year British Airways Ltd transferred its scheduled services from Stapleford Abbotts but it was not a successful move and in February 1937 the airline moved to Heston after Gatwick became waterlogged yet again.

On October 1 1937, No 19 Elementary & Reserve Flying Training School was formed and to fulfil the contract extra flying instructors were recruited. The school had Tiger Moths and Hawker Harts and was housed in No 1 hangar. The formation of the school necessitated building an operational block, parachute store, machine-gun butts and buildings to house the pupils and staff. The school also undertook the training of RAF VR pilots.

The *Daily Express* Air Display was held here on June 25 1938 and a large crowd attended to see the aircraft which included the Battles, Blenheims, Whitleys, Lysanders and Hurricanes of No 3 (F) Squadron.

In September 1938 Airports was given a contract to train direct entry officers at No 19 E & RFTS. To meet these extra duties the school was provided with 16 Miles Magisters. A further 12 instructors were engaged and a Bellman hangar was erected to house the additional aircraft. This now meant that flying continued throughout the week but weekends were still the busiest time.

On September 1 1939 all reservists were called up and there was a reorganisation of the schools. Some ceased to operate, No 19 E & RFTS was one of them, and the aircraft, instructors and ground crews were transferred to No 18 EFTS which formed on September 3 at Fairoaks. By this time, all civilian flying had ceased and Airports Ltd was engaged in the modification of Whitleys.

Following the outbreak of war, the airport fell silent and although it was placed under RAF control no flying units arrived. During the early part of 1940 representatives of the newly formed BOAC, Air France and Customs officials visited Gatwick with a view to establishing Gatwick as the London Civil Terminal.

The Air Ministry agreed, with the proviso that if the airfield was required the airlines would vacate on 24 hours' notice. Accordingly work went ahead with the airlines but doubt was cast in February when No 92 Squadron from Croydon set up a training section at Gatwick. This unit was in the process of converting from Blenheims to Spitfires and continued to train at Gatwick.

The detachment from 92 Squadron returned to Croydon in May, for things were now moving fast. With the swift advance of the Germans across Europe time was running out for the airlines and a number of expected routes had by now been overrun. Their fate was sealed in May when the headquarters of No 70 Wing, with its two squadrons, Nos 18 and 57, arrived at the end of the month. This wing had been withdrawn from France earlier in the month, having suffered heavy losses. During their stay at Gatwick both units received replacement aircraft, Blenheim IVs, and other equipment.

On June 11, No 57 Squadron moved to Wyton and the following day No 18 moved to West Raynham leaving the wing HQ to administer the aerodrome. On June 14, No 53 Squadron arrived with its Blenheim IVs and they were the first ones to be billeted in the racecourse grandstand. That same month No 98 Squadron arrived from France. Its homecoming was a tragic one for on June 17 the SS *Lancastrian* which was carrying most of No 98's personnel was bombed and sunk while crossing the English Channel. Among those lost were 90 airmen belonging to No 98 Squadron.

On July 3 No 53 Squadron moved to Detling and at the end of the month 98 Squadron was transferred to Coastal Command and subsequently served as a general reconnaissance squadron in Iceland. It was disbanded there in July 1941.

By this time work was in progress to improve the aerodrome facilities and to strengthen the defences. In September 1940 a battery of light anti-aircraft guns was installed. On September 3, No 26 Squadron arrived with its Westland Lysanders and the station started a long association with the Army Co-operation Command. On September 18, No 141 Squadron arrived from Biggin Hill with its Boulton Paul Defiants, which were now used as night fighters. At their time of arrival at Gatwick many pilots had not yet completed sufficient hours night flying in Defiants to carry out night patrols. Accordingly, night training flights were carried out. The squadron was also engaged in night patrols, but without success. No 141 moved to Drem on October 22.

December saw the arrival of No 157 Light Anti-Aircraft Battery to relieve the resident battery. Poor weather rendered the airfield unserviceable during the latter half of the month.

In January 1941, the control of the station was transferred from No 11 Group Fighter Command to No 71 Group Army Co-operation Command. This left only 26 Squadron as the resident unit. It spent time on exercises with the Army and provided aircraft for the calibration of anti-aircraft defence. The squadron had by now re-equipped with Lysander Mark IIIs for which 20mm cannon were held in store in case of invasion. The squadron was also equipped to spray gas, for which purpose it had been supplied with 47 250-lb gas charges.

In February 1941, 'C' Flight went to Old Sarum where it underwent a conversion course on Curtiss Tomahawks. This aircraft had been rejected as a fighter by the RAF and it was now thought that it could replace the Lysander following its poor showing as an Army support aircraft. During February the squadron carried out a few coastal patrols with the Tomahawks and on March 14, the AOC-in-C, Sir Arthur Barratt, with the C-in-C Home Forces, Lieutenant-General A. Brooke, visited 26 Squadron to watch comparative trials between the Lysander and the Tomahawk. But the Tomahawks brought many problems and there were many accidents caused by the malfunction of the Allison engine. Training continued with both aircraft, the practice gas spray sorties being carried out with the Lysanders.

In late September 1940, 'A' Flight of No 239 Squadron arrived at Gatwick to undertake anti-aircraft calibration duties and it was joined by the rest of the squadron on January 22 1941. Throughout the spring and summer the squadron was engaged in training which culminated in three Army exercises in August. Meanwhile, No 26 Squadron had also spent the summer working up to operations and during July had been to Weston Zoyland for a week's air-firing practice.

In August, No 71 Group Army Co-operation Command was disbanded in favour of Army co-operation wings which were directly associated with the local Army commands. No 35 Wing was formed at Gatwick and took command of the two resident squadrons.

In September 1941 work on a number of gun emplacements, and the laying of wire mesh army track runways was completed. The following month No 803 Road

Construction Company arrived from Iceland to improve the runways.

On November 22 1941, No 26 Squadron moved to Manston only to return again by the end of the month. January 1942 saw the arrival of the North American Mustang which was allocated to No 26 Squadron for Army co-operation assessment. During February, 26 Squadron returned to Weston Zoyland for a two-week training period during which it was involved in many accidents. On its return from Weston Zoyland on February 23, 'A' Flight began to re-equip with Mustangs and immediately began training them. By May it was operational with them and carried out its first *Rhubarbs.* That same month 239 Squadron commenced its conversion onto Mustangs and moved to Abbotsinch during the first two weeks of the month. After only a few days it moved to Detling on May 19, only to return to Gatwick at the end of the month.

Two squadrons were formed at Gatwick in June, No 63 with Mustangs and No 171 with Tomahawks. His Royal Highness the Duke of Kent visited the squadrons during June. Both squadrons left Gatwick in July, No 171 moved to Odiham on July 11 and on July 16, 63 moved out to Catterick.

No 35 Wing, using four Mustang squadrons, provided tactical reconnaissance in support of the Dieppe landings—Operation *Jubilee*—on August 19, and the resident Gatwick squadrons played an active part. It was apparent almost from the start that it was not going to be easy and by the end of the day No 26 Squadron had lost five aircraft. No 239 lost two and many were damaged. Two days after the operation, Marshal of the Royal Air Force, Viscount Trenchard, visited the station to congratulate the squadrons on the part they played in Operation *Jubilee*.

No 171 Squadron returned to Gatwick on August 25 and immediately began to re-equip with Mustangs. At the end of the month, No 239 Squadron departed for Twinwood Farm. No 171 continued with training and on September 10 moved to Weston Zoyland. Ten days later the squadron returned and flew its first interceptor patrols in October. The squadron's first mission over France took place in mid-November when two aircraft flew on a photo-reconnaissance mission. Interceptor patrols were carried out until early December, when, on December 7, No 171 moved to Hartford Bridge. Two days later the Hurricanes of No 175 arrived from Harrowbeer. This squadron had been withdrawn

from the fighter role to become an Army co-operation unit and continued its training at Gatwick. It moved to Odiham in mid-January.

During the winter months a number of squadrons sent detachments to Gatwick to gain operational experience. No 4 Squadron was one and another visiting squadron was No 309 (Polish), which was detached to No 35 Wing from mid-December to mid-January 1943. On January 12, No 26 departed to Detling, thus ending a stay of over two years.

In February some of the station personnel were detached to take part in Exercise *Spartan* and were subsequently absorbed into the newly formed Tactical Air Force.

March saw the arrival of No 655 (AOP) Squadron with its Austers but it departed after a month's stay. Early April saw the arrival of No 123 Airfield with Nos 26 and 239 Squadrons. Their return visit was for an intensive seven-week training programme which involved new techniques. They were joined on April 8 by the Hawker Typhoon 1Bs of No 183 Squadron. All the squadron was accommodated under canvas.

During its stay, 183 Squadron flew a few patrols and also mounted its first raid, when, operating from Ford, it bombed the power station at Yainville. The squadron moved to Lasham on May 3. The two remaining squadrons also departed in May, on May 21 No 26 returned to Detling and 239 went to Fairlop. Two days later, No 123 Airfield moved to Odiham and was joined the following month by No 35 Wing.

With the formation of the 2nd Tactical Air Force many specialist supporting units were raised. Two of these units were at Gatwick. In May No 403 Repair and Salvage Unit arrived for a three-week stay and it was followed by No 404 Aircraft Stores Park, which only remained a week. The airfield passed to the control of No 11 Group in June after the Army Co-operation Command was absorbed into the Tactical Air Force.

During the first week of July 1943, No 129 Airfield arrived at Gatwick with a Canadian squadron, No 414. All the airfield and squadron personnel were accommodated under canvas. On July 30, No 414 Squadron moved to Weston Zoyland, only to return to Gatwick on August 10, but two days later moved to Ashford in Kent. With the departure of No 129 Airfield Gatwick was reduced to a Care and Maintenance basis. During this period No

2875 Squadron, RAF Regiment arrived with No 2306 Squadron and was housed at Gatwick for a few weeks.

Many aircraft, fighters and bombers, returning from raids on occupied Europe, sought shelter at Gatwick. In order to assist such aircraft a new series of homing beacons, known as *Darkie*, was introduced. Gatwick was chosen as the site for one of these beacons, which came into operation in early October. During the middle of the month two Spitfire IX squadrons arrived, No 19 from Weston Zoyland and No 65 from Ashford. Both squadrons flew escort duties and sorties during their stay. Both left for Gravesend on October 24. They had been replaced by No 430 (RCAF) Squadron which had arrived from Ashford on October 15. The Canadians were to see the winter out at Gatwick.

During its stay the unit was engaged in regular photographic and offensive sorties. These winter months were relatively quiet and this enabled the relaying of the Sommerfeld tracking to the runways. From January 5 to 18 1944, the Canadians were at No 15 Armament Practice Camp, Peterhead, Scotland and from February 9 to 25 took part in Exercise *Eagle* at Clifton, Yorkshire.

On March 6 1944, No 168 Squadron arrived and it also carried out a number of photographic missions. At the end of the month both units moved to Odiham.

By now there was a great build-up of forces for the planned invasion and Gatwick was to play its part. No 35 Wing with Nos 2 and 4 Squadrons arrived at Gatwick on April 4 from Sawbridgeworth. A few days later they were joined by 268 Squadron. All three squadrons operated in the reconnaissance role.

On D-Day June 6 1944 the two Mustang squadrons, Nos 2 and 268, were engaged in spotting for the naval bombardment of coastal targets. Then they flew photographic and tactical reconnaissance missions. The Spitfires of No 4 Squadron were less successful, for the cloud made high-level photography impossible. They had to wait five days before they were able to operate over the battle area. On July 27 the Wing moved to Odiham.

No 36 Wing was immediately replaced by three Spitfire IX squadrons, Nos 80, 229 and 274. These arrived during the last week of June and took part in a number of sweeps and escort duties. They left Gatwick in early July. No 229 moved to Tangmere on July 1 and Nos 80 and 274 went

to West Malling on July 5.

The flying bomb menace then began and in an effort to protect London against the V1s a balloon barrage was erected. This was subsequently extended to the south, resulting in the neighbouring Redhill Aerodrome and the advanced landing ground at Horn being totally obstructed. The balloon barrage came to within 2,000 yds of Gatwick. No squadrons operated from the airfield during this period.

On August 27 two non-combatant squadrons arrived. They were Nos 116 and 287, both of which arrived from North Weald. They were joined by No 1 Aircraft Delivery Unit and No 49 Maintenance Unit. No 116 Calibration Squadron was equipped with Ansons, Oxfords and Hurricanes and was engaged in anti-aircraft calibration duties. It had a number of flights situated at airfields around the country. The unit moved to Redhill on September 5. The second squadron, No 287, provided aircraft to co-operate with other units. It moved to Redhill on January 20 1945. No 1 ADU, along with an element of No 49 MU, also moved to Redhill.

In January 1945, No 1337 Wing SHAEF was formed at Gatwick and on February 1 the station was taken over by the SHAEF disarmament unit. Following the ending of hostilities in Europe Gatwick became the satellite of Dunsfold. In June, No 103 Air Disarmament Wing arrived and took over control of Gatwick from the SHAEF unit, which moved to the Continent.

Over the next few months there was a gradual run-down of RAF activities. During this period the station housed No 85 Group Communications Squadron and a detachment of No 84 Group Communications Squadron. Also, a number of units returned to Gatwick to be disbanded. A personnel holding unit arrived but made only a short stay. A release centre was also set up. Finally, the station was derequisitioned on August 31 1946.

The airfield was then returned to the Ministry of Civil Aviation, but despite its active wartime service Gatwick still lacked hard runways, which did nothing to attract civilian operators.

During the period 1946 to 1956 the companies at Gatwick included Horton Airways, Ciros Aviation Ltd and also Airwork Ltd, which used the hangars and technical installations for the repair and servicing of naval Sea Hornets and Seafires.

In the 1950s Gatwick was chosen to be-

Top *Dilapidated Vickers Viking, G-AJFT, at Gatwick on February 3 1968.* **Above** *BAC 111-201, G-ASJJ, of British United at Gatwick.*

come London's second airport and in March 1956 all companies moved out and Gatwick closed for reconstruction work.

When the new airport opened two years later it possessed a single 7,000 ft runway and a large apron. There were also new terminal buildings which were connected to a new railway station and covered walkways from the buildings to the aircraft loading bays. The new airport was opened by HM The Queen on June 9 1958. The

Queen, who was accompanied by HRH Prince Philip, arrived in a Heron of the Queen's Flight.

The formation of British United Airways in 1960 brought a marked increase in both scheduled and charter business. There was also an upsurge in inclusive tours and to cope with the increase two additional piers were added. As the number of aircraft increased the airport expanded to accommodate the larger types then coming into

Top left *An aerial view of London Airport Gatwick, looking west (photographed October 1980). Gatwick is the sixth busiest international airport in the world, handling 10.5 million passengers a year.* **Left** *An aerial view of Gatwick, looking north and showing a good view of the old Beehive in the foreground. The Beehive is used as a general office and training centre by the British Airport Authority and various operators at Gatwick. It is the subject of a preservation order and it is possible that in future it could well become the basis of a commercial aviation museum.*

Above *The Airlink Sikorsky helicopter takes off from London Gatwick on its way to London Heathrow Airport.*

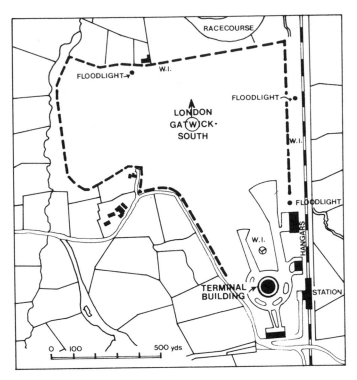

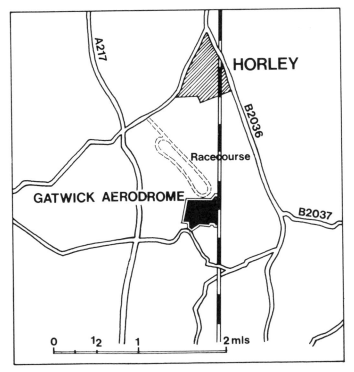

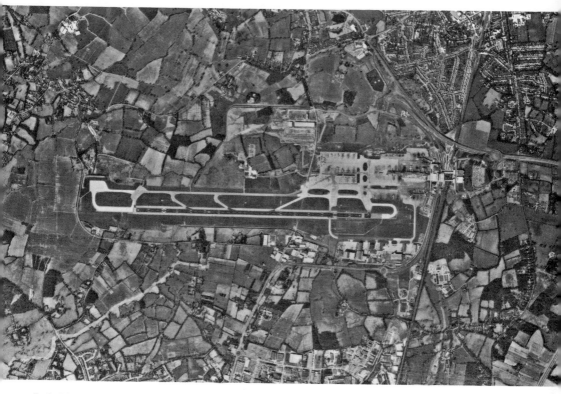

Left *Maps of Gatwick.*

Above *Aerial view of Gatwick airport circa 1978.*

service and runway was extended, first to 8,200 ft in 1964 and later to 10,000 ft.

Improvement continued to be made at the airport and in 1977 another major development began, involving a vast terminal extension, multi-storey car park and a direct access road to the new motorway. Still further expansion is planned for the 1980s, involving a second terminal building.

Gatwick is a popular airport for many inclusive tour operators, and it is home of the Golden Lion, British Caledonian. This company, from its humble beginning with a single DC-7 in 1961, plays a considerable part in the total movements at Gatwick and now operates fleets of DC-10-30, Boeing 707-320C and BAC 1-11 aircraft. It has three Airbus A310s on order for delivery in 1984 with options on more for later.

British Caledonian is Europe's largest private enterprise scheduled airline. Caledonian House, Crawley is the group's new headquarters office block near London Airport—Gatwick. The company also offers maintenance support service to the world's airlines through British Caledonian Airways Engineering Division and the centrepiece of the 27 acre maintenance base is a purpose-built DC-10-30 engineering facility which became operational in January 1980. This is complemented by two further hangar installations and enables the engineering section to handle up to five aircraft simultaneously in weather-protected conditions.

British Caledonian Airways also operates the Gatwick-Heathrow Airlink helicopter service with a 28-seat Sikorsky S-61N helicopter leased from the British Airports Authority. The service has been licensed to operate until 1984 when it is expected that the M25 motorway will be completed between the two airports.

The rapid growth of traffic has affected the counties surrounding the airport in various ways—housing and employment being just two. The airport will continue to expand as the growth in leisure travel increases, and Gatwick stands poised at the crossroads.

Gravesend (Chalk), Kent

178/TQ665720. East of Gravesend between the A226 and A2

During the early 1930s Captain Edgar Percival, an Australian aviator, used a piece of land to the west side of Thong Lane as a landing ground, and it was this early beginning that led to the construction of Gravesend Airport, which officially opened on that site on October 12 1932, with Alan Cobham's National Aviation Day Display team in attendance, Sir Alan Cobham giving demonstrations with three-engined 'Ferry' aircraft.

The airfield was sited just south of Chalk village between the A226 and A2 roads and covered 148 acres, although only a part of this area was put down to grass. It overlooked the River Thames but since it was 250 ft above sea level it was above the river fog. Construction of the aerodrome began early in 1932. Two hangars, a club house, a control tower, fuel and oil stores and all the necessary ancillaries were sited on the eastern side close to Thong Lane.

Prior to the official opening the Gravesend Aviation company had been formed in June by two pilots, T.A.B. Ternan of London and W.A.C. Kingham of Beckenham, with local builder Mr Herbert Gooding as managing director. Mr A.D. Carroll was the first chief flying instructor. Also, a rally was held at the site on August 25 when at least 20 light aircraft put in an appearance for the Press. At this time there were only four resident aircraft for instructional purposes, two Moths, an Avro Avian and a Desoutter. These belonged to the Gravesend School of Flying, which was run along Service lines and offered instruction up to commercial pilot standard.

November saw a Fokker air-liner, *PH-AEZ* of KLM, land at Gravesend with ten passengers. The KLM officials who were aboard were well pleased with the airport layout. With his money tied up in the airport, Herbert Gooding tried to promote it in all possible ways. KLM was one, and it again used the airport on February 24 1933, when a snow storm made it impossible to reach Croydon airport. Other companies were then encouraged to use Gravesend as an emergency landing ground and it became styled London East—Gravesend. At that time Croydon was the main airport for London but it often became shrouded by fog. Airliners of KLM, Deutsche Lufthansa, Sabena and Swissair did in fact use Gravesend when Croydon was closed by unfavourable weather conditions. However, none of the companies became fully established here as had been hoped for by Herbert Gooding.

On Easter Sunday, April 16 1933, the Aviation Air Days display team again visited Gravesend but the event was marred when the wing tip of Captain Mackay's aircraft struck Harry Sharp and he suffered back and arm injuries.

The flying school became busy with the better weather, but tragedy struck on June 1 1933, when Mr R. Fortescue, a 22-year-old pupil of the flying school took off in Moth *G-AAKX* and was never seen again. He was last seen heading in a westerly direction.

July 1933 saw the arrival of the Royal Air Force when three Hawker Audax aircraft and an Atlas used the airport as a base during exercises.

For the rest of the year the flying school continued to flourish and negotiations began with KLM. A new main hangar, 130 ft × 125 ft was erected and this was completed by the summer of 1934. However, the Dutch airline did not use the airport as its London terminal, and the writing was on the wall, although, in spite of the difficulties, flying continued.

Percival, who had been at the site with sales and servicing facilities since the company's formation in 1932, had been successful with his three-seat low wing monoplane, which was test-flown from West Malling, and works were then set up at Gravesend, which became the first factory airfield of Percival Aircraft Ltd. He had rented space in the hangars and production began on 24 aircraft. In fact 22 Gulls were built and these included those flown by Jean Batten *(G-ADPR)*, Amy Mollison *(G-ADZO)* and Sir Charles Kingsford-Smith *(G-ACJV)*, when setting new records for flights to Africa, Australia and South America. The Mew Gull, which emerged from the Percival stable in March 1934, was an instant winner and proved to be just about the fastest single-engined racing aircraft of the 1930s.

Sadly, Gravesend could not accommodate the success of the Percival Aircraft Company and it moved to Luton in October 1936. Here the company went on to produce many Proctors and Prentices.

Essex Aero Ltd moved in after the Percival Company had left and they specialised in tuning and converting aircraft. During this period several aircraft made their maiden flights from Gravesend, including the prototype Short Scion

G-ACJI and the sole CLW Curlew, *G-ADYU* which was test-flown in September 1936. Amy Mollison had decided to use Gravesend and in 1936 made a second flight to the Cape which broke all records for the return flight and the round trip. In 1936 she and her husband were divorced.

Another to visit the Gravesend scene was the little Dutch Scheldemusch. This was a single-bay pusher biplane and two of the aircraft visited Gravesend in 1937. *PH-AMA*, piloted by R.G. Doig, crashed there in March 1937. The pilot was unhurt but it stopped plans to build the Scheldemusch under licence. The second aircraft, *PH-AMG*, arrived in May and it somehow survived the war but its fate is unknown.

Airports Limited who already owned Gatwick, purchased Gravesend, found it unprofitable and offered it to Gravesend Council for use as a municipal airport, but a figure could not be agreed. So, in October 1937, arrangements were made with the Air Ministry for Gravesend to become a training school under the rearmament programme. No 20 Elementary and Reserve Flying Training School was formed and a contract was also obtained to teach Royal Navy pupils to fly.

Early in 1939 Gravesend was at the centre of the record-breaking flight from England

to Cape Town and back. *G-AEXF* took-off and landed at Gravesend.

With the outbreak of the Second World War the civil flying ceased and No 20 ERFTS moved away. The airfield was requisitioned by the Air Ministry to become a satellite station of Biggin Hill and many squadrons were detached here from the parent station during the early months of the war. Aircrew members were accommodated in the control tower as well as at Cobham Hall. Ground crews were accommodated in the Laughing Waters roadhouse on the A2 road and in local commandeered houses.

For some unknown reason the station was to have two decoy airfields, one at Cliffe Marshes and a 'QX'-site at Luddesdown. Records do not show if they served any purpose.

No 32 Squadron moved in during January 1940 and spent three months at Gravesend. The Hurricanes of No 56 Squadron then arrived on May 10 but after only two days they moved out. They were replaced by No 610 'County of Chester' Squadron which arrived on May 26. This unit was equipped with Spitfires and took part in the Dunkirk evacuation, during which time the squadron lost two Commanding Officers, Squadron Leaders Franks and Smith. In July No 610 moved to Biggin Hill and it was replaced by No 604 'County of Middlesex' Squadron equipped with Blenheim Mk IFs. Numerous night patrols were carried out but no contact was made

Hurricanes of No 501 Squadron taking off at Gravesend in August 1940.

with the enemy. During this period No 72 Squadron spent a week at Gravesend on detachment from Biggin Hill.

On July 27 1940, No 501 'County of Gloucester' Squadron moved in to Gravesend. This was an Auxiliary Air Force unit flying Hurricanes and at this stage of the war many of the pilots were the original Auxiliary members. Amongst the members were two Sergeant Pilots, J.H. 'Ginger' Lacey and D.A.S. McKay who went on to achieve fame. Both survived the war.

On July 29, the Squadron engaged a large formation of Ju 87s and escorting Bf 109s. No 501 claimed six of the enemy shot down and six damaged. Hawkinge was used as a forward airfield and No 501 would move there each day just after first light. As the pace of the battle increased, the squadron, like all the others in No 11 Group was being stretched to the limit. The bombing of Hawkinge had temporarily closed the airfield and from August 12 the squadron operated from Gravesend. But by 0400 hours on August 15 the 12 Hurricanes were back at Hawkinge. The action continued and hectic dog fights were carried out over Southern Kent. On September 2, bombs fell on Gravesend aerodrome, injuring two soldiers. That same day 501 Squadron lost four aircraft. Three pilots, Pilot Officer S. Skalski and Sergeants W.B. Henn and H.C. Adams, were injured, and Flying Officer A.T.

Luftwaffe target photograph of Gravesend, 1940.

Rose-Price was killed on the day that he joined 501 Squadron when his Hurricane, *L1578*, was shot down near Ashford.

The squadron was early into battle on the morning of September 6 when its members engaged a force of approximately 100 enemy aircraft over Ashford. During the ensuing battle they lost three pilots. Pilot Officer H.C. Adams in Hurricane *V6612* crashed at 0900 hours at Clavertye and Sergeant C.V. Houghton in Hurricane *V6646* and Sergeant G.W. Pearson in Hurricane *P3516* were both shot down in combat over the Ashford area at 0900 hours.

The Hurricanes of 501 Squadron moved out on September 10 and they were replaced the following day by the Spitfires of No 66 Squadron. They remained only a few weeks, during which time the squadron continued the action with daily interception patrols, either from the small bumpy grass airfield at Gravesend or Hawkinge. The Battle of Britain was now over and both 501 and 66 Squadrons had been heavily involved in the fight for survival.

On October 7 1940, No 421 Flight was formed at Gravesend on the personal instigation of Winston Churchill. The flight was formed from a nucleus of per-

Lysander IIIA of No 227 Squadron, Air Sea Rescue, at Gravesend, 1943.

sonnel from No 66 Squadron and the aircraft were coded *LZ* the same as 66 Squadron, but a hyphen was placed between the L and the Z. The role of this special flight was to patrol the sky high over the channel to report any build-up of the Luftwaffe. No 421 Flight moved to West Malling on October 30. Also, at the end of the month, No 66 Squadron moved out and was replaced by No 141 Squadron. This was a night fighter unit flying Defiants and it was joined shortly afterwards by the Hurricanes of No 85 Squadron under Squadron Leader Peter Townsend. This unit did not remain very long and when it moved out on January 1 1941 it was replaced by another Defiant squadron, No 264, but this unit remained only ten days.

In November 1940 Gravesend became a self-accounting station and more suitable buildings were erected during the winter. At the end of April 1941 the Defiants of No 141 Squadron left and for the rest of the year various Spitfire squadrons were in and out of the station: No 74 May-July, No 72 July, No 609 July to September, No 92 September to October and No 72 October 1941 to March 1942. During 1942 the station became very busy, with no fewer than 14 fighter squadrons

posted in and out: No 401 March to June, No 124 May to June, Nos 111, 71 and 350 June to July, Nos 401 and 124 July, Nos 65 and 133 July to August, No 71 August to September, Nos 124 and 232 a week in August, No 165 August to November and No 65 August to September. All of these units were equipped with Spitfires. In December 1942, No 277 Squadron arrived and remained until it moved out with Nos 19, 65 and 122 Squadrons on April 15 1944.

During 1942 and 1943 the area of the airfield was increased to enable both the north-south and east-west runways to be considerably lengthened—the north-south to 5,100 ft and the east-west to 5,400 ft. Also, Sommerfield steel tracking was laid and Drem runway lighting installed. Fuel storage at this time was for up to 32,000 gallons of aviation and 1,500 of MT spirit and 400 gallons of oil. The station could now support three squadrons and it switched from defensive to offensive operations. The Gravesend squadrons joined the Biggin Hill Wing with sweeps into occupied Europe.

Gravesend remained a busy fighter station until June 1944. Over the next two years, Nos 181, 245, 174, 247, 193, 275 and 266 Squadrons, flying Typhoon 1Bs, Nos 2, 4, 19, 65 and 122 Squadrons flying Mustangs and Nos 132, 306 and 64 Squadrons flying Spitfires all spent time at Gravesend before being replaced in mid-

Gravesend control tower, originally built in March 1935 and photographed here in June 1965 shortly before demolition.

April 1944 by Nos 21, 464 (RAAF) and 487 (RNZAF) Squadrons which arrived from Hunsdon. These three units comprised 140 Wing in the 2nd Tactical Air Force and were equipped with Mosquito FB VIs. They were mainly occupied with intruder activity, their principal task being to bomb and machine-gun tactical targets and to soften up Northern France for the approaching invasion. Individual aircraft sometimes flew three sorties in a night. The normal tactics were to cross the English Channel at 5,000 ft then dive through the coastal gun belt to an operational patrol height of 1,500 to 2,000 ft.

The Second Tactical Air Force threw its weight against enemy lines of communications, having been specially trained in night harassing techniques. On the morning of June 5, No 464 Squadron diarist wrote: 'A chilly morning with high wind, however, an air of expectancy pervades the squadron—something seems to indicate that we have not long to wait.' How right they were, for that night the Gravesend squadrons put up maximum effort, but they found little traffic on the roads of northern France as the enemy had not yet awoken to the invasion. However, they did manage to attack some bridge, rail and road junctions. The Gravesend squadrons did an excellent job and they continued to support Operation *Overlord*. The Mosquito patrols came into their own when the Bostons and Mitchells were withdrawn from this task for daylight sorties over the Pas de Calais area. However, Hitler had other plans and he launched

Operation *Rumpelkammer*. The first flying bombs (V1s) were launched against Britain on June 12 1944 and the first one fell on Swanscombe, Kent, at 0418 hours on June 13.

The V1s put an end to flying at Gravesend. They made flying operations too hazardous, for the airfield was directly in the line of fire. Therefore, it was found necessary to use Dunsfold airfield for operations, but this was only temporary, and on June 18 the three resident Mosquito squadrons moved to tented quarters at Thorney Island, Hants. After this sudden, enforced closure the station then became non-operational and it was surrounded by a heavy balloon barrage for the duration of the war. Gravesend was the control centre for guidance of aircraft through the balloon defences.

The war over, the airfield was put on a Care and Maintenance basis, but like so many airfields, its future looked bleak. Essex Aero had remained throughout the war years and had maintained a small factory on the airfield for making self-sealing aircraft petrol tanks. After the war the company purchased two Walruses and two Sea Otters but these were either sold or cannibalised for spare parts. In spite of its Ministry contracts, Essex Aero went into liquidation in March 1956 and Gravesend closed to flying. The Air Ministry relinquished control in June 1956 and within two years a large private housing estate began to engulf the area of the airfield.

Today, there is no longer any trace of the aerodrome, for much of the site is built-up and is part of River View Park estate, two schools, playing fields and a sports centre having been constructed on most of the airfield's wartime extensions. The 14 pilots who died during the Battle of Britain whilst flying from Gravesend are commemorated on a plaque in the Thong Lane Sports Centre.

With a little foresight one might today have been able to enjoy a pint, had, for example, the control tower been converted into an attractive public house. A positive link with the past would have been retained.

Today, when one stands at River View Park estate surveying the sea of houses, it is hard to imagine this land was once the scene of so much pioneering aviation activity in bygone years.

Hainault Farm (Fairlop), Essex

See Fairlop

Hanworth Park (Feltham), Middlesex

See Feltham

Hatfield (Chiswick), Hertfordshire

166/TL206090. East of St Albans on the A1, to the north of the junction with the A414

In 1930, Captain de Havilland purchased some 150 acres of farmland near Hatfield, which gave its name to the airfield and was to become renowned throughout the world.

The de Havilland company had outgrown its premises at Stag Lane and the move started in the early 1930s. At first the aerodrome occupied the northern part of the area and was separated from the remainder of the site by a stream. This was eventually culverted, but for several years a weight restriction was imposed on passing aircraft and vehicles. A hangar, club house and petrol installation were

Below *DH87 Hornet Moth at Hatfield.* **Bottom** *DH 86A,* L7596 G-ADJY, *seen on the apron at Hatfield.*

Above *The DH 84 Dragon, '146' of the 1930s. This aircraft became a successful feeder-liner operating on the shorter routes. The better known DH 89 Rapide was developed from the DH 84.*

Below *The DH 88 Comet Racer, winner of the famous 1934 England to Australia air race. Experience in the design and construction of this aircraft was invaluable to de Havilland when they conceived the Mosquito.*

DH 93 Don, L2391, seen here at Hatfield.

constructed on the south-east edge of the
site. Initially de Havilland moved only a
flying school to Hatfield but by 1934 a
new factory and offices had been built on
the edge of the airfield and production of
the Dragon light transport aircraft and
Tiger Moth trainer was well underway.

The de Havilland Flying School used
Gipsy Moths for civil pupils and DH 9s for
annual refresher courses for the RAF
Reserve. The aerodrome was sited on the
west side of Hatfield town and it had
obstructions on both sides of it. On the
east side was a 75 ft high aircraft factory
chimney and on the west side were 200 ft
high radio station masts.

During the expansion period of the
RAF in the mid-1930s the flying school
became No 1 Elementary & Reserve Flying
Training School and at the outbreak of
the Second World War in September 1939,
No 1 Elementary Flying Training School
formed that same month from No 1 E&
RFTS. There were also changes for de
Havilland's, which once again turned to
military aircraft. The Rapide was in production and with the coming of war it was
destined to see military service on a large
scale. In 1941 the DH 89B Dominie, a
military version of the Rapide, was
introduced and applied to military
Rapides. The aircraft played two roles,

one as a wireless and navigation 'flying
classroom' and the other as an eight-
to-ten-seat communications aircraft. It
was extensively used by the ATA for the
recovery of the ferry pilots.

It was here they produced one of the
most famous aircraft of the war—the
Mosquito—a twin-engined, high-speed
fighter-bomber made out of wood—and
in 1943 Dominie production was transferred to Brush Coachworks at Loughborough so that the Hatfield factory was
free to concentrate on full-scale production of the Mosquito. Twenty-one
were built in 1941, 389 in 1942, 806 in
1943, 1,203 in 1944 and 635 in 1945.
Production was halted in early war years
by the air raids and in 1940 so many hours
were being lost that people were asked to
continue work after the alert siren sounded
and only stop when imminent danger was
broadcast over the loudspeakers.

On October 3 1941, a single Ju 88 caused
a great deal of havoc during a daylight
raid. The German aircraft was from Laon
airfield in France and was detailed to bomb
Reading but visibility was poor and he
chanced upon Hatfield. As the intruder
came in low, at about 60 ft, he was hit by
small arms fire which set his starboard
engine ablaze. On his second attack just
before 11.30 am he dropped four large
HE bombs and machine-gunned workers
as they ran for shelter. Twenty-one people
were killed and 70 wounded. The Ju 88
crashed at Hertfordbury.

The Mosquito was also built at the de Havilland Leavesden plant and by Standard Motors, Percival and Airspeed. No fewer than 4,444 Mosquitoes had been built in the United Kingdom up to VJ-Day in August 1945. As a bomber of wooden construction the Mosquito was unique. The first deliveries of the Mosquito Mk I to the RAF were made in mid-1941 and they were operated by the Photographic Development Unit at Benson.

It is ironic that Mosquito development was formally cancelled by MAP and only the farsightedness of Geoffrey de Havilland and his design team won the day. After an uphill struggle an official order for 50 bomber-reconnaissance aircraft reached de Havilland on March 1 1940. This small order reflected the lack of interest in the aircraft. On November 25 1940 the first prototype, *W4050*, made its maiden flight at Hatfield with Geoffrey de Havilland at the controls. The flight trials left the doubters open mouthed and by July 1941 the de Havilland company was faced with production programmes out of all proportion to what had previously been handled. The Mosquito had many roles, as a photo-reconnaissance aircraft, fighter and fighter-bomber. It excelled itself in all of them.

From 1940 to 1942 Hatfield housed No 5 Ferry Pilot Pool and it was there that Amy Johnson was based as an Air Transport Auxiliary ferry pilot. They were first to learn of her death on Sunday January 5 1941. Amy had set off from Squires Gate, Blackpool to deliver Airspeed Oxford *V3540* to Kidlington at Oxford. This should have been a routine flight of about one hour's duration. However, nearly three hours after Amy's being overdue at her destination, the Oxford was reported down in the Thames Estuary, just off the Kent coast, in the freezing sea, nearly 100 miles off course. Ever since Amy's Oxford hit the water there has been speculation as to how she came to grief and whether she died alone. It is true to say that Amy took off alone and that the Oxford carried sufficient fuel for 4½ hours flying. Amy's crash still remains one of the unsolved mysteries of the Second World War.

Throughout this period the flying school continued to operate and Hatfield was a very busy airfield with training and test flying. To ease the congested circuit a landing ground was brought into use at Holywell Hyde in 1942 and in early April 1943 the entire unit moved there. Hatfield was now clear of training aircraft and was able to concentrate on test-flying the products of the factory, which was a vital factor in equipping the Royal Air Force.

During the war Hatfield was the centre of a double-cross sabotage. The Germans considered the de Havilland factory a prime target because of the construction of the Mosquito. So, in December 1942, agent *Zigzag* was dropped near Ely by parachute. Eddie Chapman, a safe-blower who had been in prison in Jersey when the Germans took over the island was agent *Zigzag*. Plans were laid to make *Zigzag*'s story sound convincing when he told it to the Germans on his return to Germany. He and a Major Ryde selected the power house as their target during a daylight recce of the factory. Then on January 2 1943 they were driven to the south side of the airfield by a Special Branch officer for the purpose of breaking into the airfield. They successfully made it to the powerhouse, which proved it was feasible to go through with their plan. *Zigzag* had not been supplied with any explosives by the Germans so it was decided that he should steal some in order not to arouse their suspicions. He successfully burgled a quarry at Sevenoaks. The next step was to carry through the last stage of the plan. When the shifts changed at midnight on January 29, Maskelyne, an illusionist used by the Secret Service as a camouflage expert, blew out part of the power house roof and let off smoke bombs. For the benefit of a German reconnaissance aircraft, which was allowed over the factory, pieces of transformer were scattered on the ground. The factory workers were told a mysterious

Above left *DH 95 Flamingo* R2765 Lady of Hendon. *Only three were built for No 24 Squadron.*

Left *DH 98 Mosquito T III*, RR299, *at Hatfield in the markings of No 601 Squadron. Nicknamed 'The Wooden Wonder', this unique high speed fighter-bomber performed a wide range of duties during the Second World War.*

Below *Vampire line-up at Hatfield.*

explosion had occurred in the power room. The plan had been well laid and carried out successfully.

After the war the runway was built and it came into service in 1947. It was 6,000 ft, paved with a tarmacadam surface and had 500 ft half-width extensions at either end. In its peacetime role the Hatfield factory produced both civil and military aircraft. In the military sphere the jet-powered Vampire was sold in large numbers to the Royal Air Force and Royal Navy. In the civil field the company designed and built the world's first jet airliner, the Comet, which first flew in 1949. When it entered service with BOAC it cut international flight times by half. The Nimrod, currently in service with the Royal Air Force is a direct descendant of the Comet.

On August 22 1950 it was a new kind of

The DH 106 Comet—the world's first jet airliner, which first flew in 1949. The Nimrod, currently in service with the RAF, is a direct descendant of the Comet and bears out the soundness of the original design.

Venom that lifted from Hatfield's runway. This was the prototype Venom night fighter and it had been built at de Havilland's own expense, like the Vampire night fighter before it. The first production NF 2, *WL804*, flew from Hatfield on March 4 1952. It was not until the latter part of 1953 that the first operational squadron,

DH 112 Venom FB Mk I on a flight from Hatfield.

Top *DH 108 TG283, which was converted from a DH 100 Vampire, seen here at Hatfield.*
Above *The first Super Trident 3, G-BAJL/B-268 seen here at Hatfield before leaving for China on August 22 1975.*

No 23 at Coltishall in Norfolk, began to re-equip with Venom NF 2s where they replaced Vampire NF 10s.

In 1960, at the time the Trident was being designed, the de Havilland Aircraft Company merged with the Hawker Siddeley Group. The Trident entered service with BEA in 1963 and was the most advanced airliner of its type, but never the success the company hoped it would be. In June 1970 the people's Republic of China took delivery of four ex-Pakistan International Airlines aircraft. The following year the Hatfield sales team was invited to China. The first order, for six Trident 2Es, worth £20 million, was

received on August 23 1971. A year later a further order for six Trident 2Es was placed with options for a further batch to be placed within three months. These options were confirmed on November 11.

Further changes took place in 1977 when Hawker Siddeley Aviation, Hawker Siddeley Dynamics, British Aircraft Corporation and Scottish Aviation merged to become British Aerospace. The corporation was divided into two groups, Aircraft and Dynamics. Hatfield became the headquarters of the Hatfield-Chester Division of the Aircraft Group, Chester having been de Havilland's main factory in the north of the country.

Over the years the site expanded and it now occupies a total of nearly 1,600 acres. This comprises the factory itself with buildings occupying nearly 1,500,000 sq ft and the airfield with its 6,000 ft paved runway, taxiways, engine running bay and three wind tunnels. In addition about 600 acres are still farmed.

With over 100 departments at British Aerospace Hatfield, the work-force numbers over 4,000—a team of men and women who are skilled in their work. This long-established factory is capable of complete aircraft manufacturing programmes from design and mock-up stage to final assembly and flight test. Hatfield is the major assembly for the BAe146 and component manufacturer for the A300, A310 and HS125.

Also housed here is the Hatfield Division of the British Aerospace Dynamics Group, best known for its work on Blue Steel and whose current projects include the Sky Flash, Sea Eagle and Sea Skua air-launched

weapons systems. With 2,500 employees this division has extensive research, design and test facilities. The Sky Flash is the main armament of the Phantom interceptors of the Royal Air Force and is being supplied to the Swedish Air Force for the Saab Viggen JA37 interceptor. It is also the main armament of the Tornado Air Defence Variant. Sea Eagle is an all-weather air-launched sea-skimming anti-ship missile with an air-breathing turbine engine for long range operation. It has an active radar homing head and is a fire-and-forget weapon. Sea Eagle will enter service in the mid-1980s with the Royal Air Force and Royal Navy and will arm Buccaneer, Tornado and Sea Harrier aircraft. Sea Skua is a helicopter-launched medium-range all-weather sea-skimming anti-ship missile. Four Sea Skuas can be carried by a Westland Navy Lynx helicopter, and in this form Sea Skua entered service with the Royal Navy in 1981. Chiswick, with 100 employees, is part of the Hatfield Division and this small specialist factory

Left *Aerial view of Hatfield taken mid-1940, looking north.* **Below left** *Contrasting view of Hatfield, also looking north, in 1980.*

Below *DH (HS) 125 prototype built at Hatfield. Photograph shows roll-out of G-ARYA.*

Above *Four Sky Flash air-to-air missiles on the Tornado Air Defence Variant. Sky Flash is in full production by British Aerospace Dynamics Group. It is the most advanced weapon of its type in production.*

Left *Sea Skua undergoing trials on a Westland/Aerospatiale Lynx.*

Below *Original design office based at Stag Lane and now at Hatfield as the DH Museum.*

Above right *Production of Britain's new generation Feedliner, the BAe 146. Final assembly is carried out at the company's Hatfield factory which produces three aircraft a month.*

Right *BAe 146 on 'First Hop' at Hatfield on September 2 1981. The BAe Feedliner is a short-range 70-109 seat airliner.*

produces advanced weighing systems and small high-precision components.

Today Hatfield has a world-wide reputation for the design and production of civil airliners. Serving as a reminder from those far-off days, a wooden hut, the original design office of the de Havilland Aircraft Company, at Stag Lane, stands on the perimeter of the old grass field that used to be Hatfield Aerodrome. Today, it houses the de Havilland Museum.

The new feederliner, the BAe146, was unveiled to the aviation world on May 20 1981 with a fanfare from an RAF band. The aircraft is powered by four Avco Lycoming ALF 502R-3 turbofans and the first production aircraft 001 was appropriately registered *G-SSSH* in view of its low noise level. As stated, the BAe146 is assembled at Hatfield while four other British Aerospace facilities supply parts. The centre fuselage is built at Bristol, the rear fuselage at Manchester, the fin at Brough and the engine pylons at Prestwick. Hatfield builds the front fuselage and flight deck. Two risk-sharing partners also supply parts—Avco Aero-structures at Nashville supplies the wing boxes and Saab-Scania at Linkoping, Sweden the tailplane and all movable control surfaces. Hatfield is a very important and busy site and the 146 should carry them well into the 1990s for it is the finest aircraft since the Dakota. The 146 is a likely choice for

RAF transport. Also, modified versions of the ultra-quiet £6 million jet could later be bought for the Royal Family's use, replacing the ageing Andovers of the Queen's Flight.

Hatfield today is part of the Hatfield-Chester Division of the Aircraft Group of British Aerospace. As such it is the centre of British Aerospace's civil aircraft activities and its future role will continue in this sphere.

Heathrow, London

176/TQ075755. West of London, with access from the A4 and M4

In 1929 Fairey Aviation Company Limited was on the lookout for a new site and it purchased for £15,000, a 150-acre area of land near Harmondsworth, just north-east of Stanwell, Middlesex. There, a private aerodrome was laid out. The landing area of smooth turf was laid down by C.D. Hunter's company which specialised in 'Hunterised' greensward. During this period Northolt continued to be used for flight-testing some aircraft. The new aerodrome became Fairey's flight-testing

centre for the autumn of 1930, when they moved in from Northolt. Variously known as Harmondsworth, or the Great West aerodrome and later as Heathrow it remained in use by Fairey until 1944, when it was requisitioned by the Air Ministry.

The aerodrome had been surveyed in 1942 and found suitable as a bomber airfield with the usual triangular pattern of runways. Work did not begin until 1944 and it was now decided the airfield was for use by American B-29 Superfortress bombers. The war ended before the airfield could be put to military use. The formal reason believed to have been given for the requisitioning of the aerodrome has since been questioned—no B-29s were used in the European theatre of war. It was then decided to replan the aerodrome for civil purposes and a committee was formed to decide the runway pattern. The committee had to take into account the fact that aircraft must be able to land or take off in any possible wind direction with a 4 mph crosswind. Their decisions resulted in the runway pattern known as the Star of David.

Below *Fairey Hendon night bomber, K1695. Three Fairey Gordons in the background. Photographed at Fairey's at the Great West Aerodrome circa 1930.*

Above right *Fairey IIIF Mk IV (M) two-seat General Purpose biplane (570 hp Napier 'Lion XI' engine) at the Great West Aerodrome circa 1930.* **Right** *The prototype English Electric Canberra PR 3, VX181, being prepared at Heathrow for its record-breaking trip to Australia on January 27 1953.* **Below right** *Avro 689 Tudor 5 G-AKCC at London Heathrow on April 6 1950 before its proving flight to Johannesburg. The aircraft was named* President Kruger.

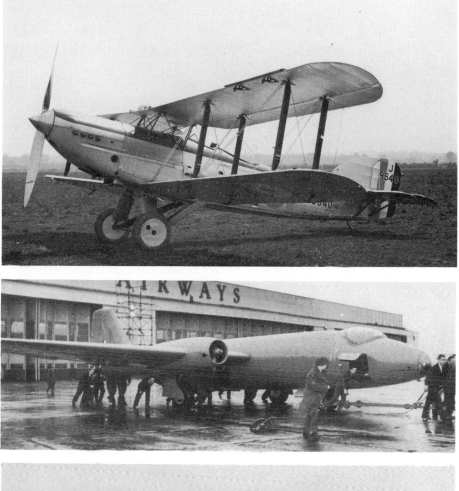

Fairey had been given alternative accommodation and during this reconstruction period Fairey Aviation moved to Heston, which had been specially developed, but this was soon to prove unsuitable as a flight-test centre. The work continued at Heathrow and by the end of 1945 the first runway and some primitive buildings had been completed. On January 1 1946 the site was handed over by the Air Ministry to the civil aviation authorities. That same day a British South American Airways Starlight, a 13-seat Lancastrian, took off on a proving flight to Buenos Aires. Regular services of BOAC and Quantas started on May 27 and Heathrow Airport was formally opened on May 31 1946.

By 1947, all three runways in the first triangle had been completed. Work continued on the second triangle phase and by 1950 the runway structure was almost complete, but Runway 3 had been

On May 16 1955, Lufthansa began regular service to London. The photograph shows the Convair CV-340 after landing at Heathrow.

abandoned to allow development in the central area. Runways 4, 6 and 7 were later to be taken out to provide more aircraft parking space. The ever-changing trends in aircraft design meant almost continual constructional development to keep pace with the ever-increasing volume of traffic.

London Heathrow as we know it today began to take shape in 1950 and work began in the centre of the airport on a new

Prototype Tu-104 seen here at London Airport March 1956. It brought General Serov. In the background are two DC3s.

control tower, passenger building (now Terminal 2) and office building (Queen's Building). At 08.35 hours on January 27 1953, Canberra *VX181*, with Flight Lieutenant L.M. Whittington as pilot and Flight Lieutenant J.A. Brown as navigator, took off from Heathrow and arrived at Darwin, Australia at 06.44 hours the following morning. The total time for this record-breaking trip was 22 hours 9 minutes, whilst the flying time was 19 hours 1 minute. By the end of 1953, passenger traffic had topped one million per annum for the first time.

On June 15 1954 a statue to Alcock and Brown was unveiled on the 35th anniversary of the first non-stop trans-Atlantic flight. October 1954 saw a further increase in air traffic when Northolt airport closed to civil flying and all operations were transferred to Heathrow. Many historic events were seen in 1955, one being the arrival of the de Havilland Comet 3 at the end of a round-the-world flight. Group Captain John Cunningham was at the controls.

By the end of 1955 the first phase of permanent buildings was complete and these buildings were officially opened by HM The Queen on December 16 of that year. The airport continued to expand and in 1957 the Millbourn report recommended the construction of Terminals 1 and 3 and the pier, or finger-and-gate system of routing passengers to their aircraft.

The airport expanded by leaps and bounds and in December 1968 the Cargo Terminal on the south side was opened. The following year both Terminals 1 and 3 were completed and in operation. All

passenger terminals are now equipped with pier and air-jetty systems.

The M4 motorway with spur to Heathrow Central opened in March 1965 and May 1969 saw 350 competitors in the Daily Mail Trans-Atlantic Race pass through Heathrow. By the end of the following year passenger throughput had exceeded 15½ million and aircraft movement had reached 270,302.

Further efforts were made to improve the country's principal airport link with the capital and in 1971 work started to extend the Piccadilly Underground line from its terminus at Hounslow West to the Heathrow Central area, via Hatton Cross on the south side of the airport. The 3½-mile tunnel was opened in July 1975. The underground station next to the control tower is linked to the terminals by subways equipped with moving walkways.

The airport continues to grow and it is interesting to note that passenger throughput in 1977 was 23,775,605, yet aircraft movements were only 265,014, less than in 1970, but with over eight million more passengers. During May 1978 talks were underway for a fourth terminal.

Heathrow is the world's busiest airport in terms of international traffic. In total terms Heathrow ranks as the fourth busiest airport. The peak rate of landings and takeoffs recorded during a complete hour, between 1100-1200 hours was 80 aircraft movements on September 10 1976. The passenger throughput in 1980 was 27,770,643.

The airport covers 2,819 acres and nearly 57,000 people are employed there. There are 69 airline companies operating out of Heathrow. The growth by the airlines and the airport to meet their needs

BOAC Boeing 707 G-APFL at Heathrow.

Left *Aerial view of Heathrow in 1980.*

Above *Concorde welcomes Eastern Airways Dakota* G-AMPO *at Heathrow on Sunday, April 26 1981.*

Below *A Boeing 747 of Singapore Airlines landing at London Heathrow.*

Above *A DC-9 of KLM Royal Dutch Airlines takes off from London Heathrow.*

Below *An Alitalia Airbus Industrie A300B4 Airbus at London Heathrow in July 1980.*

Concordes awaiting their passengers at Terminal 3, Heathrow (about 1976).

has been tremendous. A typical example is Swissair, which was formed in March 1931 by a merger of Balair and Ad Astra, and from the outset played a significant part in developing air travel. In 1932 it became the first European airline to operate the Lockheed Orion, a single-engined low-wing monoplane. It carried four passengers and cruised at 162 mph, 60 mph faster than any of its contemporaries.

In 1934 the twin engined Curtiss Condor entered service with Swissair. To look after the 15 or 16 passengers, Swissair employed the first air hostesses in Europe.

At the outbreak of the Second World War, Swissair's fleet consisted of five DC-3s, three DC-2s, a Dragon Rapide DH 89, a Fokker F VIIa and a Compte AC4, totalling 163 seats. Scheduled services were suspended during the war and were resumed in July 1945. Four years later the company opened a route to New York with four-engined DC-4s but these were soon replaced by larger, pressurised DC-6Bs.

With the larger aircraft came new routes and in the 1950s ones to South America and to Tokyo via South-East Asia were set up. The DC-6Bs were followed on long haul routes by DC-7s, while concurrently the network was built up in Europe and the Middle East. Destinations in all parts of Africa were added in the 1960s. Thus

Swissair's network now extends to all continents except Australia.

In 1960 the airline put its first jet aircraft into service. Its present all-jet fleet comprises two Boeing 747Bs, 11 DC-10-30s, four DC-8-62s, seven DC-9-81s, 12 DC-9-51s, 12 DC-9-32s and one DC-9-33F all-cargo aircraft. On order are ten A310 Airbuses for delivery between 1983 and 1987. Swissair has remained independent of state control and receives no government subsidy. Seventy-six per cent of its share capital is in private hands, and only 24 per cent in the hands of government institutions and local authorities. With the exception of 1961, Swissair has regularly paid dividends of between 4 per cent and 10 per cent to its shareholders. Swissair is just one of the companies that operates out of Heathrow and it continues to expand. By 1987 the fleet will be five DC-9-32s, six DC-9-51s, 15 DC-9-81s, ten A310s, 12 DC-10-30s, four B-747s and two B747 combis, a total of 54 aircraft. As the airlines expand, so do the airports.

At present runway No 1 28R/10L is 12,800 ft; No 2 05/23 is 7,734 ft and No 5 28L/10R is 12,800 ft. All runways are 150 ft wide and Nos 1 and 5 have paved shoulders 75 ft wide along original lengths and 25 ft wide on extensions. The perimeter road is 9.3 miles long. An inch of snow at Heathrow means they have 3,000 tons to clear, so to do the job they keep 28 snow-

ploughs, 14 snow sweepers, four snow blowers, four gritters and seven de-icers on stand-by. For an airfield that came too late in the Second World War it has made up for it since. Designed after the war to deal with 100,000 passengers per year it now copes with 28 million.

Top A Swissair Convair 990 Coronado seen parked on the apron in front of the control tower at Heathrow. In the mid-1960s the Coronado operated regularly between London and Zurich.

Above *A Swissair DC-10 landing at London Heathrow (circa mid-1970).*

Hendon, Middlesex

176/TQ215905. Between Edgware and Hendon on the south side of the M1 motorway

In 1909 a small and ultimately unsuccessful monoplane was constructed in Colindale by Messrs Everett and Edgcumbe, and a

shed was erected to house it in a field at the end of Colindale Avenue.

January of 1910 saw a newly-qualified British pilot, Claude Grahame-White, testing a Farman biplane from the same field, and on April 29 Louis Paulhan took

Austin Whippet, G-EAPE, and Sopwith Pup, G-EBAZ, *outside the hangars at Hendon, May 21 1923.*

off from it to make the first flight from London to Manchester within 24 hours. Grahame-White, his rival, had already failed once, and on this occasion he made the first recorded night flight in an unsuccessful attempt to overtake Paulhan. Although the Frenchman won the race, the honours were divided equally. Grahame White had used Wormwood Scrubs as a base for his Manchester flights, but he subsequently moved to Hendon and became involved in the company which was about to develop the field as the London Aerodrome. By October 1910 an open space two miles in circumference had been cleared. Three of the eight sheds then in being were occupied by the Valkyrie canard monoplanes of Horatio Barber's Aeronautical Syndicate, two contained the Bleriot School's aircraft, and the remainder were for the use of the aerodrome company.

The following year Grahame-White started a school, offering a complete flying course for 50 guineas on monoplanes or biplanes, or 75 guineas on both. In August 1911 Grahame-White Aviation Ltd, with backing from the Dunlop company, bought the aerodrome and began to turn it into a social venue to rival Ascot and Henley. Races and displays were held every week-end, and in the first year of operation

these events raised £11,000. During this period a flying school was established when Blackburn School moved here from Filey Sands, Yorkshire.

As a result of Grahame-White's urgent pleas for government recognition of the aeroplane as a vehicle for war, a military flying display was held at Hendon on May 12 1911 under the direction of the Parliamentary Aerial Defence Committee. Hendon was the site of many 'firsts', notably the first air mail service in Britain, operated from September 9-18 1911. Gustav Hamel carried over 100,000 letters and cards between Hendon and Windsor as part of the celebrations to mark the coronation of George V. The first Aerial Derby, an 80-mile round-London race was flown on September 20 1912 and witnessed by an estimated half million spectators around the course plus some 45,000 paying customers at Hendon. The first aerobatic and parachuting displays in Britain were held here, and in November 1913 the first inverted flying and loops were performed by British fliers, G.L. Temple and B.C. Hucks respectively. A passenger-carrying record was set up by the Grahame-White 'Charabanc' biplane on October 2 1913, when it flew for almost 20 minutes with nine persons aboard.

From June 1913, night flying displays took place, the aircraft being outlined with electric bulbs. Grahame-White had organised a demonstration to Members of Parliament of the possible military uses of aircraft as early as May 1911, and a popular item

in the night displays was the 'bombing' of a set piece, usually a mock ship or fort, in the centre of the airfield.

However, these light-hearted activities foreshadowed the use of military aircraft in earnest, and by the end of 1914 the three local aircraft factories, Handley Page at Cricklewood, the Aircraft Manufacturing Company at Colindale, and the Grahame-White works at Hendon Aerodrome, were all producing aircraft for the Services. When war was declared on August 4 1914, Hendon aerodrome together with Grahame-White's aircraft and facilities was requisitioned under the Defence of the Realm Act and Hendon was designated a Royal Naval Air Service Station.

The five flying schools at Hendon at the beginning of the war were contracted to train pilots for the Services; the Grahame-White school, the largest and longest-lived of the five, trained more than 490 pilots, and notable Hendon graduates included fighter 'aces' Mannock, Ball and Warneford, all destined to win the Victoria Cross.

Meanwhile the RNAS established a delivery centre for new aircraft on the aerodrome. This became No 2 Aircraft Acceptance Park and received DH 9s from Aircraft Manufacturing Co, Waring & Gillow and Berwick; DH 9as from the Aircraft Manufacturing Co; Camels from Hooper and Nieuport and Handley Page aircraft. By this time, 14 storage sheds had been erected to accommodate the aeroplanes. Forward-looking as usual, the RNAS also set up a flight for the defence of London, using a miscellany of types, which included Farman biplanes, Caudron

DH 54 Highclere, G-EBKI, *with King George V at Hendon, June 1925.*

G IIIs and a Deperdussin monoplane. No reconnoitering German aircraft were brought down in this early phase of operational flying, but a tragic casualty was Richard Gates, co-founder and former manager of the London Aerodrome, who died in a landing accident in October 1914.

By September of 1915 the only aircraft operating in defence of London were four RNAS BE 2cs flown by specially-trained pilots and divided between Hendon and Chingford. In February of 1915 some aircraft were sent from Hendon to join in raids on German submarine bases in Belgium from Dover and Dunkirk. The RFC used Hendon between February and May 1916, basing a pair of BE 2cs here on anti-airship duties, and thereafter the airfield ceased operational duties, concentrating instead on training. The RFC's School of Instruction, 18 Wing, absorbed the existing schools in September 1916 and functioned until the end of hostilities. Somewhat surprisingly, civilian students, including women, had continued to use the schools alongside military students up to this point.

Hendon in its other capacity, as a centre of aircraft manufacture, produced about a seventh of the 55,000 aircraft built in Britain over the four years of war. Besides the Grahame-White works on Aerodrome Road and Airco (de Havilland) on the Edgware Road, Handley Page established a factory in Kingsbury to assemble 0/100 and 0/400 bombers. The prototype 0/100 was towed with wings folded along Colindale Avenue to Hendon Aerodrome on the night of December 9 1915, with Frederick Handley Page himself climbing trees along the route to saw off obstructing branches in the face of protests from the unfortunate owners of the trees. The giant machine, built to fulfil the RNAS' requirement for a heavy bomber, began test-flying two days later. Subsequent Handley Page bombers were tested at the new Cricklewood aerodrome and flown to Hendon for storage. Some of these would be used

by the RAF on passenger and courier services during the peace negotiations of early 1919.

Aircraft types built at Hendon during the First World War included Airco DH2s, 4s, 5s, 6s, 9s and 9As and BE 2cs, Avro 504Ks and Farman 'Longhorn' trainers. In the latter part of the war the Grahame-White works were building Avro and de Havilland types under licence, and these were joined in 1917 by the products of the British Aerial Transport Co, whose aircraft were built in Willesden and flown from Hendon.

The Grahame-White Company had rapidly expanded and to accommodate the new growth a new factory was erected in 1916. On December 4 1917 Their Majesties King George V and Queen Mary visited the works.

Beardmore 'Inflexible', J7557, on show at the Hendon Air Display in 1928. On the left is Supermarine S5 N219 Schneider Trophy machine.

Vickers Virginia at Hendon, June 13 1934.

Also in 1917, an experiment of fundamental historical importance took place at Hendon, when an Avro 504 flown by Flight Commander R.E. Penny, RNAS, was successfully launched from a compressed air catapult on the airfield. This device was to revolutionise the operation of aircraft from ships at sea.

In December 1918, a month after the Armistice, the newly-formed No 1 (Communications) Squadron began ferrying officials and documents between Hendon and Paris for the Versailles conference. Handley Page 0/400s carried passengers, and DH 4s mail. This unit moved to Kenley in May 1919, by which time the 0/400s stored at Hendon were also beginning to disperse, leaving the aerodrome once more in civil hands but still under military ownership. Claude Grahame-White, failing to sell any new aircraft in the tiny post-war market, turned his factory over to car bodies and furniture. With typical ingenuity Grahame-White designed a two-seat runabout car, the 'Buckboard' and turned his huge work force to producing it. By January 1919 over 100 cars were leaving Hendon each week. He retained a dozen Avro 504s and two DH 6s for joy-riding purposes, but results were disappointing and the company stopped flying in 1920, although the airfield was still the venue for races. The year 1919 saw Hendon briefly in use as an airport, with BAT operating a very short-lived London-Birmingham service and a London-Amsterdam route which lasted until early 1920, while the Airco-owned Aircraft Transport and Travel used Hendon as a maintenance and air taxi base. ATT ceased operations in December 1920. Another user of the field was the Skywrit-

ing Corporation, whose smoke-generator-equipped SE 5as were based here from 1922, first experiments having taken place at Hendon in 1919.

A turning-point in Hendon's fortunes was 1920, for that year the RAF Tournament took place. This spectacular and fashionable event, known subsequently as the Pageant and finally as the Display, was staged annually until 1937, when the latest high-performance aircraft needed more space than Hendon could provide. Over the years, the show was seen by over 4,000,000 spectators and raised more than £150,000 for RAF charities. The 1920s and 1930s were the golden years for Hendon. The tournaments thrilled thousands of spectators and did much for RAF training. In 1939 Hendon put on just one of the many Empire Air Day displays staged around the country.

By 1925, when the airfield was sold to the RAF, the only tenants were the London Flying Club and the Skywriting Corporation. De Havilland's had moved to Stag Lane in 1920, and Handley Page had transferred entirely to Cricklewood within weeks of the Armistice. Jack Savage's Skywriters stayed on alongside RAF squadrons until 1932. January 1927 saw the arrival of 600 (City of London) Squadron and 601 (County of London) Squadron, both units of the Auxiliary Air Force. They were joined in 1930 by some of the red, blue and silver aircraft flown by Prince Edward, Prince of Wales, and by his brother, Prince Albert. This 'Royal Flight', which reached a total of four aircraft in 1933, was down to one Airspeed Envoy when it moved to RAF Benson in September 1939. No 24 (Communications)

Squadron arrived from Northolt in July 1933, and was to stay right through the Second World War. The unit was involved with flying high-ranking officers, Ministers of State and important civil servants about the country.

Two more auxiliary squadrons were based at Hendon during the 1930s; No 604 (County of Middlesex) was formed here on March 17 1930 and departed for North Weald in September 1939, while No 611 (West Lancashire) formed at Hendon on February 10 1936 and moved to Liverpool two months later. Nos 600, 601 and 604 had all originally been bomber squadrons, and changed to fighters in 1934, whereas No 611 was a fighter unit from the outset. No 600 went to Kenley in September 1938, and No 601 left for Biggin Hill a year later, leaving no operational aircraft at Hendon at the beginning of the war.

During the Second World War Hendon housed many fighter squadrons including the Hurricanes of 257 Squadron from May to July 1940 and 504 Squadron from September 5 to 26, 1940. The day before, Colindale Underground Station was destroyed by enemy aircraft. On October 7 1940 No 24 Squadron hangar was destroyed by an oil bomb.

No 1 Camouflage Unit arrived on November 11 and that same day 250 lb bombs dropped in the east camp, on the airfield and in the west camp.

March 3 1941 saw No 1416 Flight form and it moved to Benson on September 9 1941. Meanwhile No 116 Squadron had moved in on April 20 1941 and after one year moved to Heston.

No 1 Camouflage Unit moved to Stapleford Tawney on June 1 1942. No 510 Squadron formed from 'A' Flight of No 24 Squadron on October 15 1942. Two other squadrons to form at Hendon were No 512 on June 18, 1943 and No 575 on February 1 1944. Both units were equipped with Dakotas and moved to Broadwell during February 1944.

In April 1944, No 510 Squadron was redesignated the Metropolitan Communications Squadron. On June 30 a flying bomb hit a wing of Colindale Hospital and four airmen were killed. Another flying bomb exploded in front of a brick barrack block in the south-east corner of the airfield on August 3. Nine airmen were killed and 25 injured. In addition to the block, five huts were damaged beyond repair.

On July 7 1944, Hendon ceased to be administered by 44 Group and came under the command of ACC No 116 Wing which moved in from Hendon Hall to No 2 Mess at Hendon. During October 1944 the 50 Dakotas of the USATC moved to Bovingdon.

By the autumn of 1945 all units had moved out. This included the Air Ambulance Unit and its training unit which had been based at Hendon since 1942 and had carried out much air ambulance work. Only No 24 Squadron now remained at Hendon. The comings and goings of VIPs

Vickers Wellington (prototype, K4049) at Hendon RAF Display in 1935.

and other officers were flown by No 24 Squadron throughout the war years with various aircraft. The unit moved to Bassingbourn on February 25 1946 and with the departure of the resident unit, flying ceased at Hendon.

Flying resumed when Nos 601 and 604 Squadrons re-formed at Hendon with Spitfires. Both units moved out at the end of March 1949 and once again flying ceased. The station then housed the Metropolitan Communications Squadron but there was no room for expansion and the airfield was considered too small for modern aircraft. Over the next few years housing development gradually encroached upon the airfield until it became unsafe for flying. In November 1957 the Metropolitan Communications Squadron moved to Northolt and the airfield closed with its departure.

Today Hendon aerodrome has almost disappeared. The RAF main gate still shows the flag and one hangar is still in use as the Royal Air Force Museum. The museum was established in 1963 and opened by HM the Queen in 1972. The Museum building is sited on ten acres of the historic former airfield at Hendon. The aircraft hall displays some 40 aircraft from the museum's total collection of over 150 machines. The past is kept alive and a visit to the Royal Air Force Museum and the Battle of Britain and Bomber Command Museums is well worth it.

Henley-on-Thames (Crazies Farm), Berkshire

175/SU795824. 7 miles north-east of Reading

This was another small grass airfield just west of London that had very few facilities and could hardly be called an aerodrome. It opened in the early part of July 1940 as a Relief Landing Ground for White Waltham and the Tiger Moths of No 13 Elementary Flying Training School used it in that role until December 1940.

The airfield then became an RLG for Woodley and from February 3 1941 to September 21 1942 the Magisters of No 8 EFTS were frequent visitors.

During 1944 the circuit at Woodley became very congested and the Tiger Moths of No 10 Flying Instructors' School made use of Henley during this period.

In mid-August 1944, No 529 Squadron moved in from Halton where it had formed from No 1448 Flight (Radar Calibration Duties) on June 15 1943. The unit operated Oxfords, Hornet Moths, Rota Autogyros, and in May 1945 a Hoverfly 1. (It was the first RAF squadron to use one operationally.) No 529 Squadron disbanded at Henley on October 20 1945 and the tiny airfield then closed.

Heston, Middlesex

176/TQ118781. North-east of Heathrow Airport

Heston Aerodrome was the brainchild of Sir Nigel Norman and Alan Muntz, both private pilots and members of auxiliary RAF squadrons. Throughout the 1920s they had travelled around Europe and upon their return began to put their ideas into practice. They purchased land near the village of Cranford and by the end of 1928 work had begun on turning the land into an aerodrome.

The aerodrome was named Heston and it officially opened on July 6 1929. The controlling authority was Airwork Ltd, which had been formed by Norman and Muntz to run and operate the aerodrome. It had been carefully designed and some of the hangars were built along the lines of shops where aircraft were displayed for sale.

The main complex contained the control tower, traffic offices, Heston Aero Club house, a restaurant and a small hotel on the east section. The west section housed the Airwork flying school. Heston was the first Aerodrome in Britain to feature an all-concrete apron and an all-concrete hangar which measured 100 ft × 80 ft at its base. It was also the first private aerodrome to have a Customs post, established in 1931. Heston had floodlights and night flying became a regular feature. The Lorenz blind landing system was introduced here in 1936.

Heston quickly grew in popularity and only a few weeks after it had opened the Household Brigade Flying Club moved in from Brooklands. In 1931 Heston was the venue for the start and finish of the King's Cup Air Race. On April 12 of that year Captain Neville Stack and Mr J.P. Chaplin flew their Vickers-Napier 'Vivid' Mail Carrier from Heston to Berlin in 5 hours

Opposite page *Captain Neville Stack and Mr J.P. Chaplin in front of their Vickers-Napier Mail Carrier,* G-EBPY, *that flew from Heston-Berlin-Heston on April 12 1931.*

Junkers F 13, G-ABDC, *of Personal Flying Services Ltd, Heston, 1930-1933.*

8 minutes. The return journey was done in 5 hours 22 minutes.

By 1934 Heston had become an important aerodrome and commercial airlines were well established. The first resident airline was Spartan Air Lines. Others followed and they included United Airways, Jersey Airways and Commercial Air Hire Ltd.

The year 1934 saw the formation of Heston Aircraft Company Ltd in March of that year. This company was formed from the ashes of the folded Comper Aircraft Company. The new company built several aircraft, including the Type 5 Racer, Hordern-Richmond Autoplane and after the war the Heston AOP. Other companies based at Heston included the Carden-Baynes Aircraft Company Ltd, which built the little twin pusher Bee.

British Airways Ltd, formed on January 1 1936 by the merger of Spartan Airlines and United Airways, used Heston as its London terminus until the summer of that year, when it moved to the newly opened Gatwick. However, Gatwick became waterlogged and in February 1937 British Airways moved back to Heston where it remained until the outbreak of war.

Throughout this period the aerodrome continued to expand and the main hangar was completed in 1935. The new Customs and Immigration building was opened in 1938. That same year the Government took an interest and the Secretary of State

for Air purchased Heston and adjoining land with the intention of extending the aerodrome. However, the gathering war clouds over Europe brought these good intentions to an abrupt end. A page in the airfield's history was written when the Prime Minister, Neville Chamberlain, came here with his little piece of paper containing 'Peace in our time' on September 30 1938.

At the outbreak of the Second World War the airfield was requisitioned by the RAF, becoming a satellite of Northolt under No 11 Group, Fighter Command. During September the Heston Flight was formed and this later became the very important Photographic Development Unit under Sidney Cotton. It is ironic that Cotton should have had an uphill struggle to get this special unit started.

Before the start of the Second World War, the German Colonel-General Baron von Fritsch commented that: 'The next war will be won by the military organisation with the most efficient photographic reconnaissance.' How right he was. Cotton knew this also and he told Tedder that photographic intelligence would have one of the most important roles in the war. Cotton asked for Spitfires but on September 21, two Mk IV long-nosed Blenheims arrived at Heston. There was ample evidence that the Blenheim was unsuitable yet he had to use it. Then he had tea with Air Chief Marshal Lord Dowding at Stanmore and the next day two Spitfires landed

Ford 5AT-C Trimotor, G-ABHO, *at Heston in 1934.*

at Heston. Cotton's team took out the guns and gun fittings and got rid of all excess weight. In this way they increased the speed of these two Spitfires from 360 to 396 mph. But their presence at Heston soon got around and Air Marshal Richard Peck wanted to know how Cotton had got new aircraft without reference to the Air Ministry.

By the end of October Cotton had two aircraft capable of a cruising speed of close on 400 mph with a range of 1,250 miles at 30,000 ft, fitted with the best photographic equipment available. He had gathered a first-class team, but it had been hard work and it was still an uphill fight to prove his point. During the phoney war period one Spitfire from Heston was detached to an airfield at Seclin, near Lille, France, during the early part of 1940 and got some perfect pictures from 33,000 ft. Meanwhile, back at Heston the other Spitfire that Dowding had lent Cotton was in daily use for training purposes. Cotton cried out for more aircraft and materials and the neglect in laying the foundations for such a unit is unbelievable when one considers that by the end of the war the Allied Central Interpretation Unit employed about 550 officers and 2,000 other ranks.

It was also unbelievable that the photographs the Cotton team were taking in the Spitfire evoked little interest at the Air Ministry. There were further complications because no specialist organisation existed to interpret the photographs and extract intelligence from them. With the Air Ministry, Cotton was banging his head against a brick wall and they made it very difficult for him. Cotton knew he was right. The RAF had photographed 2,500 sq miles of enemy territory in three months for the loss of 40 aircraft, mostly Blenheims. The French had photographed 6,000 sq miles of enemy territory in three months for the loss of 60 aircraft. The Spitfire detachment from Heston had photographed 5,000 sq miles of enemy territory *in three flights* without loss. On January 26 1940, Cotton took those figures into Peck's office and at long last priority was given to modifying the new Spitfires. The first one arrived at Heston on February 7. Also, several pilots were posted in, but the flight was not over for Cotton, who still had to work hard against mountains of red tape.

The Air Ministry continually made it difficult for Cotton even after he had done a good job. At 11.00 am on February 10, Shorty Longbottom took off from Heston for Wilhelmshaven. At 3.20 pm that afternoon he was safely back having photographed Wilhelmshaven and Emden from more than five miles up. The reason for the mission was the *Tirpitz,* a vital target, yet inter-Service jealousies held up the correct interpretation of the prints for some 36 hours. This was frustrating for Cotton. At the start of operations the Heston Flight was designated No 2 Camouflage Unit but on July 8 1940 its name was

changed to No 1 Photographic Reconnaissance Unit.

September 1940 saw the airfield come under attack and a parachute mine exploded outside the main hangar, bringing down the roof and damaging or destroying 17 aircraft, including Sidney Cotton's Lockheed *G-AFTL* and five PR Spitfires. Heston was now receiving its fair share of bombing and to safeguard No 1 PRU it was transferred to Benson in December 1940. With its departure the airfield was transferred to No 81 Group (Training) and No 53 OTU formed on February 20 1941 with an establishment of Spitfires. This unit remained only a few months and on July 1 it moved to Llandow.

No 1422 Flight formed on May 12 1941 for Turbinlite development. This unit had an establishment of Bostons/Havocs, Spitfires and Hurricanes. Later additions to this unit were Mosquitoes, Ansons and a Wellington. No 1422 Flight disbanded here on January 25 1943. No 61 Operational Training Unit formed at Heston on June 9 1941. This unit was a Spitfire OTU and its code letters were HX. The unit also had on strength a few Harvards and Magisters.

April 1942 saw the departure of 61 OTU to Rednal and with its departure the airfield was transferred back to 11 Group. It then became an operational fighter station and for two years was used by a succession of squadrons, most of them equipped with

Aerial oblique view of Heston, June 17 1941, looking west.

Spitfires. The first fighter squadron to arrive was No 316 (Polish) Squadron which arrived on April 22. It moved out on July 30 1942.

Other squadrons which remained at Heston were No 116 from April 1942 to December 1943, No 302, which arrived May 7 1942 and was in and out three times more before finally departing to Perranporth on June 20 1943, No 303, which had three visits between February and June 1943 and No 306, which made three visits between September 1943 and April 1944. No 308 also made three visits, arriving for the first in July 1942 and departing after its last visit on October 29 1943. No 315 was in and out twice from November 1943 to April 1944. No 317 made a three weeks' stay during June 1943 and No 350 a two weeks' stay during March 1943. No 515 Squadron, equipped with Defiants, arrived on October 29 1942 and departed on May 31 1943. No 129 Squadron with its Spitfires and Mustangs stayed the last two weeks in March 1944.

During their stay at Heston some of the squadrons took part in Operation *Jubilee* in August 1942 and in numerous *Ramrods* and *Circus* operations. Together with Northolt, No 131 Airfield, Heston was designated No 133 Airfield and the squadrons were absorbed into the 2nd Tactical Air Force and brought up to three-squadron strength. The Polish squadrons with their Spitfires were present until April 1944 when the fighter squadrons moved south to Coolham, Sussex in preparation for the invasion.

Some American units were based at Heston for a short period and the first unit, the 27th Air Transport Group arrived in May 1943. By the spring of 1944 a number of other units flying a variety of aircraft in the communications and transport role had arrived. The last of these American units left in October 1944.

Meanwhile, as part of the invasion build-up Heston became a forward airfield in the Tangmere Sector of No 11 Fighter Group on February 2 1944, but this was for only a few months and it was then relegated to being a satellite for Northolt in June 1944.

During 1944 two RAF communications units were also present. The Allied Expeditionary Air Force had formed on December 13 1943 with a variety of aircraft which included Spitfires. This unit was joined in May 1944 by No 85 Group Communications Squadron which was flying Oxfords, Austers and Spitfires.

In October 1944 the various communications units moved out to allow work on the airfield in preparation for the transfer of Fairey Aviation from its base at Heathrow. Three 'T2' Type hangars were erected on the site of the bombed hangar for Fairey's use and on January 13 1945 Heston was transferred to the Director General of Civil Aviation for operation on behalf of the Ministry of Aircraft Production.

During the summer of 1945, No 701 Royal Navy Communications Squadron arrived and this unit had a variety of aircraft, including Harvards and Seafires. It remained until December 1946 and by now the fate of the airfield had been decided. There was a possibility of it becoming London's international airport but this fate befell nearby Heathrow, where more surrounding land was available for expansion. The opening of Heathrow was the death knell for Heston and on March 13 1946, Lord Winston, Minister of Civil Aviation, announced the airfield's closure. Flying ceased a few months afterwards. The airfield had proved unsuitable as a flight-test centre for Fairey's and it moved the final assembly, production and flight-testing departments to White Waltham, near Maidenhead. The move was completed by November 1947.

Part of the airfield was returned to agricultural use and in December 1978 the control tower and adjoining buildings were demolished. However, some buildings still stand, including the three 'T2' hangars and those on the east wing and are now in use as warehouses. The M4 motorway cuts across the site and it is covered by housing estates and factories.

Holywell Hyde (Panshanger), Hertfordshire

See Panshanger

Hornchurch (Sutton's Farm), Essex

177/TQ530845. Between Hornchurch and Rainham off the A125

During 1915 some land around Sutton's Farm was requisitioned by the Government from Mr Tom Crawford and made into an airfield. It was named Sutton's Farm and by October of that year two small canvas hangars had been erected just to the west of the farmhouse on the edge of the landing area.

The first aircraft to arrive was a BE 2c flown by 2nd Lieutenant H. MacD. O'Malley of No 13 Squadron Royal Flying Corps, who arrived on October 3 1915. Five days later Lieutenant E.W. Powell flew in with a second BE 2c. Facilities were very simple and to enable flying to take place at night there was a primitive petrol tin flare path 300 yds long.

By 1916, Sutton's Farm was part of the 18th Wing, which included all the air defences of London. At first each station was allocated two aircraft but by March of that year Sutton's Farm was the base for part of No 39 (Home Defence) Squadron, one flight being here, one flight at Hainault Farm and the third flight at North Weald Bassett with headquarters at Woodford in Essex. These three aerodromes were selected to cover the east of London and at Sutton's Farm work got under way for the construction of permanent wooden hangars, workshops, and living accommodation.

On March 16, 2nd Lieutenant Brandon was patrolling between Hainault Farm and Sutton's Farm when the Zeppelin *L 15* appeared. Brandon fired and scored hits. The Purfleet guns then engaged the Zeppelin and it was doomed. The *L 15* crashed into the sea at Knock Deep 15 miles north of Margate. Then, on May 16, Lieutenant W. Leefe-Robinson attacked another Zeppelin but without visible result.

It was on the night of September 2/3 that this same pilot made history, not only for 39 Squadron and the little aerodrome but for the Royal Flying Corps. Leefe-Robinson attacked the airship Schutte-Lanz *SL 11* and brought it down in flames over Cuffley, Herts, at 2.25 hours. This brought Leefe-Robinson overnight fame and a Victoria Cross was awarded to the gallant pilot. Sadly, he himself was shot down on April 5 1917 over the Western Front and taken prisoner. He died of influenza just after the war and was buried in the tiny cemetery of All Saints, Harrow Weald. This first victory was quickly followed by two more Zeppelins being destroyed on the night of September 23/24. 2nd Lieutenants Brandon and Sowrey made it a hat trick by downing Zeppelins *L 33* and *L 32*. They were awarded the DSO.

The enemy now switched to aeroplanes and new bombing operations were begun by twin-engined Gotha aircraft. To counter this new threat BE 12s and SE 5s replaced earlier machines at Sutton's Farm. Also, No 46 Squadron was withdrawn from France in July 1917 to Sutton's Farm to defend London and Essex. With 46 Squadron came great pilots like Major Philip Babington and J.T.B. McCudden. In August, 46 Squadron moved to St Marie Cappel and the following month the detached flight of No 39 Squadron moved to North Weald. They were replaced on a more permanent basis by No 78 Squadron which moved in with Sopwith Camels on September 20 1917. This was the first complete squadron to make Sutton's Farm its base.

In early April 1918, No 78 was joined by No 189 (Night Training) Squadron which moved in from Ripon. By this time the permanent buildings were nearly all completed. After the Armistice was signed in November the Night Training Squadron disbanded, on March 1 1919. No 78 Squadron re-equipped with Sopwith Snipes only to disband in December 1919.

Sutton's Farm was not retained by the RAF, the buildings and hangars were demolished and the land returned to its original state. By 1921 the station had disappeared but for a few scattered sheds in use by the farmer.

In 1922 it was decided to raise 15 new squadrons for home defence and in November of that year a visit was made to Sutton's Farm to establish its suitability as a permanent aerodrome. Mr Crawford, having only recently recovered his land

from the Government was in no mood to give it back. A further search was made in the area for an alternative site but to no avail. The owners, New College, Oxford agreed to sell 120 acres of their land but insisted that Mr Tom Crawford be allowed to retain some farmland and that the northern boundary of the landing ground should be 300 yds south of the farmhouse. Under peacetime conditions the Air Ministry agreed to these terms and the building of a permanent aerodrome commenced. The technical and domestic areas of the new airfield were in the north-western corner of the site, the landing area extending over the location of most of the buildings of the former aerodrome. Initially two hangars were erected, both 'A' Type, in an arc with a wide gap between them which was partly filled in the mid-1930s by the construction of a 'C' Type (Gabled). This was a seven-bay version and the space left for its eventual extension to a ten-bay was never occupied.

On April 1 1928 the new Royal Air Force station opened as RAF Sutton's Farm with the arrival of No 111 Squadron under Squadron Leader Keith Park, MC, DFC, who, 12 years later, would be fighting the Battle of Britain as Air Officer Commanding No 11 (F) Group, of which this airfield was a vital sector.

The station was renamed RAF Hornchurch on June 1 1928 and in January 1929 General Italo Balbo, Chief of the Regia Aeronautica landed with 11 aircraft after a non-stop flight from Rome.

Squadron Leader L.H. Slatter, OBE, DSC, DFC, then Wing Commander E.R. Manning, DSO, MC, became station commanders in succession as Hornchurch increased in importance. It became a two-squadron station with the re-forming of No 54 Squadron on January 15 1930.

The 1930s saw Air Defence of Great Britain exercises, and practice flying for the Hendon Pageants by the local fighter squadrons. No 111 Squadron moved out on July 12 1934, to be replaced by No 65 Squadron, which re-formed at Hornchurch on August 1 1934. A year later, in September 1935, Hornchurch added a third squadron with the arrival of No 74 Squadron. All three squadrons were equipped with Gauntlets.

In 1936, Hornchurch became part of No 11 Group in the newly-formed Fighter Command. Hornchurch was to play a major part and be a sector headquarters. By 1938 Nos 54 and 65 had re-equipped with the Gloster Gladiator, the RAF's last biplane fighter. In March of that year 54 Squadron received the Spitfire. Home defence exercises were held in August 1938 between Eastland and Westland and the station was very busy with VIP visitors, the Secretary of State for Air and the Secretary for War, all wanting to see a Spitfire display. On August 11, with the war clouds now thickening, No 54 Squadron moved down to Rochford to practice evacuation of Hornchurch in the event of German bombing. By the end of the month all buildings had been camouflaged and regulars and reservists recalled. From September 1 the operations room was manned continuously.

In December, Group Captain C.A. Bouchier, OBE, DFC (former CO of 54 Squadron) replaced Group Captain Nicholas as station commander. The first offensive patrol over France from Hornchurch was mounted by 12 Spitfires each from Nos 54 and 74 squadrons on May 21. It was the next day that the station claimed its first victory when a Ju 88 was shot down over Flushing by the Spitfires of No 65 Squadron. On May 25 1940, No 19 Squadron put in an appearance for Dunkirk cover but it was brief and on June 6 its Spitfires returned to Duxford.

June 27 1940 was a momentous day for the station when HM King George VI came to Hornchurch specially to present decorations to five officers. Squadron Leader J.A. Leathart of 54 Squadron received the DSO, Flight Lieutenant A.C. 'Al' Deere of 54 Squadron the DFC, Flight Lieutenant A.G. 'Sailor' Malon of No 74 Squadron the DFC, Flight Lieutenant R.R. Stanford Tuck of 65 Squadron the DFC and Pilot Officer J.R. Allen of 54 Squadron the DFC.

During this period from November 14 1939 to August 14 1940, No 74 Squadron was in and out no less than five times. When Queen Wilhelmina, accompanied by Princess Juliana, Prince Bernhard and their children, crossed to Britain in a British destroyer, 74's Spitfires were on escort duty. International events moved fast. It had been a very wise move not to send any Spitfire squadrons into France. Hornchurch squadrons were involved almost daily in patrols over the battle area.

Hornchurch did not have runways, the grass landing area allowing for a 3,600 ft run from north–south, a 3,400 ft from north-east–south-west, and a 2,500 ft from south-east–north-west and east–west. A perimeter track 18 ft wide circled the landing area. There were three 'C'-

Type hangars. Petrol storage amounted to 72,000 gallons with 4,000 gallons of oil. As part of the airfield defence the whole station was surrounded by barbed wire and a few pill boxes were sited at strategic points around the perimeter. A searchlight was erected on the west side of the airfield. Also, there were four Bofors guns which were protected by a series of trenches. Being one of the early airfields, Hornchurch had a decoy airfield at Bulphan. This was equipped with dummy flarepath 'Q'-site lighting and with dummy Hurricanes. It was used until early 1942 but it was not particularly useful.

Hornchurch suffered at least 20 separate bombing attacks during the Battle of Britain, the most serious being on August 31. While the airfield was under attack the squadron was scrambled and eight Spitfires got airborne. Three of 54's Spitfires were hit as they were taking off, but miraculously all three pilots escaped serious injury. Flight Lieutenant Deere had one wing and his prop torn off and he was blown along the aerodrome for about 200 yds upside down. He was helped from the aircraft by Pilot Officer Edsall who had suffered a similar fate except that he was the right way up. The third member of the section was Sergeant Davis who was blasted into the air and crashed two fields away.

At precisely 1800 hours the station came under attack again for the second time that day. Most of the bombs fell wide but two Spitfires on the ground were destroyed and one airman was killed.

On October 15 the operations room on the station was moved to more spacious accommodation at Lamborne Hall, Romford where it remained for the duration of the war.

Squadrons based at Hornchurch during 1940 were No 41, which put in three visits, arriving back for its third on September 3 and staying out the winter months here; No 54, which also put in three visits, departing to Catterick on September 3; No 64, which arrived mid-November and moved out at the end of January 1941; No 65, there from June 5 to August 28 (it also had a two-month stay during the Spring); No 74, there from June 25 to August 14 when it moved up to Wittering; No 92, there for two days during May and then a week in June; No 222, there from May 28 to June 4 then again during the Battle of Britain from August 29 to November 11 and Nos 264 and 266, which arrived in mid-August but departed before the end of the month. They were replaced by 600

Squadron whose Blenheims arrived from Manston on August 28 and moved out on September 12. No 603 Squadron arrived from Turnhouse on August 27 and departed December 3. All units except 264 with Defiants and 600 with Blenheims were equipped with Spitfires.

Having won the Battle of Britain the RAF turned to attacking enemy barges being assembled at the invasion ports along the Channel coast. The first offensive operation from Hornchurch took place on January 7 1941 when Nos 41 and 64 Squadrons escorted six Blenheim light bombers to attack installations in France. This first *Circus* operation was a complete success and was accomplished without any loss whatsoever. On January 27, No 611 arrived to complete the Hornchurch Wing—consisting of three Spitfire squadrons, Nos 41, 64 and 611. The latter remained until May and returned again on June 16.

In early 1941 the aerodrome was heavily guarded against possible invasion, which at that time was still considered a strong possibility. The 70th Essex Regiment provided sentries and ground defence units with 258 men. A heavy 4.5 in anti-aircraft detachment of the Royal Artillery was positioned on the west side of the airfield. Eight Bofors guns manned by the 109th Canadian Light Anti-Aircraft Battery and RAF Ground Defence using Vickers machine-guns were sited in pillboxes and gun pits to give protection against low-flying aircraft. These were backed up by a mobile force which consisted of three light

Spitfire IIA, P7666: EB-Z, named Observer Corps, seen here at Hornchurch with Squadron Leader D.O. Finlay. Aircraft was transferred to 54 Squadron in late February 1941.

tanks and four RAF manned armoured trucks. In reserve were 680 officers and men of the 10th Essex Regiment camped a mile to the east at Hacton House.

By mid-1941 the last remnants of Sutton's Farm on the north-east side had been demolished to make way for additional Spitfire dispersals. No 64 Squadron, which had departed at the end of January paid two visits during this period, moving to Turnhouse in mid-May. No 54 Squadron put in three appearances, its last being on June 13. It left Hornchurch for good when it moved to Martlesham Heath on August 4 1941. It was replaced that same day by 403 (RCAF) Squadron but the Canadians did not remain for very long and after three weeks moved to Debden. An unusual mission was carried out from Hornchurch on August 19 when an artificial leg was dropped over St Omer, France, for Wing Commander Douglas Bader who had been shot down and captured, minus a leg, earlier that month. This operation was carried out during a normal fighter sweep into France.

The build-up of Allied resources continued. No 411 (RCAF) Squadron arrived on November 19 to replace 603 Squadron, which had been at Hornchurch for the past

Tea and 'Wads' at Hornchurch, 1941.

five months and 611 Squadron, which had also been here for about the same period. No 313 (Czech) Squadron arrived on December 15. The Wing now consisted of Nos 411, 313 and 64 Squadrons. The latter had returned in November. All units flew the Spitfire VB which was armed with two 20 mm cannons and four .303 machine-guns.

By June 1942, Wing Commander 'Paddy' Finucane was Wing Leader. Tragically his Spitfire was hit by ground fire and he was lost in the Channel. Many squadrons were in and out during summer and autumn, these included No 64 twice, No 81 May 15 to July 17, No 122 three times returning for its fourth visit in December, No 132 a week during October, No 154 June 7 to July 27 and No 313 there from early March until the end of April. No 340 (Free French) Squadron arrived from Westhampnett on July 28 and remained until September 23. It was replaced by the Australians of No 453 Squadron, which arrived that same day. The Aussies were now in the front line but were still equipped with the Spitfire VB aircraft. Some squadrons of Fighter Command had been rearmed with Spitfire IX aircraft. These were able to engage Fw 190s on fairly even terms.

The winter months had seen a change in tactics and the vast air armadas of the spring had given way to small compact units each day. Sweeps and small *Ramrods*

against airfields were timed to preoccupy enemy forces while the main force attacked the primary target. During October, No 453 flew 404 hours on 311 sorties. The greater part was applied to protective patrols off the North Foreland and in the Thames Estuary. These kind of sorties gave the squadrons little chance to distinguish themselves but this defensive flying was necessary as the Germans sent fighters and fighter-bombers on hit-and-run raids very much like our own *Rhubarb* operations. In cloudy weather, when it was difficult for fighters to operate, small numbers of German long-range bombers operated in daylight over widespread areas of England. As these intruders could approach anywhere on a broad front, they were difficult to oppose.

Low cloud and thick ground have severely limited all flying during November and this, together with the seasonal decline in offensive activities made this a very quiet period. On December 7, No 453 moved to Martlesham. The following day it was replaced by 350 Squadron.

The attacks on the continent continued throughout 1943. In March Nos 64 and 350 Squadrons moved out and were replaced by 453 Squadron on March 27. It began to re-equip with Spitfire IXs and this meant it could operate on a far wider range of tasks than previously. Within a week the Australians were ready. On April 5 they gave withdrawal cover to a large American force returning from Antwerp, but it was not until three days later that for the first time in five months the Australians actually came face to face with the enemy. The Hornchurch Wing was near Abbeville when the ground control warned Wing Commander J.R. Ratten, who was leading the wing, that enemy aircraft approached. Soon afterwards six Fw 190s were seen but these quickly dived into the clouds. Soon afterwards eight more Fw 190s appeared. Ratten instructed No 122 Squadron to remain up-sun at 27,000 ft while the Australians dived down to attack. In a brief encounter both Ratten and Flight Lieutenant Andrews damaged an enemy aircraft. Only half the section got anywhere near to firing their guns as the enemy quickly dived into cloud. No 453 re-formed, climbed swiftly, crossed out of France over the Somme Estuary and headed home.

The Australians were now keen for action but the German fighter pilots became ever more reluctant to do battle. During April the Australians flew 12 more offensive operations. At the end of the month they were joined by 222 Squadron which flew in from Martlesham. It joined in as part of the Hornchurch Wing on the offensive operations which were mostly in conjunction with bomber or dive-bomber formations.

May was busy but saw little success. On May 3 a tragic and costly failure occurred. The members of No 453 Squadron were detailed as target-support fighters for an attack by 11 Venturas of No 487 Squadron (RNZAF) against a power house at Amsterdam. Just 30 miles from the Dutch coast No 453 Squadron was

recalled. The bombers and their close escort flew on and were met by approximately 60 enemy fighters. The *Ramrod* formation was split up and all except one of the bombers were shot down.

A little compensation was had on May 8 when Sergeant Williams of 122 Squadron shot down, near Pitsea, one of six Ju 88s which were making medium-level forays in the Thames Estuary. The Hornchurch Wing continued to be active throughout May. On May 14 the Wing again gave cover to the American Fortresses. Small formations had attacked Courtrai and Antwerp and the Hornchurch Wing covered the withdrawal of the second operation. Ratten was advised by radio that the Fortresses and their close escort of American Thunderbolts were already heavily engaged by enemy fighters, so he led Nos 122 and 453 Squadrons between Antwerp and Flushing to pick up straggling bombers

Below *RAF Hornchurch 'C' Type hangar, the main central with two 'C1' Types either side. In the late 1950s the Ford Motor Company used the hangars to store cars from their nearby Dagenham factory, but had ceased by the time this photograph was taken in March 1962. Note aerial masts either side of the watch office. The central iron staff attached to the hangar was the wind sock mast.*

Right *RAF Hornchurch Main Guard Room (September 1962), now passed into history.*

which were being fiercely attacked. Instructing 453 to remain as top cover, Ratten
led 122 Squadron down and split up the
enemy fighters, keeping them engaged in
dog fights until the bombers had safely
withdrawn. *Ramrods, Sweeps, Circuses*,
and withdrawal support continued through
out May and June. The American daylight
operations against western France had
broadened the front on which Fighter
Command based its offensive.

On June 20, the Americans made a very
heavy attack against the Huls chemical
works and the Hornchurch Wing gave withdrawal support. The Wing made rendezvous near Rotterdam just as one of the
leading bombers was shot down. The Spitfires dived down and the Fw 190s fell back.
The Wing then rejoined the American
Fortresses and escorted them safely back
to Ipswich. In this skirmish with the enemy

the Australians lost their first pilot in
combat for over six months and only the
seventh during the whole year of the
squadron's existence.

No 453 flew its last sortie from Hornchurch on June 27 and the following day
it was transferred to Ibsley and No 10
Group. No 453 Squadron was immediately
replaced by 129 Squadron. In August it
was joined by 239 Squadron. This unit was
equipped with Mustangs but it remained
only a few weeks before moving to Ayr.
October saw the arrival of 485 Squadron
but it also remained only a few weeks
before moving to Drem. At the end of
November 66 Squadron arrived. It was
joined at the end of December by 350
Squadron. These units remained throughout the winter months.

The New Year saw the arrival of 504
Squadron and in March No 349 replaced

Nos 66 and 350 Squadrons. Hornchurch was now coming to the end of its role, for the fighter squadrons were moving nearer to the invasion beaches. On April 4, 222 Squadron said goodbye for the last time and a week later No 349 moved out. At the end of the month No 504 departed. It was immediately replaced by Nos 229 and 274 Squadrons. On May 6, No 80 Squadron arrived. Two weeks later Nos 80, 229 and 274 Squadrons moved to Detling.

The Hornchurch operations room was stood down now the squadrons had gone. In the event it was a wise move with the arrival of the V1 flying bombs, as balloon cables and anti-aircraft guns would have made it difficult for fighters to use the airfield. A great many V1s landed in the area. Hornchurch became the home of a repair unit engaged on restoring vital buildings. The Air Ministry then turned Hornchurch into a great marshalling area for personnel in transit to and from the battle front. In December of 1944 almost 2,000 officers and men passed through. In March 1945, many Italian 'co-operators' worked at the station and after VE-Day returning ex-prisoners of war passed through Hornchurch.

During the winter months, from mid-November to mid-February, a detachment from 278 Squadron operated from here on air-sea rescue duties. Also, from mid-November 1944, No 567 Squadron operated from the airfield with a few Martinets. They moved to Hawkinge on June 16 1945. During this period No 116 Squadron arrived in May and disbanded here on May 26. No 287 Squadron also arrived in early May and it moved to Bradwell Bay on June 15. Its glorious days as a fighter station were now over and in June the station was transferred to Technical Training Command. The transit unit and Personnel Despatch Centre closed in 1947 and the aerodrome was reduced to a Care and Maintenance basis.

On July 1 1948, No 17 Reserve Flying School formed at Hornchurch with an establishment of Tiger Moths and Anson 22s. For the next few years flying continued with the school right up until it disbanded on July 31 1953. The station now had a role as an Aircrew Selection Centre, formed April 1 1952 and operated as such for the next decade. The Aircrew Selection Centre then moved to Biggin Hill where it was renamed the Officers and Aircrew Selection Centre.

The station finally closed with the disbandment of the holding party on July 1,

1962. The following year the airfield was put up for auction and it was sold for £517,000. The actual airfield became the East London quarry of Hoveringham Gravels and the technical site was bought by a property company for development. When the gravel was exhausted the quarry became a refuse tip—a sad end for such a distinguished and historically important front-line airfield.

Today all the buildings have been demolished and replaced by a housing estate. The only links with those unforgettable days and nights of two wars are the roads named after the pilots of Sutton's Farm and RAF Hornchurch. Mitchell Junior School stands on part of SHQ and rightly takes its name after the late R.J. Mitchell's fighter which was such a common sight during the dark days of the 1940s in the Hornchurch area. West Havering School is built on part of the site where once stood the officers' mess, and today Wing Commander Robert R. Stanford Tuck, DSO, DFC, RAF (Rtd), sits on the board of this school. Airfield Way now follows the same route as the one-time perimeter track which passed the hangars, apron and watch office.

Horne, Surrey

187/TQ332435. Between Redhill and East Grinstead just west of the A22

This was one of the advanced landing grounds established in the south of England prior to the invasion of occupied Europe in 1944. It was situated a few miles to the north-east of Gatwick and was one of the most northerly of the ALGs. It housed three Spitfire squadrons, Nos 130, 303 and 402, which arrived on April 30 and May 1. They all departed on June 18 and 19 and the grass airfield reverted back to its former use.

Hounslow, Middlesex

176/TQ120745. South-east of Heathrow Airport between the A315 and A314

Standing on, or near, Hounslow Heath, this civil airfield had been in existence for some time before it was taken over by the RFC for training purposes in August 1914. It was a training depot station for single-seater fighters and a 6th Brigade landing ground, 1st class.

The site covered an area of 266 acres, of which 27 acres were occupied by the station buildings, which were grouped in the north-western corner. The maximum dimensions were 1,100 yds × 1,100 yds. It was

Major W.C. Barker, VC, with captured German Fokker D VII at Hounslow aerodrome, April 1919.

a mile from Hounslow Junction railway station and the general surroundings of the site were enclosed and difficult with many trees and buildings.

No 10 Squadron arrived on April 1 1915 but after only six days it moved to Netheravon. It was replaced a week later by No 15 Squadron which arrived from Farnborough with a few BE 2cs. After a month this unit moved to Dover.

No 24 Squadron was formed at Hounslow on September 1 1915 with a motley collection of aircraft but these were soon traded in for twelve Vickers FB 5s. By the time the squadron went to St Omer, France, in February 1916 it had converted to DH 2s. On November 5, 1915, No 27 Squadron formed here with a few Martinsydes and moved to Dover before the end of the year.

On January 29 1916, No 19 Reserve Squadron formed at Hounslow under the command of Major T.C.R. Higgins as a home defence night fighter training squadron and sent a detachment of BE 2cs to various aerodromes around London, replacing those previously supplied by

various squadrons. On April 15 1916, it became 39 Squadron and all detachments were concentrated on aerodromes to the east of London. No 39 Squadron moved out during August having been replaced by No 52 Squadron, which had formed at Hounslow on May 15 1916 with BE 2cs.

No 18 Wing formed on March 23 1916 under Lieutenant Colonel H. Holt to include all air defence detachments in the London area and in May of that year Hounslow was one of seven airfields specifically designated for the air defence of London.

November 1917 saw the arrival of Nos 19 and 42 Training Squadrons, also No 18 Wing Aeroplane Repair Section which remained until August 1919.

No 85 Squadron arrived from Norwich at the end of November 1917 with SE 5As. Two weeks later it was joined by No 87 Squadron with its Avro 504Ks. Both units remained at Hounslow over the winter months as they prepared for their move to France. No 87 moved to St Omer on April 23 1918, followed a month later by No 85 Squadron. It was replaced by No 62 Squadron but this unit moved out in June and two months later Hounslow became No 42 Training Depot Station. In March 1919 No 107 Squadron arrived from

One of the first London-Paris Air Expresses. The aircraft was a DH 4A and the journey took 2½ hours. Pilot E.H. Lawford, passenger G.M. Stevenson-Reece. Seen here at Hounslow, August 25 1919.

Maubeuge, France but it disbanded on June 30 1919. The following month No 42 TDS disbanded and that same month the site returned to civil use.

Despite its poor position Hounslow became Britain's first terminal airport and was considered to be busy with four cross-Channel services a day. One firm which operated out of Hounslow was Aircraft Transport and Travel Limited which made the first (but unsuccessful) newspaper flight to Bournemouth in the DH 9 *C6054*. Up until February 18 1920, Hounslow was the only Customs airport for London but its glory was short-lived for it was reclaimed by the Army and was closed to air traffic on March 28 1920.

Today it lives in the shadow of Heathrow Airport and is back once again as Hounslow Heath.

Hunsdon, Hertfordshire

167/TL426138. Adjacent to the B180 about three miles north-west of Harlow

Work first started on Hunsdon Aerodrome on October 9 1940, when two runways were sited. The station headquarters was officially opened on February 22 1941 in No 11 Group and the first flying unit to arrive was No 85 Squadron, which arrived from Debden on May 3 1941. A detachment of No 242 Squadron, commanded by Squadron Leader Whitney Straight moved in on May 8 for operational night flying and training, equipped with 12 Hurricanes. At this time Wing Commander G.D. Harvey, DFC, was the Commanding Officer of the station but was relieved by Wing Commander P.W. Townsend, DSO, DFC on May 21 1941.

After its arrival No 85 Squadron began converting from Hurricanes to Havocs and in July it was joined by No 1451 Turbinlite Havoc Flight. On August 10 No 3 Squadron arrived and there was a great deal of activity at Hunsdon with these three units engaged in operational training and night defence operations, including the defence of London during enemy raids. During this period a decoy airfield at Braughing had been in use for Hunsdon but it had served little purpose.

On July 1 1942, No 1530 Beam Approach Training Flight formed at Hunsdon, moving to Wittering on November 23 1942. In

THE AIRFIELDS

Right *A crew from 410 Squadron at Hunsdon, December 17 1943. Teamed for more than a year, Flying Officer Vernon Williams, 24-year-old observer, and Flying Officer Rayne D. Schultz, the 20-year-old pilot (whose home is at Bashaw, Alberta), were the crew of 'N for Nuts', the Mosquito which destroyed three Dornier 217s in one night off the coast of East Anglia.*

Below *Flying Officers L.E. Fownes of Baddeck, Victoria City, Nova Scotia, navigator, and R.E. Britten of Arichat, Richmond City, pilot, hold a clean-up session in front of their tent at Hunsdon on August 1 1944. They flew RCAF 409 'Nighthawk' Squadron Mosquitoes on patrols over the beachhead in Normandy, and are seen here living under canvas readying for the day when they will move closer to the battlefronts in France.*

September 1942, No 1451 Flight was re-numbered to No 530 Squadron and received an establishment of Hurricane night fighters.

By 1943 there was less need for night fighter squadrons patrolling the skies over the United Kingdom, so for the remainder of the war period the resident squadrons were almost entirely engaged in intruder attacks on occupied Europe using Mosquitoes. On January 25 1943, No 530 Squadron disbanded. No 85 Squadron moved to West Malling on May 13 1943 and the following day No 3 Squadron also moved to West Malling. It was immediately replaced by No 157 Squadron which moved in from Bradwell Bay. No 515 Squadron joined the resident unit on June 1. This unit was equipped with Beaufighters. November 9 saw the departure of No 157 Squadron and the arrival of the Canadians by way of 410 Squadron.

December was a very busy month and saw many changes. On December 15, No 515 moved to Little Snoring. Two weeks later the Canadians moved to Castle Camps. On December 31 three squadrons, Nos 21, 464 (RAAF) and 487 (RNZAF), equipped with Mosquito VIs, arrived from Sculthorpe, Norfolk. Hunsdon is best

remembered for these three light-bomber squadrons, for they carried out the attack on the Amiens prison under the leadership of Group Captain P.C. Pickard. On February 18 1944, Nos 464 and 487 Squadrons attacked Amiens prison to release French patriots. Mosquitoes of No 21 Squadron acted as reserve and did not bomb. The prison walls were breached and 258 prisoners were able to escape, including over half the patriots who were awaiting execution. Group Captain Pickard was killed when his aircraft was shot down near the target area by Fw 190s.

During the latter part of April 1944, Nos 21, 464 and 487 squadrons moved to Gravesend. On April 29 No 410 Squadron returned and it continued the intruder attacks. The station played a very active

Here are the weapons that made the Mosquito one of the most formidable night fighters in the sky. They are 20 mm cannons, four of which were carried, being checked over by 409 RCAF 'Night-hawk' Squadron armourers LAC Jack Peachell, of Winnipeg left, and Corporal Ozzie Shaw of Windsor, Ontario, right, chief armourer for the squadron. Hunsdon, August 1 1944.

role in the operations for the invasion of Normandy, and five personnel were mentioned in despatches on June 8 1944.

At 22.35 hours on the evening of June 14 1944 Flight Lieutenant Walter Dinsdale and his radar-operator Jack Dunn, took off in their Mosquito XIII, *HK476*: 'O' Orange, and set course for Fighter Pool No 1, at the Beachead Area. They arrived and started to orbit. The weather was good, with a few broken clouds and for some time no enemy actions were being reported. Then they were vectored south, following the Seine river where bandits were reported about. Pilot Officer Dunn was busy watching for any sign of activity in his radar scope while Flight Lieutenant Dinsdale scanned the sky for any sign of visual contact. Vectored 280 degrees they experienced heavy *Window* on the screen of the aircraft's radar. Several contacts were obtained simultaneously. Suddenly Dinsdale's controller calmly announced: 'Bandits in your immediate area' and from the blip on his radar screen he vectored Dinsdale onto it, closing quite rapidly on the target. By now Dinsdale's navigator had got a fix on his radar screen: 'Bandit dead ahead and closing fast'. In fact, the target was moving so slowly that when Dinsdale saw it he had to put down wheels and flaps to avoid overshooting. When he got visual contact, he was at a range of 2,000 ft from the unidentified aircraft, flying at 11,000 ft. It was 23.35 hours then, exactly one hour after take-off.

Closing to 1,000 ft, Dinsdale positioned the Mossie behind and under the target and identified it, with the aid of Ross Night Glasses, as a Junkers 88 with a glider bomb attached to the top of the fuselage. They speculated that the target must be an airborne launching platform for V1 buzz bombs.

While this strange flying monster of Hauptmann Rudat's unit was lumbering slowly in the direction of the concentration shipping on the Normandy beachhead, the Mossie closed in further to 750 ft, astern slightly below. Knowing that the 'bomb' was located on top of the Junkers, Dinsdale aimed at the starboard wing. The first burst of 32 rounds caused a terrific explosion as the cockpit and port wing burst into flames immediately. The enemy aircraft banked slowly to port, then went down suddenly in a steep diving turn, burning fiercely and leaving a trail of sparks all the way down. A lot of debris flew back in the direction of the Mosquito but they were fortunate in not having any

The outdoor barber does a flourishing business at RCAF 409 'Nighthawk' Squadron's tent site at Hunsdon on August 1 1944. Here LAC J.H. Connop of Bragcreek, Alberta, wields the shears on LAC J.H. Demers of Montreal.

of it strike their aircraft.

At 23.40 hours the enemy aircraft hit the ground with a terrific explosion some 25 miles to the south-east of Caen, lighting up the whole countryside. Dinsdale landed at base at 02.00 hours and immediately filled out the official form 'F' personal combat report and claimed this enemy aircraft as destroyed. They stuck to their story that they had shot down a Junkers operating as an airborne launching pad for a V1.

The next day Flight Lieutenant Dinsdale and Pilot Officer Dunn were called to London for further debriefing. Obviously there was great interest in this first report of another possible Hitler secret weapon. It was only a few days later that a Mistel was observed flying in the daytime and the true nature of this weapon was revealed to the Canadian night fighter pilots. They had shot down the first German 'piggyback' flying bomb—incorporating an Me 109 mounted on an explosive-laden Ju 88. Dinsdale described the piggyback as: 'An awkward thing which lumbered along at about 150 miles an hour. I recognised it as a Ju 88 but couldn't figure out what the thing on top was,' he said. Flight Lieutenant Dinsdale and Pilot Officer Dunn were the first RAF fighters of the Second World War to shoot down a Mistel.

On June 17 1944, No 410 Squadron

moved to Zeals, Wiltshire. The following day No 409 Squadron RCAF arrived and remained until August 23. Among the squadrons based at Hunsdon over the next few months were No 29 (June 1944 to February 1945), No 264 (July 1944 to August 1944), No 418 (August 1944 to November 1944), No 219 (August 1944 to October 1944), No 410 (September 1944), No 488 (RNZAF) (October 1944 to November 1944), and No 151 (November 1944 to March 1945). By the spring of 1945 all these Mosquito squadrons had moved to more advanced bases in England or France and were replaced during the first week of March by Nos 154 and 611 with Mustangs and 501 Squadron with Tempests.

At the end of March No 154 disbanded, having been replaced by two Canadian units, Nos 441 and 442, both flying North American Mustang Mk IIIs. During this period the resident squadrons took part in long-range bomber escort missions. The last of the Mustang units, Nos 441 and 442 left on May 16 1945. Three days later the station was reduced to a Care and Maintenance basis. Hunsdon was finally abandoned on July 21 1947.

Very little of the aerodrome remains today, the main and secondary runway and the perimeter track are apparent. There are a few buildings standing.

Joyce Green, Kent

177/TQ540773. Between Dartford and the River Thames

In 1911 Messrs Vickers Ltd acquired part of Franks Farm for the construction of an airfield from which to test aircraft then going into production at their Erith works. The land formed part of Dartford Salt Marshes and it was a most unsuitable site for there were numerous drainage ditches, six or more feet in width across the whole area. However, work went ahead and boards were put over the ditches. Hangars and workshops were then erected at the southern end of the landing area. The River Darent formed the western boundary, the River Thames the northern and to the east lay the sewage works. A slight undershoot presented many hazards.

The first aircraft to use the airfield was a Robert Esnault-Pelterie (REP) Monoplane No 1 which was manufactured under licence to the design of the famous French aviation pioneer. It was piloted by Captain Herbert F. Wood. There was very little flying over the next two years and as flying increased so did the accidents.

At the outbreak of war in 1914 Vickers was engaged with the development of seaplanes. Joyce Green was taken over as an air defence airfield and work began to extend the aerodrome facilities to house a permanent RFC unit under the auspices of No 6 Wing, which was responsible for training stations in the south-east of England. Hangars, workshops and ground staff quarters were erected at the northern end of the landing field alongside the Long Reach Tavern. The work was completed early in 1915 and the first service occupant to arrive was No 10 Reserve Squadron with a variety of aircraft which included Henry Farman, Vickers FB 5 and FB 9, DH 2 and FE 8 machines. The role of this unit was to receive pupils from preliminary training schools for final training for their wings. Each course consisted of about 20 pupils and lasted two to three weeks. This included time spent at Lydd where aerial gunnery was practised on the ranges at Hythe. On gaining their wings the young pilots would get a 48-hour leave pass and then be posted off to war. August 1915 saw the arrival of the 'Wireless Testing Park' from Brooklands.

Throughout the rest of the year the training continued but changes were in the wind. The matter of air defence had been a hit and miss affair, for throughout 1915 War Office orders forbad pilots to be ordered to fly unless it seemed very likely that the enemy could be found and engaged. Early in October changes took place after the Admiralty had shed its responsibility for the defence of London. The War Office accepted the responsibility and seven BE 2cs were temporarily attached from No 5 Wing to home defence stations. Joyce Green received one BE 2c together with an SE 4a from No 6 Wing. However, it was not a very satisfactory arrangement and by the end of October all the aeroplanes that had been filling in on home defence duties had gone about their official duties overseas. London was again without any aeroplane defence. Gradually the Army took over control of the guns and searchlights around London. To support the defence of the capital the Directorate of Military Aeronautics ordered two BE 2cs with experienced night flying pilots to be permanently attached to each of the ten aerodromes circling London. These were Croydon, Chingford, Hainault Farm, Sutton's Farm, Hounslow, Hendon, Wimbledon Common, Northolt, Farningham and Joyce Green.

Mid-April 1915 saw further improvements in home defence when No 39 Home Defence Squadron was formed, bringing together all units and detachments detailed for anti-Zeppelin duties in the London area. After the formation of this squadron it was decided to concentrate its strength to the north-east of London. This reorganisation brought to an end Joyce Green's active involvement as an anti-Zeppelin station. Training, testing and wireless experiments continued from Joyce Green, but the prevalent mists made take-off and landing very difficult. At least one pilot managed to force-land a DH 2 in the nearby sewage works.

During the early part of February 1917 the Wireless Testing Park moved to the newly opened Biggin Hill. On March 22, Lieutenant J.B. McCudden arrived to take up his new post as wing fighting instructor. During May, No 10 Reserve Squadron moved out to Tern Hill in Shropshire and was replaced by No 63 Reserve Squadron. This unit was equipped with 504Ks and Camels and at the end of May it became No 63 Training Squadron.

On May 25 the Germans mounted the first of their daylight Gotha raids but they did not reach London, due to bad weather, so they bombed Folkestone. They attacked again on June 13 and July 7 and McCudden was airborne in his Sopwith Pup, which now had a Lewis gun on the top wing. 2nd Lieutenant W.G. Salmon was killed during the latter raid when he crashed at Slade Green. Several spectators were arrested at the scene of the crash for having removed the dead pilot's goggles and other items. They were later fined. Salmon was given a hero's funeral with full military honours at Dartford. On July 12 1917 McCudden returned to France to join 66 Squadron.

During this period Vickers was invited by the Air Board to submit designs for a twin-engined night bomber. The prototype, later christened the Vimy, was first flown by Gordon Bell on November 30 1917. The final prototype, powered by two 360 hp Rolls-Royce Eagles was tested at Martlesham Heath in October 1918. With the Vimy it was planned to bomb Berlin and so finish the war. This, however, was not to be for the war ended a few weeks later.

No 63 Training Squadron had moved to Redcar in Yorkshire during the first week of October 1918 and the station was run down, leaving only a pilots' pool. Vickers continued to operate from its end of the field and with the coming of peace it changed to commercial aviation. But the firm was not to remain for very long since Joyce Green had many drawbacks as an aerodrome and after a final public display at Whitsun 1919, Vickers moved all further aircraft construction and testing to its site at Brooklands. In December 1919 the pilots' pool moved out and Joyce Green closed.

Between the wars the land was farmed and the hangars and buildings used by the farmer. During the Second World War the site of the old RFC camp was again used for military purposes when a gun site was set up on a pillbox close to the river bank.

Today, almost all traces of the old aerodrome have been erased and the land is again under the plough. The Long Reach Tavern has also been removed and it is difficult to imagine that the site was once a busy aerodrome.

Kenley, Surrey
187/TQ328580. South of Croydon off the A22

This aerodrome was constructed on a small site on Kenley Common and was only a few miles south-east of Croydon aerodrome. Kenley opened in the summer of 1917 as No 7 Aircraft Acceptance Park and was equipped with no less than 14 hangars, each 170 ft long by 80 ft wide and constructed in pairs. Many kinds of aircraft were received at No 7 AAP: DH 9s from Cubitt, Short and Whitehead; Dolphins from Darracq and Sopwith; Camels from Hooper; RE 8s from Napier; Salamanders from Sopwith; SE 5s from Vickers (Crayford); and Handley Page aircraft from the Croydon Assembly. The main duty of No 7 AAP was to prepare these machines for issue to operational units.

From the summer of 1918 several squadrons were in residence, No 88 with F 2Bs, No 108 flying DH 9s and No 110 flying DH 9as. No 91 Squadron flying Dolphins re-formed at Kenley and so did No 95 but this unit did not have any aircraft, and it disbanded after a few weeks. Nos 108 and 110 had moved to Kenley for mobilisation as day-bomber squadrons and then, in August, moved to France. By November 1918 all units except No 91 had moved out. No 91 Squadron remained over the winter months and it moved out on July 3 1919. Meanwhile, in April of that year, No 1 (Communications) Squadron had arrived from Hendon. This unit maintained a regular service between Kenley and Paris

Top *Bulldog K1678 of No 23 Squadron at Kenley, 1931.* **Above** *Bulldogs of No 32 Squadron, Kenley, on exercise in 1932. Left to right: K1606, K1617 and K1690.* **Top right** *Fairey Hendon of No 38 Squadron at Kenley.* **Above right** *Gloster Gladiator K6149, of No 3 Squadron at Kenley in 1935.*

where the peace conference was being held. It remained until September 1919.

Kenley was selected for retention as a permanent RAF station and was partly reconstructed in the early 1920s, although it appears to have continued as an active flying station and housed squadrons until September 1932. No 84 Squadron was here

during January 1920, but this unit had no aircraft and it disbanded before the end of the month. No 24 (Communications) Squadron re-formed at Kenley on April 1, 1920. This unit had Avro 504s, DH 9s and F 2Bs. It was to have a long association with Kenley. No 39 Squadron arrived with its DH 9as on January 18 1922 but this was

merely a cadre unit and it was only after its move to Spitalgate, Lincolnshire in February 1923 that it became established as a day-bomber squadron.

It was replaced by the Snipes of No 32 Squadron which re-formed at Kenley on April 1 1923. A year later No 13 Squadron re-formed with an establishment of Bristol F 2Bs. On June 30 1924 it moved to Andover and 32 Squadron to Bircham Newton but the latter returned on August 5 to become the main resident unit. No 24 Squadron moved to Northolt during the latter part of January 1927.

No 23 Squadron arrived from Henlow on February 6 1927. This unit was equipped with Gloster Gamecocks. Douglas Bader joined 23 Squadron at Kenley in August 1930 and the following year he lost his legs in a flying accident while at Woodley aerodrome, near Reading. No 23 Squadron moved to Biggin Hill on September 17 1932. Four days later No 32 Squadron moved to Biggin Hill whilst Kenley closed for further reconstruction. By 1934 the work was complete and in May Station HQ and Nos 3 and 17 Squadrons arrived from Upavon. On September 3 1936, No 46 Squadron re-formed at Kenley with an establishment of Gloster Gauntlets. It remained just over a year, moving to Digby, Lincolnshire on November 15 1937.

Earlier in the year No 80 Squadron had re-formed on March 3 1937 with Gauntlets and moved out a week later to Henlow. The build-up continued and on June 1 1937, No 615 Squadron formed at Kenley. It moved to Old Sarum at the end of August 1938 only to return again a week later. October saw the arrival and departure of No 600 Squadron with its Demons.

During May 1939, No 3 Squadron, now equipped with Hurricanes, moved to Biggin Hill and No 17 Squadron with its Gauntlets moved to North Weald. By August the aerodrome was mainly out of commis-

sion due to the laying of two concrete runways. While this work was in progress some flying continued. The Gauntlets of No 615 Squadron remained and they did not move out until September 2 1939. Also, No 56 Elementary and Reserve Flying Training School had formed on August 24 1939 but this was hastily closed the following month when war was declared, after only six Tiger Moths and three Harts had been received.

The site work was carried out by Constable, Hart & Co. The airfield was considerably extended and three pairs of hangars were demolished to allow the runways and perimeter track to be laid. The two runways running north-west–south-east and north-east–south-west measured

Below *Hawker Hind, K4644, at Kenley.* **Bottom** *Hawker Hector, K8105, of No 615 Squadron at Kenley.*

3,000 ft and 3,600 ft respectively. Off the perimeter track were 12 concrete pens—three aircraft per pen—for dispersed aircraft. Fuel storage totalled 35,000 gallons of aviation spirit, 8,000 gallons of motor fuel and 2,500 gallons of oil. Small arms ammunition amounted to 1¼ million rounds.

The aerodrome defence consisted of four 40 mm Bofors guns manned by the 31st Light Anti-Aircraft Battery, two 3 in guns manned by the 148th Light Anti-Aircraft Battery and a few Lewis guns.

Along the north side of the airfield was a parachute and cable installation. This device fired salvos of chutes about 600 ft into the air, where they dangled attached to cables in the path of low flying aircraft (it was hoped).

On May 8 1940, the Hurricanes of 253 Squadron arrived, but after only two weeks they moved to Kirton-in-Lindsey, Lincolnshire. Their replacements were No 64 Squadron which arrived on May 16 and Nos 3 and 615 Squadrons which flew in on May 20. No 3 Squadron had arrived straight from Merville, France, but it did not remain very long and after only three days moved to Wick. The following day No 17 Squadron returned. Its stay was also very brief, for on June 6 its Hurricanes moved to Hawkinge. At this period of the war Croydon was used as a satellite.

Kenley was established as Sector HQ of 'B' Sector in No 11 Group, Fighter Command. Gatwick and Redhill were emergency satellites.

The airfield was attacked on August 18 at 1.15 pm by about 40 Do 17s escorted by Bf 109s. Entry was still made despite a salvo from the parachute and cable installation bringing down one Dornier which crashed just outside the airfield boundary. The station suffered considerable damage. Three hangars, equipment stores, four Hurricanes on the ground and a Blenheim were destroyed. Four other aircraft were damaged. All communications were cut. Nine were killed and ten injured.

The day after the raid the Spitfires of No 64 Squadron were posted out of the front line to Yorkshire, and were replaced immediately by the Spitfires of No 616 Squadron. At the end of August No 615 Squadron moved to Prestwick in exchange with the Hurricanes of 253 Squadron. On September 3, 616 was pulled out of the front line and posted to Coltishall. During the previous 15-day period of fighting four pilots were killed, five were wounded and one became a prisoner of war. The com-

mission of one officer was terminated and another was posted away from the squadron. Out of the original 20 pilots only eight flew back to Coltishall, although some of the wounded pilots made it back on the squadron to fight again. No 616 was immediately replaced by 66 Squadron from Coltishall.

On September 4, No 253 Squadron shot down six Bf 110s without loss. Five days later it destroyed a further five Ju 88s. On September 11, No 66 Squadron was posted away and replaced by 511 Squadron.

The airfield was bombed on many occasions, particularly during the period of the Battle of Britain and it suffered considerable damage and casualties. It was again attacked on October 17 and nine aircraft on the ground were hit. During November, Kenley was at the receiving end of a night-bombing attack during which two were killed and damage sustained to a hangar, living quarters and offices. In the autumn of 1940 Shoreham and Redhill became satellites.

On December 17 1940, No 615 arrived back at Kenley with its Hurricanes. It was followed early in the New Year by the Hurricanes of No 1 Squadron replacing 253 Squadron, which moved into Yorkshire. The squadrons continued to operate and in 1941 they went on the offensive by attacking targets in enemy-occupied Europe. These low-level flights over France were known by the code name *Rhubarb*. The idea was to take full advantage of low cloud and poor visibility to get into France then let down below the cloud to search for targets, aircraft on the ground, rolling stock, military vehicles and the like. The *Rhubarb* operations were not liked and presented serious hazards. Apart from the flak the main hazard was to let down over unknown territory with no accurate knowledge of the cloud base. The risk was too great for the damage inflicted and hundreds of fighter pilots were lost on *Rhubarb* operations.

Circus operations were introduced in January 1941 and Kenley squadrons took part in these. The object of these daylight excursions was to escort a small number of Blenheim bombers to short-range targets in France. *Circuses* also gave problems, the main one being that far too many fighters would escort the handful of Blenheims. It was not unknown for 12 squadrons, in the various roles of close-escort, escort-cover, high-cover and top-cover wings to be allocated for only ten Blenheims. With so many fighters the rendezvous between

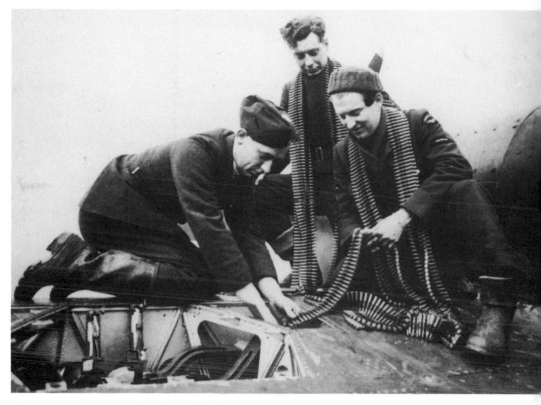

Above *Armourers of 402 (RCAF) Squadron at work at Kenley.*

Left Brad Walker—a fighter pilot of No 402 (RCAF) Squadron who flew with the Kenley Wing.

bomber and fighter forces over Beachy Head, Pevensey Bay or Selsey Bill were often very dangerous.

The squadrons housed at Kenley during the first half of the year were Nos 1, 258, 302 and 312. All were Hurricane squadrons and they were replaced in July by Nos 452 and 602 Squadrons which were equipped with Spitfires. In September the Station HQ at High House, Whyteleafe Road moved to Peterswood in Torwood Lane. The following month the New Zealanders arrived by way of 485 Squadron. This was also a Spitfire unit.

At the beginning of 1942, Group Captain F.V. Beamish became Officer Commanding. He was a man much admired by everyone on the station. He frequently flew with the wing and was the first to spot the German battleships as they raced up the Channel in February 1942. On March 28

the Kenley Wing engaged enemy fighters and Group Captain Beamish and three others were lost. March saw the return of 602 Squadron after its six weeks' spell at Redhill, and the departure of 452 Squadron.

On May 14 1942, No 402 (RCAF) arrived from Fairwood Common, South Wales. At the end of May it moved out and was replaced in early June by 611 Squadron which arrived from Drem, but after only ten days it was posted to Martlesham Heath.

On July 8, No 616 arrived back at Kenley where it had taken such a mauling in the Battle of Britain. A week later in flew 350 Squadron but before the end of the month both squadrons had been posted away. They were immediately replaced by the Spitfires of 111 Squadron.

In August, 402 Squadron returned and that same month No 308 Fighter Squadron, USAAF arrived. This was also a Spitfire unit but after only a few weeks it departed to be replaced by No 4 FS, 52nd FG, also with Spitfires. This unit remained only a few weeks.

No 401 Squadron arrived on September 24. Then, in October, 14 aircraft of 421

Squadron arrived, but they only stayed two days. No 412 Squadron arrived on November 2 and the Canadian Kenley Wing formed on November 25. 412 Squadron remained for the rest of the year and on January 28 1943 moved to Angle, South Wales. Six days previously No 401 Squadron had moved up into Yorkshire.

No 416 Squadron took its place on February 1. These were all squadrons of the Royal Canadian Air Force and they formed a Canadian Spitfire Wing for a number of months. From March 1943 the wing was led by Wing Commander 'Johnnie' Johnson. The RCAF squadrons that flew from here during the period from March 1943 to April 1944 were 402, 403, 411, 416 and 421. During this period *Ramrods* were the chief operations. One RAF fighter squadron, No 165, had operated out of Kenley, from August 8 to September 17 1943 to escort B-26s and B-17s over France. Otherwise, all units were Canadian. No 127 (RCAF) Airfield was formed on July 12 1943, moving out to its summer quarters at Lashenden in August and arriving back in mid-October. This inapt name was subsequently altered to 127 Wing.

Above *This photograph does not look much like a Church Service; but actually that is what it is. In the dispersal hut of 403 Squadron at Kenley on March 3 1943. Notice that the pilots are wearing their Mae Wests ready to run to their aircraft in case an alarm should sound, or in case they should be ordered suddenly on a sweep. Almost all of the aircrew are wearing Battledress, for the squadron is at readiness. The Service was taken by Squadron Leader F.K. Belton, Protestant padre.*

Above right *Flight Lieutenant Hugh C. Godefroy had destroyed four enemy aircraft during his flying career when this photograph was taken on April 6 1943, and was on his second tour of operations.*

Right *Pilot Officer D.H. Dover saves labour by using his bicycle to take his parachute out to his aircraft. He has taken part in many recent operations with 403 'Wolf' Squadron. Kenley, April 30 1943.*

Over the past few months the Kenley Sector had played a large part in the onslaught on Europe but its job was now

Above left *An informal group of some 416 (City of Oshawa) Squadron pilots outside their dispersal hut on one of the first fine days for some time. Taken at Kenley on May 24 1943.*

Left *This picture is worth a gander or two! In fact, there are several which appear to be the targets for potential 'pranging' by Flight Lieutenant Bob Middlemiss, hatchet aloft, and three ground crew members of 403 Canadian 'Wolf' Squadron. Apparently, the boys have Christmas dinner in mind. Taken at Kenley on December 13 1943.*

Above *Supermarine Spitfire Mk V, W3834, a presentation aircraft inscribed* Corps of Imperial Frontiersmen, *with No 401(F) Squadron, seen here at Kenley in 1943.*

done and on March 4 1944 it was absorbed by Biggin Hill. The last operation from Kenley was carried out on March 13 1944 when Nos 403, 416 and 421 Squadrons escorted bombers to Namur in Belgium. On April 16 and 17 No 127 Wing with the last three Canadian squadrons, Nos 403, 416 and 421 moved to Tangmere. Kenley was thereafter administered by a holding party. In all, the Sector had claimed 603 enemy aircraft plus 231 probably destroyed.

Kenley became inactive and was closed to flying in June as a result of the balloon barrage flown in the area as a counter to the German flying bombs. On June 28 a flying bomb fell just south of the station, doing considerable damage to houses and the station cinema.

Kenley was transferred to No 46 Group, Transport Command on July 1 1945. It became HQ of No 61 Group, Reserve Command in October 1946. For the next 18 months Kenley was used as a store for captured German and Japanese equipment. This included V1s and V2s. During this period a small group of German PoWs was housed on the Group's HQ side of the aerodrome. They did menial tasks which included redecorating the buildings, including the station church.

During the period 1946/47 Westminster Airways operated a passenger service from the aerodrome. It shared the only available hangar with No 61 Group Communications Flight, which was housed at Kenley.

Throughout the 1950s the Tiger Moths and Austers of two auxiliary air observation post flights, Nos 1957 and 1960 (661 Squadron) maintained the flying link. Also present for shorter periods were No 143 Gliding School and London University Air Squadron. In 1951 the first Battle of Britain film, *Angels one five*, was filmed

Above *Fighter pilots of No 403 'Wolf' Squadron, RCAF, are shown at the salute as they march past Air Vice Marshal W.F. Dickson, GB, DSO, OBE, AFC, of the RAF, at Kenley on February 1 1944. Spitfires line the parade square for the ceremony of the presentation of the 'Wolf' Squadron crest, which was personally approved and signed by the King and which includes the crown, a wolf with bared fangs and the squadron motto: 'Stalk and Strike'. On Air Vice Marshal Dickson's right is Group Captain William B. MacBrien, of Ottawa, officer commanding a sector of two Canadian fighter wings in Britain. Behind them is Flight Lieutenant Emmanual Galitzine, DFC, personal aide to AVM Dickson.*

Below *North American Harvard T 1, N7015, at Kenley.*

entirely at Kenley. The clock was again wound back in the late summer of 1955 when Kenley became the location for the making of the film *Reach for the Sky*. Kenneth More played the part of Douglas Bader and Kenley once again relived some of its great moments.

RAF Kenley was eventually closed on May 1 1959, but an air cadets gliding school continued to use the airfield. Also, from 1959 to 1964 the airfield was used by various Reserve flights. The sole occupant in 1964 was No 605 Mobile Signals Unit, which had arrived on September 26 1963. After it moved out on February 21 1966 the station was placed on Care and Maintenance.

The sole remaining pair of First World War hangars was completely destroyed by fire in October 1978. Today, Kenley is still in military use, for the whole of the technical site is under Army control. The Army also occupies the RAF married quarters. Kenley is officially designated an emergency landing airfield and is still used by the Air Training Corps for gliding instruction.

Kings Hill (West Malling), Kent

See West Malling

Langley (Parlaunt Park or Slough), Buckinghamshire

176/TQ025795. East of Slough

In 1936 Hawker Aircraft Ltd expanded from its Kingston base and purchased land at Langley on which a factory and airfield were built. By the end of 1938 the factory was completed and producing one Hurricane a day, rising to a peak of five a day in 1942. During 1941/42 a few Typhoons were built at Langley.

Few bombs fell on or near the works and a Hurricane was allocated for defence but with no record of any results.

The site continued in use after the war but since it was only a few miles from London Airport and lacked runways, Sea Fury testing was hampered.

Hawker Aircraft's rearrangement of sites took place in 1950 when the flight-test facilities available at Langley's grass airfield were no longer suitable for the

Below *LA610, ex-Tempest III completed as Fury on prototype and seen here at Langley Aerodrome.* **Bottom** *Avro York Star Speed, G-AHEZ, seen here at Langley early post-war.*

new breed of aircraft. In that year the company acquired the tenancy of the runwayed Dunsfold airfield. Langley was replaced by the Kingston factory and the site vacated.

Leavesden, Hertfordshire

166/TL095003. North-west of Watford, north of the A41 between the A41 and the A405

The history of the airfield at Leavesden goes back to 1940 and the early days of the war. Prior to this, the site was called the King George V Playing Fields, known locally as 'Mile Field' because of its approximate dimensions in either direction. As part of the vast wartime expansion in aviation this 300-acre site was purchased from the local council by the government of the day and a 3,033 ft long runway was laid, together with workshops and hangars. The premises were leased to two organisations—London Aircraft Productions (LAP) and the Second Aircraft Group (SAG)—the latter came under the general administration of the de Havilland Company, the Hatfield-based company who administered the factory area.

During the Second World War, both Halifax bombers and Mosquito fighter-bombers were built at Leavesden. So that they could take off from the relatively short runway, the final assembly of heavy equipment was carried out at secondary and final assembly factories elsewhere in the country. Records show that over 4,000 Mosquito aircraft were assembled at Leavesden during the war years.

As the war ended, these activities ceased and in 1946 Leavesden became the service department for civil repairs of de Havilland aircraft. The repair and servicing of DH Gipsy engines was a good introduction into the engine business. Leavesden was reorganised and expanded to become the de Havilland Engine Company.

The transition of Leavesden to the manufacture of the jet engine was a progressive one involving new techniques and

Aerial view of Leavesden with the Rolls-Royce Small Engine Division complex top left.

new equipment. When the lease of the Stonegrove works expired in 1954, Leavesden was equipped and ready to take the full production load of both piston engine and gas turbine manufacture.

Then, with the re-forming of the aircraft industry, management of Leavesden changed from de Havilland to Hawker Siddeley, to Bristol Siddeley and finally to Rolls-Royce. But the nature of the work carried out here has changed little over the years.

The 300-acre site, on which is situated the Rolls-Royce Aero Division Leavesden and Leavesden Aerodrome, is still owned by the Ministry of Defence and leased to Rolls-Royce through the Property Services Agency, which is, in effect, the Government's estate agent. Rolls-Royce Leavesden designs, develops, manufactures and overhauls a range of gas turbine engines for civil and military helicopters used worldwide. The engines power 81 per cent of Royal Navy helicopters, 99 per cent of British Army helicopters and 100 per cent of all Royal Air Force helicopters. Twenty-three other military and civil customers operate engines produced and supported by Rolls-Royce Leavesden, which is one of the three main production plants in the Rolls-Royce Aero Division. Rolls-Royce Leavesden employs over 3,000 people including 160 at its Manor Road, Hatfield engine test and development facility. The men and women of Rolls-Royce Leavesden make a product which is vital to the world of aviation—and to the economy of Britain, the jet engine.

There are two main factory areas at the Leavesden site; experimental and development area where engines are designed and developed, and the production build and machine shops. Parts for the giant RB211 for the wide-bodied airliner market and the RB199, powerplant of the multi-role Tornado, are also manufactured at Leavesden.

Leavesden Airfield is not just used for Rolls-Royce Aero Division's comings and goings. It is a publicly licensed aerodrome run by Rolls-Royce but open for all aircraft operators. It mainly serves executive, commercial and private flyers of light and medium aircraft. The airfield is fully equipped with some of the most advanced navigational and landing aids. Not only do the air traffic controllers check the movement of aircraft arriving or departing at Leavesden, they also provide assistance and information to aircraft flying over their airspace. These advantages are greatly appreciated by the travelling executive and the business commuter using the facilities at Leavesden.

Leysdown, Kent

178/TR040698. On the east side of the Isle of Sheppey

It was perhaps not surprising that the Isle of Sheppey was one of the first places in England to become connected with aviation. In January 1909, Mr Albert Eustace Short, who, with Mr Hugh Oswald Short, had been appointed Aeronautical Engineer to the Aero Club of the United Kingdom in the ballooning days, visited the brothers Wilbur and Orville Wright at their flying ground at Pau, in France. Having received instructions to construct Wright machines in this country, he returned, hunted for a flying ground, and settled upon Leysdown.

The ballooning members of the Aero Club (not yet Royal) endorsed this choice as they knew from experience that Sheppey was flat country, comparatively free of trees and other obstacles. Most balloon ascents were made from the neighbourhood of London and most winds were westerly, the north and south shores of the Thames estuary were therefore well known to this community of amateur aeronauts.

The brothers Wright having also reported favourably as to its suitability, in February, the club decided to acquire 400 acres of marsh ground between Leysdown and Shellness Point for its aeroplane experiments. It also took over a small hotel in Leysdown village and a house called Mussell Manor, to accommodate its members.

During the following month, Eustace Short was joined at Leysdown by his brother, Horace Leonard Short, and they at once erected workshops, two sheds for aeroplanes, and bungalows for their workmen. In addition, several private sheds were quickly put up to house members' private machines, the leading pioneer being Frank McClean (later Lieutenant-Colonel Sir Francis McClean, AFC), Ernest Pitman, J.T.C. Moore-Brabazon (later Lieutenant-Colonel Moore-Brabazon, MC, MP), the Hon Maurice Egerton (later Lord Egerton of Tatton), Percy Grace, Cecil Grace (subsequently drowned in the Channel), and the Hon Charles Rolls (subsequently killed at Bournemouth).

From the outset Moore-Brabazon became one of the most enthusiastic of the little band, and on February 27 1909 on a Voisin 'pusher' brought from France, called the *Bird of Passage*, he flew five kilometres. The following day he flew several short distances, and would have continued with others, but, unfortunately, while taxying, the propeller-shaft broke off and the airscrew buried itself in the ground.

Flying was taken up in earnest during April of that year, and so much progress in turning in the air was made that on October 30 Moore-Brabazon, on the second biplane designed and built on the spot by Horace Short, and fitted with a 40-60 Green engine, accomplished at an average height of 20 ft the first circular mile ever flown on a British aeroplane. The time taken was 2 minutes 36¼ seconds. For this he was awarded a prize of £1,000 by the *Daily Mail*. On November 4, on the same machine, he flew 3½ miles.

During the summer, McClean and the Hon C.S. Rolls were flying Wright biplanes built by Short Brothers under licence to Wright Brothers, the American pioneers. In August, McClean, on Short No 1 was catapulted into the air, but the machine was fitted with an old motor-car engine and could not sustain flight. On November 2, however, the first successful straight flight on this machine was made, followed by another the next day. On November 6, whilst landing, the machine was rather badly damaged.

About this time Pitman was flying a Voisin, and others were making short hops. Several members ordered machines from the Short firm during the autumn, and McClean and others built bungalows for living accommodation near the hangars.

Captain J.W. Dunne arrived at Leysdown during the latter part of 1909, erected a shed, and arranged with the Short brothers to construct to his drawings an inherently stable tailless biplane, with V-shaped wings. This was the first attempt in England to build a power-driven stable aeroplane, though Mr Jose Weiss had already built man-carrying gliders which were quite stable.

The flying ground was somewhat rough for wheeled undercarriages. The Wright biplanes were launched off a rail by a catapult and so escaped this trouble. Accidents due to landing on bumpy ground were quite frequent until one of Messrs Short's workmen hit on the idea of burning the grass in the hollows, which thus showed up in the air.

By the end of the year it was found that the flying ground was rather too low-lying

for all-the-year-round use. A new site was needed and McClean purchased a large tract of ground near Eastchurch and gave the free use of it to members of the Aero Club in return for a fixed rent of one shilling per year from the club. Shortly afterwards the Short brothers removed their factory from Leysdown to Eastchurch.

Between the wars the site at Leysdown was used as a landing ground but it had no facilities and the controlling authority was the Officer Commanding, RAF Station, Eastchurch.

London Colney, Hertfordshire

166/TL180020. Approximately 5 miles south-west of Hatfield

Situated two miles from Radlett railway station, London Colney was established as a second class landing ground and covered an area of 212 acres. The surroundings were undulating and somewhat heavily wooded. It came under the south-east area and was used by 44 Squadron.

In the spring of 1916 a training aerodrome was established on the site. It was provided with wooden flight sheds and hutted accommodation and the first unit to be based at London Colney was the newly formed 56 Squadron, which arrived from Gosport on July 4 1916. On December 22 1916 the Sopwith Pups of 54 Squadron arrived, but two days later they moved to St Omer, France. Major Blonfield took over as Commanding Officer at London Colney on February 6, 1917 and he began to build 56 Squadron into a fighting unit. After using a variety of training aeroplanes the squadron became the first to receive SE 5 fighters when these were issued in March 1917. The first flying officer was Captain Albert Ball, the RCF's leading ace, with 36 victories. Ball went on a tour of the training squadrons to find suitable pilots for the squadron. Many of those he chose later became outstanding fighter pilots. At 11.55 hours on April 7 1917, No 56 Squadron flew to St Omer where it stayed for lunch before flying on to its assigned station at Vert Galant. Ball was killed on May 8 1917 flying with the squadron.

No 56 Squadron was replaced by No 56 Training Squadron, which had formed here on February 7 1917, flying a mixed bag of aeroplanes. This was the second such unit to form here, as 45 Reserve Squadron had been created on November 2 1916, but it had moved to South Carlton,

Lincolnshire, a few days later. Another short-term resident was 27 Training Squadron, which was re-formed on March 22 1918 but soon transferred up to Eastburn. On July 10 1917 No 74 Squadron arrived from Northolt with Avro 504Ks and SE 5As. It was joined by 92 Squadron on September 1 but this unit remained only a few days and during the middle of the month it moved to Chattis Hill. No 74 Squadron remained throughout the winter months and worked up with SE 5s before moving to Goldhanger on March 25 1918. As part of the reorganisation of training in the RAF in the summer of 1918 and on July 15 of that year No 56 Training Squadron expanded into No 41 Training Depot Station. It was flying Avro 504Ks and Sopwith Snipes. After the Armistice in November 1918 the training programme was run down and early in 1919, No 41 Training Depot Squadron disbanded. During this period a second TDS had a short stay at the aerodrome when 54 TDS arrived from Fairlop in 1918, disbanding the following year.

After the war the field was retained by the RAF and used throughout the summer and autumn of 1919 by Nos 1 and 24 Squadrons, but these were only cadre units and both had disbanded or moved else-

where to disband by November 1919. London Colney was not retained as a permanent post-war RAF station and it closed in December 1919.

The airfield was never reactivated but in the late 1920s Radlett Aerodrome opened only a mile or so just north-west of the old RFC site. Also, during the Second World War, Salisbury Hall, near to London Colney, was used for military purposes. On October 5 1939, the nucleus Mosquito design team moved to Salisbury Hall for secrecy. A hangar was erected and this was disguised as a barn. It was here, under the shadow of the old First World War site that the prototype was built under the direction of F. Plumb.

Luton, Bedfordshire

166/TL123208. South-east of Luton, some two miles from the M1, junction 10

The site was first used by the Percival Aircraft Company which moved in from Gravesend in October 1936. The grass airfield at Luton was officially opened on July 16 1938. The Vega Gull was in production and this type was developed into the Proctor, which began to appear in late 1939 to serve as an RAF communications

The control tower at Luton Airport forms the background for this photograph of Percival Provost WV614 showing a variety of stores including bombs and rockets.

Percival Gull Six, G-ADPR, *flown by Miss Jean Batten to South America. It is today in the Shuttleworth Collection at Old Warden, Bedfordshire.*

aircraft. Throughout the war years the company produced the Proctor for radio operator training.

After the outbreak of war, the airfield housed No 24 Elementary Flying Training School, which moved in from Sydenham on July 22 1940 with its Tiger Moths. In May 1941 the school began to use Barton-in-the-Clay as a relief landing ground. As the circuit became more congested Halton was taken on as a second RLG on August 18 1941. Both continued to be used right up until the school moved to Sealand on February 7 1942.

After the end of hostilities the Luton Flying Club was re-established. Aircraft production continued and the Prentice was produced after the Second World War to supersede the ageing Tiger Moth. It remained as the standard basic trainer until the arrival of the Provost. The prototype, *TV163* first flew on March 31 1946. Full-scale production of 370 was undertaken and the first deliveries were made in November 1947. The Percival Prentice went into service with the Central Flying School, RAF College at Cranwell, the FTS at Ternhill, Cottesmore and many other stations.

Then followed the Percival P 56 Provost trainer and the Cheetah-engined prototype flew on February 23 1950. After flight trials the Leonides-engined P 56 was selected and it went into full-scale production at Luton under the designation Provost T Mk 1.

By the mid-1950s the company was known as Hunting Percival, abbreviated to Hunting before becoming a part of the British Aircraft Corporation. The reorganisation brought aircraft production to an end at Luton.

In the 1950s several charter airlines began to operate out of Luton, including Eagle Aviation's three Yorks, which were resident from April 1950 to November 1952. Derby Aviaiton began scheduled services in 1959. During this period considerable improvements were made to the airport. This made other airlines look again at Luton and in 1960 Autair began charters from Luton. Autair's first scheduled service was on October 1 1963. This was a Blackpool route, later extended to Glasgow. Other routes followed but a change of policy in 1969 saw an end to all these operations, the airline adopting the name Court Line for its proposed extensive inclusive tour (IT) work. Court Line continued with BAC 1-11s until its collapse in August 1974. For a time traffic at Luton was reduced, but only for a short period, for the gap was quickly filled by airlines such as Dan-Air, Monarch and Britannia which increased their market in the holiday flight business.

The airport is still used principally for charter work. Executive and light aircraft also make considerable use of the airport. To meet the demands further development is planned to include another terminal extension and improved approach roads.

Maidenhead (White Waltham), Berkshire

See White Waltham

Maylands (Romford), Essex

177/TQ560924. North-east of Romford off the main A12

After almost a decade of non-flying in the county of Essex a small aerodrome was established at Maylands in 1928. This small sloping site adjacent to the A12 trunk road near Harold Wood was first used as a base for A.H. Matthews' Avro 504K.

On March 30 1929, the aerodrome was licensed to Inland Flying and Motor Services Ltd and from their base at Maylands they gave flying displays with their two DH 6s and two 504Ks from small fields all over the country. Those who had survived the post-war slump were now active in the pleasure flying business but their main competitor was the Brookland School of Flying which operated with two red Avro 548s.

The early 1930s saw many changes, for joyriding was now big business and on November 26 1931 the licence was taken over by Hillman's Saloon Coaches and Airways Ltd which had just formed here with two Puss Moths. E.H. Hillman was well-known locally as a bus operator who decided to move into the air taxi business. It was the start of bigger things for the little field at Maylands.

Hillman soon expanded and in 1932 he acquired two Fox Moths and opened a scheduled summer service to Clacton and Ramsgate. To mark the enlargement of the aerodrome and the growth of his airline, Hillman staged the great Essex Air Pageant on September 24 1932. It was attended by the Lord Mayor of London who arrived in a Spartan Cruiser piloted by Lieutenant-Colonel L.A. Strange. They were escorted by five Wapitis of No 600 Squadron and three Bulldogs from No 54 Squadron from nearby Hornchurch.

Hillman then took delivery of six new de Havilland DH 84 Dragons and in April 1933 began with them a scheduled service to Paris. One of his pilots was Amy Johnson. With a return fare of £5-10s-0d. Hillman undercut all his rivals. By the end of the year Hillman's Airways came into being as a separate company, the coach side of the business having been disposed of to become the forerunner of today's Green Line services. Maylands was officially licensed as a Customs aerodrome in February 1934 but it was unable to cope with the increased traffic. Therefore, in June 1934, Hillman's Airways moved to Stapleford Tawney aerodrome, a few miles to the north-west and Maylands fell by the wayside.

The site of the aerodrome was sold for development as a golf course at the beginning of 1936 but it remained in use by light aeroplanes and housed the Romford Flying Club until 1939. The end finally came on the night of February 6 1940 when incendiary bombs fell on the aerodrome and destroyed the hangars and all the club's aircraft. The airfield was never reopened to flying and today Maylands Golf Course occupies the site but one can still pick out the overgrown foundations and hangar bases.

DH Moth at Maylands, early 1930s. This aircraft was flown by Captain Glover.

Northolt, Middlesex

176/TQ100850. To the west of London on the A40, to the west of the junction with the B455

Northolt was one of the earliest military aerodromes to be built in the United Kingdom, construction having started at the beginning of 1915. The site had previously been surveyed three times since 1910 with intentions to construct an aerodrome but this came to nothing in all three cases. Lying 14 miles to the west of London on, the A40, Western Avenue, the site consisted of some 283 acres. Six flight sheds, each 200 ft × 60 ft and a twin hangar of the same size were erected, plus workshops and long wooden barrack huts. The guard room was near the gate to West End Lane.

The aerodrome, named Northolt after the nearby Northolt Junction railway station (since re-named South Ruislip), officially opened on March 1 1915 when No 4 Reserve Aeroplane Squadron arrived from Farnborough.

Northolt was designated one of the seven home defence night landing grounds, having very primitive lighting for night operations. No 18 Squadron, RFC, was formed at Northolt on May 11 1915 from No 4 Reserve Squadron, and on August 16 moved to Norwich, before moving to France in November 1915, equipped with Vickers FB 5s for fighter-reconnaissance duties.

The first recorded flights took place on the night of June 4/5 1915, when two BE 2cs took off on an anti-Zeppelin sortie. On October 12, No 11 RAS was formed. This unit was commanded by Major L. Penn-Gaskell and was responsible for training pilots in night flying for home defence duties. It was equipped with BE 2cs, Martinsydes and Curtiss JNs. It also kept two BE 2cs and crews permanently available for home defence.

During the first winter of operations the lack of drainage brought serious waterlogging problems and flying became difficult. By this period a line of hangars had been completed on the north side and it became almost impossible for aircraft to taxi from the hangars to the landing area. A quick solution was to cover an area of 8 sq acres in the middle of the aerodrome with clinker. This clinker patch lasted until 1925 when proper drainage was laid. Although the site of the 'patch' is now crossed by the north-south runway, the course of the cinder tracks can still be seen from the air, distinguished by the different colour grass.

On January 13 1916 all RASs became known as Reserve Squadrons (RS). February 1 saw the arrival of a detachment from 19 RS at Hounslow. This was a new unit just formed and on April 15 1916 it became No 39 Squadron. The following month the detachment moved out. No 40 RS was formed in July 1916 but left for Oxford on August 21.

During this period two tragic accidents occurred. On January 31 1916, Major Penn-Gaskell hit a tree on the west side of the airfield during a night take-off to intercept Zeppelins attacking the Midlands. He died four days later from his injuries. Another night take-off exactly two months later resulted in a similar fatal accident when Lieutenant John Bailey of No 11 Reserve Squadron was killed.

On December 8 1916, No 43 Squadron arrived from Netheravon equipped with Bristol Scouts. At Northolt the squadron was brought up to full strength and re-equipped with its long-awaited 1½-Strutters. Training recommenced and one of the flight commanders who joined the squadron here was Captain H.H. Balfour (later Lord Balfour of Inchrye). By the middle of January, 43 Squadron was equipped fully and ready to fly to France. Captain Balfour was detailed to take the squadron personnel by boat to France via Southampton. On January 17 the squadron left for Treizennes in France via Lympne and St Omer. Unfortunately, the first aircraft airborne, flown by Lieutenant Addis, stalled and crashed, killing him, his mechanic and Captain Balfour's little terrier dog which was also in the rear cockpit. A week later No 11 RS, by now equipped with BE 2cs, RE 7s, 1½-Strutters and a few Avros, moved to Rochford where, on February 8 1917, it became known as 98 Depot Squadron.

No 11 RS was replaced by 2 RS, an elementary training squadron which arrived from Brooklands. This unit was commanded by Captain Chadwick and was equipped with Maurice Farman Shorthorns. February 16 saw the arrival of 35 RS from Filton. This was an advanced flying training squadron and was equipped with BE 2cs, and, later, Bristol fighters. On May 31 all Reserve squadrons were renamed training squadrons.

On June 13 1917, during a daylight raid, an aircraft piloted by Captain C.H. Cole-Hamilton intercepted some Gothas over Ilford, Essex and during the ensuing fight

Captain C.H. Keevil, his observer, was killed. This was the one and only contact with the enemy by aircraft flying from Northolt in the First World War.

By this time, the Fairey Aviation Company, which had opened a factory in Hayes in the latter part of 1916, was using the aerodrome for flight-testing. Fairey was involved with the aircraft known as the Kennedy Giant, designed by J.C.H. Mac-Kenzie Kennedy who had returned to England in 1915 after working with Igor Sikorsky in Russia. The aircraft resembled the early Sikorsky giants and had a wing span of 142 ft.

Work started on the aircraft in 1916 on the understanding from the Government that no financial support would be given until it flew. The aircraft was taken by road to Northolt but it was too large for any hangar and it had to be built outside. After many problems and design changes it was ready by November 1917. The first flight of the infamous Kennedy Giant (serial No 2337) was undertaken by Lieutenant F.T. Courtney, then an instructor with No 35 TS. From the hangars he started down the slope towards the south under full throttle and managed a short hop of about 100 ft before coming to a dead stop in soft ground. No further attempts were made to fly the machine and it was eventually dumped in the north-western corner of the aerodrome where it slowly rotted away.

With the entry of the United States into the war, Northolt received many Americans for flying training and in June 1917 received a party of 40 Russian cadets. It is not recorded how the latter progressed but it is known that at least one was killed during training.

On July 1 1917, No 74 Squadron formed under the command of Major A.H. O'Hara Wood with Avro 504s. Nine days later the squadron moved to London Colney. No 35 TS moved to Oxford on December 16 and its place at Northolt was taken on the same day by No 86 Squadron. This was an advanced training squadron flying Sopwith Camels and Avro 504s.

Northolt's role as a training aerodrome was full of incidents, and crashes were frequent but usually not fatal. In 1917 there were approximately 13 fatal crashes with 16 deaths. One of the lucky ones was 'Dud' Mudge, who, on his first solo, crashed into a hangar while landing at Northolt. The nose of the Nacelle, with the pilot sitting in it, went through the wall of the hangar and he was pitched on to the floor breaking his arm. The pusher engine continued to roar at full throttle outside because the throttle control had broken in the crash.

In February 1918 the reorganisation of training squadrons underwent a review and as a result Northolt's three training squadrons, 2 TS, 4 TS and 86 Squadron were amalgamated into a single unit—No 30 Training Depot Station. The TDS had three flights and each one had a strength of 18 machines and 40 pupils, later increased to 24 machines and 60 pupils.

After the Armistice on November 11 1918 the squadrons were rapidly being disbanded and aerodromes closed. By May 1919, Northolt's career as a fighter training aerodrome ceased altogether. In June 1919 the South-Eastern Communications Flight arrived at Northolt, which was the nearest airfield to the RAF Depot (later HQ) at Uxbridge. The flight operated a refresher course for officers. On June 18 an unusual incident occurred when Lieutenant C.L. Startup and Air Mechanic Carpenter were flying at 1,000 ft over Harrow. The petrol tank of their Avro 504 burst, the aircraft caught fire and both men were forced by the blaze to climb out of their cockpits onto the wings. Somehow the pilot succeeded in retaining sufficient control to make a hurried landing. Both men were injured but survived.

In 1919 Northolt was licensed as a joint RAF/civil flying field and the Central Aircraft Company moved in to operate a flying school and a charter organisation as well as manufacturing aircraft. The company designed and built a large cabin biplane, the Centaur, the prototype being registered in July 1919 and tested in May 1920. The company finally closed in 1926.

During this period a Coastal Area flight had arrived in 1920 and in 1923 merged with the resident flight to become the Inland Area Communications Flight. Military activity had increased when No 12 Squadron was re-formed at Northolt on April 1 1923 as a bomber squadron equipped with DH 9As. No 41 Squadron was also re-formed with a single flight of Snipe aircraft and in 1924 was re-equipped with two flights of Siskins. No 12 Squadron moved to Andover in March 1924 but No 41 stayed on and re-equipped with Bulldogs in October 1931.

Meanwhile, changes had taken place on the aerodrome after a few wet winters. During one the aerodrome had been completely waterlogged and closed to RAF

flying. In 1925 proper drainage was installed and the clinker patch grassed over.

It soon became obvious that the old
accommodation was worn out, so in the
latter part of the 1920s three of the original
wooden flight sheds were demolished and
replaced by an 'A' Type hangar. New
barrack blocks and messes were built and
the landing area was enlarged.

The year 1925 saw the formation of some
of the Auxiliary Air Force squadrons and
two of these squadrons, No 600 (City of
London) and No 601 (County of London)
were both formed at Northolt on October
14 1925 as light bomber squadrons equipped
with DH 9As. The latter was commanded
by Squadron Leader Lord Edward Gros-
venor and was known as 'The Millionaires'
Squadron' (because at one time before the
war it was reputed to have six millionaire
members). These were the élite 'weekend
fliers' and their peacetime activities followed the usual auxiliary pattern—flying
training at weekends, annual camp at
Tangmere and occasional participation in
the RAF Display. Both squadrons remained based at Northolt until January 18 1927,
when a move was made to the famous
Hendon airfield which the Government
had purchased in 1925 from aviation
pioneer Claude Grahame-White.

No 24 Communication Squadron moved
in on January 15 1927 to join No 41 Squadron. No 24 maintained a training flight to
provide flying practice for pilots on the
Air Ministry staff and was involved in
flying high ranking officials and military
personnel about the country. The aircraft
used for these duties were Bristol Fighters,
Avro 504s, Fairey IIIFs, DH 9As and DH
Moths. Both the Duke of Windsor (then
Prince of Wales) and Prince George (then
Duke of Kent) learned to fly at Northolt
under the instruction of Squadron Leader
D.S. Don, CO of No 24 Squadron.

Fairey Aviation activity continued with
test-flying of the long-range monoplane in
November 1928, the Firefly 11M prototype (G-ABCN) and Fleetwind in 1929.
The following year Fairey Aviation moved
out to the Great West aerodrome (which
later became Heathrow Airport).

In July 1933, No 24 Communication
Squadron moved to Hendon. A year later
111 Squadron arrived from Hornchurch
with its Bulldog fighters. The year 1935
saw the formation of the University of
London Air Squadron, consisting of a
staff of ground and flying instructors with
accommodation at Northolt and Kensington. The CFI was also in charge of the
station flight. The equipment consisted of

No 111 Squadron at Northolt in 1938; note the prewar code letters TM *which were re-
allocated to No 504 (County of Nottingham) Squadron on outbreak of war.*

Avro Tutors and Hawker Harts. In October 1935, No 41's 12-year tenure ended when it was posted to Aden during the Italian-Abyssinian War.

On May 1 1936 the station was transferred to No 11 Group Fighter Command. At the end of that year No 23 Squadron moved in with Hawker Demon biplanes and stayed until May 16 1938, when it moved to Wittering where it re-equipped with Blenheims.

This was the expansion period for the RAF and on March 8 1937, No 213 Squadron re-formed at Northolt with Gloster Gauntlets, and on July 1 moved to Church Fenton.

No 111 Squadron made history in January 1938 when it became the first squadron in the RAF to receive the new Hawker Hurricane. As the squadron worked up on its new aircraft it was inevitable that incidents would occur. The first fatal Hurricane crash, *L1556*, flown by Flying Officer Mervyn Bocquet was on February 1. It was seen to dive straight into the ground next to the Western Avenue between Hillingdon and Ickenham. On March 19, Hurricane *L1551* force-landed at Ickenham and on July 18, *L1550* force-landed at Colnbrook. Two days later *L1549* crashed whilst approaching to land at Northolt. The crash tenders were kept very busy.

The year 1939 started badly for 111 Squadron when there were two crashes on January 17. As training continued there were further crashes and by now the war clouds were gathering. Throughout the build-up period the improvement continued with a second permanent hangar, a 'C' Type hipped—one of the earliest to be built. Five 'H' Type barrack blocks were also completed in the north-eastern corner and in 1939 two short paved runways, each of 2,400 ft were laid, making Northolt one of the few RAF airfields to be equipped with runways when war was declared in September 1939. On the outbreak of war, Northolt's resident squadrons were No 25, which had arrived from Hawkinge on August 22, No 111 and No 600, the latter having arrived at the end of August with Blenheim Ifs. On September 15 the Blenheims of 25 Squadron moved to Filton only to return again on October 4. Two days previously, No 65 Squadron had arrived and this squadron was flying Spitfires. These squadrons were replaced by a succession of units which came and went throughout 1940 (see movement table).

Movement table for squadrons at Northolt, 1939-1944

Date arrived	Date departed	Squadron No	Equipment
2.10.39	28.3.40	65	Spitfire I
4.10.39	16.1.40	25	Blenheim If
16.1.40	14.5.40	604	Blenheim If
14.2.40	8.5.40	253	Hurricane I
9.5.40	23.5.40	92	Spitfire I
13.5.40	21.5.40	111	Hurricane I
14.5.40	20.6.40	600	Blenheim If
19.5.40	6.7.40	609	Spitfire I
4.6.40	9.6.40	92	Spitfire I
18.6.40	23.7.40	1	Hurricane I
4.7.40	15.8.40	257	Hurricane I
23.7.40	1.8.40	43 (Det)	Hurricane I
1.8.40	9.9.40	1	Hurricane I
2.8.40	11.10.40	303	Hurricane I
-.8.40	9.10.40	1 RCAF	Hurricane I
26.8.40	2.9.40	17	Hurricane I
12.9.40	-.10.40	264 (B Flt)	Defiant I
9.9.40	15.12.40	229	Hurricane I
10.10.40	17.12.40	615	Hurricane I
11.10.40	23.11.40	302	Hurricane I
15.12.40	15.1.41	1	Hurricane I
17.12.40	1.5.41	601	Hurricane I
3.1.41	16.7.41	303	Spitfire I
3.4.41	7.10.41	306	Hurricane II
24.6.41	12.12.41	308	Spitfire V
16.7.41	1.4.42	315	Spitfire V
7.10.41	16.6.42	303	Spitfire V
12.12.41	22.2.42	316	Spitfire V
1.4.42	30.6.42	317	Spitfire V
16.6.42	13.3.43	306	Spitfire V
7.7.42	4.9.42	317	Spitfire V, IX
6.9.42	1.6.43	315	Spitfire V, IX
1.10.42	29.10.42	515	Defiant II
29.10.42	29.4.43	308	Spitfire V
2.2.43	5.2.43	303	Spitfire V
12.3.43	22.9.43	316	Spitfire V, IX
1.6.43	12.11.43	303	Spitfire IX
26.7.43	20.9.43	124	Spitfire VIII
21.9.43	2.12.43	317	Spitfire IX
21.9.43	1.4.44	302	Spitfire IX
29.10.43	8.3.44	308	Spitfire IX
18.12.43	1.4.44	317	Spitfire IX
15.3.44	1.4.44	308	Spitfire IX
7.4.44	4.9.44	16	Spitfire XI
7.4.44	3.9.44	140	Mosquito IX, XVI

In January 1940 Group Captain (later AVM) S.F. Vincent assumed command of the station and was at the helm during the Battle of Britain. At 43 he was an old man by RAF standards, but he had seen considerable action over the Western front during the First World War.

By this time Northolt had acquired Heston as a satellite aerodrome and in February 1940 opened a dummy aerodrome complete with wooden Hurricanes and dummy flarepath on a golf course at Barnet. This served Northolt for the next 12 months.

During early 1940 camouflage experts

Above *Squadron Leader McNab of No 1 (RCAF) Squadron at Northolt, September 1940.*

Below *Fighter pilots at Northolt during the Battle of Britain, 1940.*

arrived at Northolt to paint the hangars and buildings in the usual wavy stripes of green and black and brown, but Vincent disagreed with them, pointing out that the airfield was in the midst of suburban areas of Ruislip, Northolt, Harrow and Uxbridge, which would show up the camouflaged hangars. After much argument, Vincent won the day and each hangar was painted as two rows of houses with gardens running between. The perimeter track and runways had large black blobs representing trees and bushes and as a final effect a meandering stream was painted down each runway with a pond where they intersected. The open grass areas were marked with tar lines to represent hedges, these faithfully following the pre-1915 field patterns. Because the airfield and its buildings were so skilfully camouflaged to blend in with the surrounding area it suffered relatively little damage from enemy air attacks.

Below *King George VI inspecting No 1 (F) Squadron RCAF, at Northolt during the Battle of Britain. His Majesty is accompanied by the Squadron CO, Ernest McNab (only head showing)*

Bottom *Tea break at Northolt in 1940. Note the Sergeant in the tin hat is armed with a revolver.*

Throughout all this the improvements continued and a new section of perimeter track which looped away from the west end of the airfield was built, providing access to a number of new dispersals. A total of 13 twin dispersal pens was built on various parts of the airfield, together with huts for maintenance and aircrews. Bofors guns were placed in position, trenches dug and a detachment of the 2nd Battalion, The London Scottish Regiment took up aerodrome defence duties.

During the heat of the battle, No 303 (Kosciuszko) Squadron, the RAF's second Polish fighter squadron, was formed at Northolt on August 2 1940, and was the first to go into action. This was the start of the Polish squadrons which were to last for almost four years. No 303 Squadron moved to Leconfield in October 1940.

After a very hectic few months the year was brought to a close when No 1 Squadron replaced No 229 on December 15, and 601 replaced 615 on December 17.

As the New Year opened, Fighter Command went on the attack, and on January 3 1941, No 303 Squadron arrived. Together with Nos 1 and 601 it opened Northolt's offensive operations. No 1 Squadron moved to Kenley during mid-January and as 1941 progressed, further Polish units arrived. On April 4, No 306 arrived from Tern Hill and at the end of June No 308 arrived. By this period of the war all the squadrons based at Northolt were Polish

No 1 (F) Squadron, RCAF, in transit from Northolt after the Battle of Britain.

and with the odd exception were to remain so until April 1944. No 303 Squadron moved out on July 16 and was replaced on the same day by 315 Squadron. *Rhubarbs*, *Ramrods* and *Circuses* were now the order of the day for the Spitfire squadrons. The Polish personnel were now well established in the locality.

When the satellite at Heston gained station status in April 1942, Northolt was reduced to two squadrons with two Polish squadrons at Heston, all four operating as a Polish wing. The Northolt Spitfires became the first to fly as a wing over Germany.

A Special Service flight formed at Northolt at the end of August 1942. This unit was equipped with specially modified Spitfire IXs in an attempt to combat the high-flying Ju 86 bombers which roamed England at will at altitudes of over 40,000 ft. Six pilots were selected for this special unit and one of them was the famous Pilot Officer Prince Emmanuel Galitzine who was Russian-born. On September 10 1942, Galitzine intercepted a Ju 86R at 42,000 ft, north of Southampton, damaging the port wing—possibly the highest combat to take place during the Second World War. The flight was later incorporated in No 124 Squadron which was based at Northolt from July 1943 to September 1943.

On October 1 1942, No 515 Squadron formed at Northolt with Boulton Paul Defiants. The squadron was employed on radar jamming duties and moved to Heston at the end of the month.

In November 1943 the squadrons were absorbed into the newly formed 2nd Tactical Air Force. Northolt was designated No 131 Airfield and together with Heston formed the 18th Fighter Wing, No 84 Group, 2nd TAF. The 2nd TAF was formed to give close support and air cover to the Allied airmen in the planned invasion of Europe. Each unit was to be completely mobile and self-sufficient in maintenance, servicing, etc.

On March 25 1943, RAF Transport Command was created out of the old Ferry Command. Air Chief Marshal Sir Frederick Bowhill, who had commanded Ferry Command in Montreal, was made AOC-in-C of the new command. He established his headquarters at Stanmore and Northolt became the command's main London airfield. As the war progressed more and more use was made of the airfield by transport aircraft and in April 1944 the short north-south runway was closed so that it could be used as additional parking space. By this time work had already commenced on extending the main north-east-south-west runway. Up to this period little new construction had been carried out. A 'B1' Type hangar had been erected to the west of the main group and in 1943 14 Blister hangars were erected around the aerodrome.

On April 1 1944, the three resident Polish fighter squadrons, Nos 302, 308 and 317 moved away to Deanland, an advance landing ground near the south coast, in preparation for D-Day. This move brought to an end Northolt's days as a fighter station. The fighters were replaced by No 34 (Photo Reconnaissance) Wing which had moved to Northolt to be near SHAEF HQ. The wing was another 2nd TAF unit and consisted of three photographic reconnaissance squadrons, No 16 equipped with Spitfire XIs for high and low level reconnaissance duties, No 140 with Mosquito IXs and XVIs and No 69 equipped with Wellington XIIIs for night reconnaissance. The wing was camped out on the west end of the airfield and was completely divorced from all station facilities.

All three squadrons were heavily involved with reconnaissance duties on D-Day. No 16 Squadron was called to make low-level sorties against strongly defended targets when cloud cover prevented high-altitude photographs being taken. In consequence, 16 Squadron's casualty rate began to climb. No 16, one of the oldest squadrons in the RAF, was formed in France in 1915 at St Omer. This explains the nickname the 'Saints'. In the First World War the squadron was involved in aerial reconnaissance for the Army and pioneered the use of wireless in air-to-ground communications. Again in the Second World War it played a vital part. In September the Wing moved to Balleroy in Normandy.

During this period the Transport Command Communications Flight, operating a variety of aircraft, had moved into Northolt in March the previous year. This unit later took on strength some Avro Yorks and in May 1944—when the King inspected the station—the station flight was raised to the status of a squadron and became known as the Air Defence of Great Britain (ADGB) Communication Squadron. In June many passengers passed through the station with the addition of casualties and PoWs arriving from Normandy. At this time London was under attack from the V weapons and on July 30 1944 a V1 exploded on the south side of the airfield, fortunately causing little damage. It did not halt the expansion of the station. In November 1944, when new night lighting was installed, there were 7,506 movements during the month.

During 1944 the USAAF had used Northolt, but by December all American units had left the station. The year 1944 also saw additional activity at weekends when local ATC squadrons participated in air experience flights from Northolt.

Heavier aircraft demanded longer runways and early in 1945 a new north-west-south-east runway was initially laid in pierced steel planking (PSP). During this period the north-east-south-west runway was resurfaced and work also started on an aircraft parking apron, and passenger and freight buildings on the south side of the aerodrome.

In February 1945 five Dakotas of No 271 Squadron, 110 Wing, 46 Group, were based at Northolt to operate a scheduled passenger service to Brussels. During February the ADGB Communication Squadron moved out and that same month No 246 Squadron absorbed the VIP Flight of the Metropolitan Communications Squadron equipped with Avro Yorks. This unit received its first Douglas Skymaster in April and in November the VIP Flight was transferred to Lyneham in Wiltshire.

Above *Avro 691 Lancastrian, VN726, photographed at Northolt in March 1946 after its record flight to New Zealand. Round flight was 25,660 miles and the total time was 111 hours 37 minutes. A.E. Tebboth far right.*

Below *Aerial view of Northolt, circa 1950, when it was a main passenger airport.*

Breda Zappata, BZ308, at Northolt in September 1952.

In the immediate post-war era Northolt was the main London airport while the former RAF airfield at Heathrow was reconstructed. From February 1 1946, regular services were operated by Dakotas of the European Division of BOAC (which became British European Airways on August 1) from Northolt to Paris, Brussels and Amsterdam. On February 4 1946 Northolt became officially a civil airport on loan from the Air Ministry to the Ministry of Civil Aviation.

During this period No 1359 Flight was at Northolt servicing aircraft which included three Yorks, *LV633*, *MW100* and *MW101* and also *MW102*, Lord Mountbatten's aircraft, when major work was required. When the work started on the runway the flight was posted to Holmseley South.

By March 1946 the north-west–south-east runway, relaid in concrete, was ready for use, together with a new control tower on the north-western corner. Services developed rapidly and European operators from Northolt included Alitalia, ABA Swedish Airlines, Aer Lingus, DHY Danish Airlines and Swissair. The main aircraft were Dakotas, DC 4s and Vikings. In October 1954 the aerodrome reverted to RAF control. Since 1946 almost five million passengers had passed through Northolt on 300,000 flights. Throughout this period the RAF had continued to use the airfield and operated scheduled Dakota services to Berlin, Warsaw and Vienna.

In the mid-1950s a programme to resurface the runways and renovate the buildings was put in hand. This work was completed in mid-1957. During this period of repair the last remaining First World War hangars were demolished. In November 1957 the Metropolitan Communications Squadron arrived from Hendon and the station became part of Transport Command.

On June 1 1960, an Anson of the Bomber Command Communications Squadron suffered an engine failure on take-off and pancaked on to the Express Dairy at South Ruislip. Fortunately there was no fire and there were no serious injuries. Then, on October 25 1960, Northolt had an unexpected visitor when a Pan American Boeing 707 landed and needed every foot of the 5,500 ft runway. The aircraft was bound for Heathrow and the pilot inadvertently set up a visual approach pattern on the Harrow gasholder and the north-east–south-west runway at Northolt, mistaking those two landmarks for the Southall gas holder and runway 23L at Heathrow. The Boeing 707 was subsequently stripped of its seats and successfully flown out. On April 28 1964 a Lufthansa Boeing 707 made a similar approach but a red Very light seemed to convince the captain that he was in error and he carried out a low overshoot. As a result of these two incidents it was decided that the bigraph for Northolt should be changed from NH to NO since it was considered that the large white letters NH painted on the Harrow gasholder were too easily confused with the LH painted on the Southall gasholder.

Early in 1969 the southern taxiway was resurfaced and the building of a new education centre begun. However, on Easter Monday the sergeants' mess was gutted by fire which caused the plans for

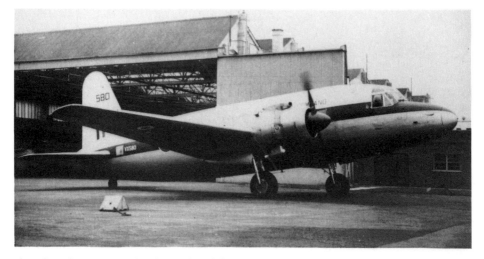

the education centre to be changed and the new building instead became the sergeants' mess.

April 1969 saw Northolt in the news again when Squadron Leader Thompson took off in a Harrier Jump Jet from North-olt on a practice run to New York as part of the *Daily Mail* Transatlantic Air Race. Six hours and 37 minutes later he landed at Floyd Bennet Naval Air Station, the first vertical take-off jet to fly the Atlantic.

Today, Northolt, as London's military aerodrome, is occupied by Nos 32 and 207 Squadrons. Both re-formed at Northolt on February 3 1969, No 32 from the Metropolitan Communications Squadron and No 207 from the Southern Communi-cations Squadron which had recently arrived from Bovingdon. No 32 Squadron operates HS 125s, Whirlwinds, Andovers and a Gazelle and is responsible for trans-porting high-ranking civilians and senior officers of all three Services. No 207 Squadron has the task of flying Strike Command staff within the UK. Northolt also supports several 'lodger' units, some of which are RAF, while some are civilian-manned. The main lodger units include No 1 Aeronautical Information Documents Unit. This unit is commanded by a Squad-ron Leader and moved to Northolt in 1956. It is responsible for the research and development, editing, compiling, printing and distribution of most of the Flight Information Publications (FLIPs) that are used by the RAF in the execution of its many and diverse flying tasks. The unit produces approximately 1,500,000 FLIPSs a year. There are also signals engineering laboratories (commanded by a civilian)

Vickers Valetta, VX580, outside the hangar at Northolt, December 12 1968.

and HQ Air Cadets London and South-East Region, responsible for the training of some 5,300 cadets. Thus Northolt today is not only an active flying station but a combination of several units each relying on the other and illustrating strength in diversity.

It is only fitting that a connection with those wartime years is still maintained today with the Polish War Memorial in Western Avenue. Situated just outside the south-eastern boundary of the aerodrome, the monument is constructed of York stone and surmounted by a bronze eagle. On the back of the monument are inscribed the words 'I have fought a good fight, I have finished my course, I have kept the faith'.

North Weald, Essex

167/TL488044. West of Chipping Ongar between the A122 and A1161

Early in 1916 an aerodrome was construct-ed on a requisitioned site west of the village of North Weald Bassett and this was occupied in August 1916 by a detachment from 39 Squadron, a home defence unit based at Woodford. On Sunday October 1 1916, 2nd Lieutenant W.J. Tempest took off from North Weald to engage enemy raiders heading for London. Nearly two hours later he found the Zeppelin *L 31* trapped in searchlight beams and success-fully shot it down over Potters Bar. Tempest was awarded an immediate DSO.

In May 1917 a new menace appeared in the shape of the giant Gotha aircraft. To combat this new threat the two detached flights of No 39 Squadron which had operated from Sutton's Farm and Hainault Farm moved into North Weald, from whence the squadron operated as a complete unit. On May 22 1918, the resident unit was joined by No 75 Squadron with its Bristol F 2Bs. At the end of October 1918, No 39 Squadron moved to France.

After the Armistice there was a rundown of the armed forces and on June 13 1919 No 75 Squadron disbanded. The Camels of No 44 Squadron then arrived on July 1 but at the end of the year the squadron disbanded leaving North Weald without a resident flying unit.

The airfield then lay dormant for several years and it was not until the obvious resurgence of militarism in Germany began to rear its ugly head that the Air Ministry decided to start an expansion of its depleted forces.

Reconstruction for North Weald began in 1926 and it reopened on September 27 1927 under Wing Commander A.G.R. Garrod with Flight Lieutenant W.M. Yool

Bristol Bulldog K2227, at North Weald on June 11 1962; it subsequently rolled on to its back.

as his adjutant. North Weald still retained a grass surface but had greatly improved facilities and accommodation, including two 'A' Type hangars in the south-east corner of the site. In common with several other fighter airfields these were widely spaced in order that a third hangar could be built between them at a later date if necessary. On October 11, No 56 (Fighter) Squadron flew in from Biggin Hill with its Armstrong-Whitworth Siskin IIIAs under Squadron Leader C.H. Elliott-Smith, AFC, to become the first of the station's resident units. All the young pilots were proud to serve with No 56 Squadron, forever associated with Captain Albert Ball and Captain J.B. McCudden who gained as a pair, two VCs, five DSOs, three Military Crosses, and a Military Medal.

On March 17 1928, No 56 Squadron, led by its new Commanding Officer, Squadron Leader A. Lees, took part in the Hendon air pageant and gave an air demonstration for the King of Afghanistan.

April 1 1928 saw the arrival of North Weald's second squadron, No 29, from Duxford. This unit was also flying Siskin IIIAs but in 1932 both squadrons re-equipped with Bristol Bulldogs. That same year both squadrons joined in a Hendon air display under North Weald's new Commanding Officer, then Wing Commander Sholto Douglas, MC, DFC.

In March 1935, No 29 Squadron re-equipped with the Hawker Demon two-

Hawker Hart, J9941, at North Weald on May 18 1964. It represented the type used by 57 Squadron in the early 1930s and a nostalgic sight it made, sitting on that airfield in silent tribute to a great era.

seat fighter and on October 4 1935 moved to Egypt during the Abyssinian crisis.

As part of the RAF's expansion programme No 151 Squadron under the command of Squadron Leader W.V. Hyde was formed, using 'B' Flight of No 56 Squadron as a nucleus, on August 4 1936. The following month saw the return of No 29 Squadron and in July 1937 it traded in its Gloster Gauntlets for the more powerful Gladiators. At the end of July No 64 Squadron arrived with its Demons but after only two weeks it returned to Martlesham Heath.

On September 30 1937, two of No 29 Squadron's Demons collided over the aerodrome, killing the occupants. On November 22 the squadron moved to Debden. By this time No 56 Squadron had received the first of its Hurricanes, but 151 Squadron had to wait until November 1938 before it was similarly equipped.

The Munich crisis brought in No 604 (County of Middlesex) Auxiliary Squadron from Hendon on September 29 1938, but early the following month it moved out.

The public's awakening interest in the threat of war was reflected in a record crowd of 16,000 for the Empire Air Day of 1939. (The first display in 1934 was attended by only 3,000.) In May No 17 Squadron arrived from Kenley and immediately exchanged its Gauntlets for No 56's Hurricanes. On September 2 they moved to their war station at Debden. They were replaced that same day by 604 Squadron with Blenheim Is, one of which was flown

by Pilot Officer John Cunningham with his gunner Jimmy Rawnsley, later to achieve fame as the top-scoring night-fighter team.

Just after war had started there was a sad mix-up which cost the life of Pilot Officer Hulton-Harrop of No 56 Squadron when Spitfires from Hornchurch mistook the Hurricanes for Me 109s in poor visibility. Pilot Officer Tommy Rose managed to bale out from his burning Hurricane and was only slightly injured. It was only on their return to North Weald that it was realised that the RAF had shot down its own aircraft. Throughout Fighter Command it became known as the Battle of Barking Creek. On October 22, No 56 Squadron began using Martlesham Heath and claimed the first squadron victory since 1918 when a Dornier 18 flying boat was damaged.

The hard winter of 1939/40 cut flying severely but in mid-January 604 Squadron left for Northolt and it was immediately replaced by the Blenheims of No 25 Squadron from Martlesham Heath.

During February, hundreds of tons of snow were removed from the runways by the station's three snowploughs and at the end of the month No 56 Squadron returned from Martlesham. On May 10 it moved to Gravesend only to return two days later and at the end of May moved to Digby, Lincolnshire, in exchange with 111 Squadron. Mid-May had seen the departure of No 151 Squadron only for it to return again after five days.

Hawker Hurricane Mk 1, L1592, of No 56 Squadron at North Weald in 1939.

When Holland, Belgium, France, Denmark and Norway were attacked and occupied that brought North Weald's fighters into the front line. North Weald occupied 400 acres between Weald Hall Lane, Church Lane and the Epping-Ongar road. At the beginning of the Second World War it was equipped with two paved runways, among the first to be laid at fighter airfields in the UK. Both runways were 50 ft wide. The north-south runway was 2,800 ft long and the east-west was 2,750 ft. North Weald, now 'E' Sector Station within No 11 Group had continually been improved. It now had four Blister hangars and four Extra Over Blister hangars as well as the two 'A' Type hangars. A perimeter track was also laid on the western

No 151 Squadron pilots at North Weald, 1940. Fourth from left, Squadron Leader E.M. Donaldson, CO; fifth from left, Wing Commander F.V. Beamish, Station Commander.

side of the airfield. Fuel supplies totalled 96,000 gallons of aviation spirit, 4,000 gallons of MT fuel and 2,000 gallons of oil. Two satellite landing grounds were provided at Hunsdon and Stapleford Tawney. North Weald also had a decoy airfield at Nazeing. This was equipped with dummy flarepath 'Q'-site lighting and with dummy Hurricanes. It was used until early 1942 but it did not have much effect and served very little purpose.

On June 4, No 111 Squadron moved to Croydon and was replaced the same day by No 56 Squadron. Mid-June saw the departure of 25 Squadron which was only to return again on September 1 under the command of Squadron Leader Mitchell. During these changes the North Weald fighters had carried out escort duties and mounted patrols over convoys and the evacuation ports. The battles raged daily and North Weald's fighters fought many a desperate battle. On Sunday August 11 No 56 Squadron lost Sergeant Ronnie Baker through a tragic error. He was attacked by a Spitfire of No 74 Squadron and shot down in the Thames Estuary. The young pilot was picked up dead by a rescue launch. North Weald became the priority target for the Luftwaffe and on Saturday August 24 about 200 bombs fell on or around the airfield. Both the officers' and airmen's married quarters were severely damaged. Nine members of the Essex Regiment, who were in a shelter which received a direct hit, were killed and ten other personnel injured. Wing Commander Beamish was everywhere, encouraging everyone by his fine example both in the air and on the ground.

On Saturday August 31, the Luftwaffe returned in force. Radar gave warning of 200 plus aircraft but nearing the coast they split into groups, one of which headed for North Weald. 56 Squadron put up 12 Hurricanes but before they could attack the Dorniers they were 'bounced' by the escorting Bf 109s and 110s, losing four of their number almost immediately. This brought the total to 11 aircraft lost in five days of hard fighting. The squadron was almost wiped out. On Sunday September 1, the seven remaining Hurricanes of 56 Squadron, now without a Commanding Officer, moved to Boscombe Down to re-form and rest. They were replaced that same day by No 249 Squadron which arrived from Boscombe led by Squadron Leader John Grandy. Also on September 1, No 151 left for Digby, Lincolnshire, it too

being without a Commanding Officer and reduced to ten serviceable aircraft.

The following day 249 was into action and it lost one of its Hurricanes. On Tuesday morning the Luftwaffe returned again. No 249 had just landed when the warning sounded and it was action stations. The Hurricanes again roared across the field to get airborne, many with their tanks only partially replenished. By the time the raiders appeared all the station's serviceable aircraft were in the air. However, 249 had a serious height disadvantage and the bombs were already falling before they could get into an attacking position. The hangars were hit and gutted by fire. The MT yard was badly damaged and many vehicles set alight. Many other buildings also received damage. Most of the bombs fell in the south-western corner of the field and although heavily cratered it was still serviceable for daytime use. More than 200 bombs hit the aerodrome area, killing two and injuring 37.

As recognition of his leadership and drive Wing Commander Francis Beamish, who had flown regularly with his units since his appointment as Station Commander in July, went to an investiture at Buckingham Palace on September 4 1940 to receive his DSO from HM King George VI. Throughout the remainder of the month Wing Commander Beamish flew operationally at every opportunity, making it very clear that he was no 'chairborne warrior'.

On October 2, the station received a visit from Sir Hugh Dowding and on the following day from Captain Balfour, the Under Secretary of State. On October 8 No 25 Squadron moved to Debden and No 257, led by Squadron Leader 'Bob' Tuck, arrived from Martlesham.

The aerodromes in the south and east were again the targets on Sunday October 27. Heavy cloud formations assisted the raiders but only one Dornier attacked North Weald. The raider came below the clouds, dropped his bombs then hurriedly dived back into cover. No 249 Squadron had taken off just prior to the attack and Pilot Officer Millington spotted the Do 17 and gave chase. Over the Thames Estuary he opened fire but he lost it in the clouds.

On Tuesday October 29, the station was caught off guard when a group of Bf 109s machine-gunned and bombed the airfield. About 45 100 kg bombs were dropped causing a great deal of damage. No 249 Squadron was just taking off when the raiders struck. The first three Hurricanes had just become airborne when a 100 kg bomb exploded below and to the right of them. Sergeant A.G. Girdwood's Hurricane took the full blast and he was blown past the other two aircraft. His Hurricane hit the ground and burst into flames. The pilot was burned to death.

On November 7, No 249 returned to Martlesham and the following day No 46 Squadron arrived from Stapleford Tawney. For the next few weeks the North Weald fighters were engaged on coastal patrols but in December, No 249 commenced flying *Rhubarbs* over France while No 46 Squadron flew north to Digby on December 14. No 56 Squadron with a new Commanding Officer, Squadron Leader H.M. Pinfold, flew in two days later to replace them. On December 22, No 403 Squadron (RCAF) arrived from Martlesham Heath. The Canadians were flying Spitfire Mk VBs. No 56 Squadron, back once again at its home station, remained until the latter part of June 1941 when it left for Martlesham.

In May 1941, No 403 Squadron moved out and No 249 Squadron left for duty in Malta. No 242 Squadron flew in from Stapleford to replace it. This was Bader's

332 Squadron Spitfire IXs at North Weald in the middle of 1944.

old unit and was now commanded by Squadron Leader W.F.P. Treacy, DSO, a former Hornchurch pilot who had returned to the UK via Spain and Portugal after being forced down in France. Alas, he was killed when another aircraft collided with his Hurricane. He was replaced by Squadron Leader Whitney-Straight, MC. On July 19 No 242 moved to Manston but it returned to North Weald in August 1942 having been re-formed in April after decimation in Java.

In June 1941 came the first of the American 'Eagle' squadrons, No 71. It flew its first operations over France in September, losing three pilots, Hillard Sidney Fenlaw, Thomas Paul McGerty and Eugene Quimby Tobin.

In July, 111 Squadron arrived from Dyce and on August 18 No 222 (Natal) Squadron took up residence. All units were actively engaged on fighter sweeps over the Continent. No 111 Squadron moved to Debden on November 1 only to return again on December 15 to replace No 71 Squadron which had moved out the previous day. However, it only remained a few days and moved out again on December 22. December also brought the second of the 'Eagle' squadrons, No 121, when it moved in on December 16. During this period the squadrons were engaged on *Circus* and *Rhubarb* operations.

At the beginning of May came the first of the Norwegian units, No 331. It was the first of many visits. At the end of May No 222 Squadron moved to Manston. Early June saw the departure of 121 Squadron and on June 19 No 332 Norwegian Squadron came as a replacement, remaining until mid-August. At the end of June No 331 moved out.

North Weald was a vital link in the defences of the nation and from 1942 up to early 1945 it was the operational base for many fighter squadrons (see movement table). After a period of relative inactivity the airfield was transferred to No 46 Group Transport Command on July 1 1945 and later that month was occupied by two Polish squadrons, No 301 and No 304 (Mazonia) Squadron with Wellington CXIIIs and Warwick CIIIs. The airfield proved to be unsuitable for these aircraft and both units moved to Chedburgh in September 1945 leaving North Weald without any flying units until 1949, when it reverted to the control of Fighter Command.

During this period from October 1945 to September 1948 the station was used as No 9 Personnel Despatch Centre and various selection boards were also established there.

On March 27 1949 No 601 (County of London) Squadron Royal Auxiliary Air Force moved in and was joined the following day by No 604 (County of Middlesex) Squadron. Both units were equipped with Spitfire LF 16es and scheduled for early re-equipment with Vampires. Both squadrons soon converted to de Havilland Vampire F 3s and in March 1950 the two Royal Auxiliary Air Force Squadrons were joined by No 72 Squadron also flying the Vampire. The next year the main runway was extended to facilitate the operation of these jet fighters.

The Vampires were replaced by Meteors in 1952 and in April 1953, No 72 Squadron left North Weald, which in October 1953 became once more a sector operations centre and the headquarters of the Metropolitan Sector.

On December 2 1953, No 111 Squadron arrived from Italy. This unit was equipped with Hawker Hunters and under the brilliant direction of its Commanding Officer, Squadron Leader Roger Topp, became the RAF's most famous aerobatic team. As the 'Black Arrows', with their 22 all-black Hunters, they thrilled thousands during their displays at Farnborough and elsewhere.

Movement table for squadrons at North Weald, 1942–1945

Date arrived	Date departed	Squadron No	Equipment
19.6.42	14.8.42	332	Spitfire V
4.5.42	30.6.42	331	Spitfire V
4.6.42	18.6.42	412	Spitfire VB
7.7.42	14.8.42	331	Spitfire V
7.7.42	1.8.42	222	Spitfire V
11.8.42	14.8.42	242	Spitfire V
20.8.42	1.9.42	242	Spitfire V
20.8.42	7.9.42	331	Spitfire V
20.8.42	5.1.44	332	Spitfire V, IX
-.9.42	-.10.42	486	Typhoon
14.9.42	2.10.42	331	Spitfire V
9.10.42	5.1.44	331	Spitfire V, IX
7.11.42	7.12.42	124	Spitfire VI
12.3.43	26.7.43	124	Spitfire VII
15.11.43	30.11.43	4	Mustang I
30.11.43	16.1.44	63	Mustang I
30.11.43	21.1.44	168	Mustang I
17.1.44	7.2.44	268	Mustang I
21.1.44	5.3.44	331	Spitfire V
22.1.44	29.2.44	2	Mustang I
3.2.44	6.3.44	168	Mustang I
20.2.44	1.3.44	268	Mustang I
21.2.44	21.3.44	332	Spitfire V
1.3.44	31.3.44	66	Spitfire IX
13.3.44	31.3.44	331	Spitfire V
27.3.44	31.3.44	332	Spitfire V
3.4.44	22.4.44	1	Spitfire IX
23.4.44	17.5.44	127	Spitfire IX
23.4.44	17.5.44	33	Spitfire IX
24.4.44	17.5.44	74	Spitfire IX
2.7.44	27.8.44	116	Oxford 1, Hurricane II, Tiger Moth
4.7.44	27.8.44	287	Oxford II, Martinet I
27.8.44	3.10.44	311	Spitfire IX
28.8.44	29.12.44	310	Spitfire IX
28.8.44	17.12.44	234	Mustang III
19.9.44	1.11.44	63	Spitfire V
4.10.44	29.12.44	313	Spitfire IX
4.11.44	30.1.45	63	Spitfire V
4.1.45	20.6.45	285	Oxford II, Hurricane II
21.1.45	3.4.45	26	Spitfire XI
10.5.45	24.5.45	130	Spitfire IX
3.7.45	5.9.45	301	Warwick III
10.7.45	6.9.45	304	Warwick III

To the deep regret of many, the Royal Auxiliary Air Force squadrons were disbanded in March 1957. In June 1958 'Treble One' squadron left North Weald and on November 15 1958 the station was reduced to Care and Maintenance status. From 1953 to 1959 the aerodrome had been the base for various Reserve flights. On September 1 1964 it was reduced to an inactive state but it received a new lease of life when it was transferred to the Army Department on January 4 1966.

During the 1960s the airfield remained

Above *Hawker Tempest 5, JN766:SA-N, of No 486 (RNZAF) Squadron at North Weald.*

Below *DH Vampire T 11, WZ458, of 414 Squadron, ATC, at North Weald on March 6 1963.*

Bottom *Meteor TT 20, WM224, with Harvard 483009 just visible behind it; North Weald Restoration Flight.*

open for light aircraft and gliders. Many air displays were also held at North Weald. At one of these air displays on June 11 1962, Bristol Bulldog *K2227*, piloted by Godfrey Auty, then Chief Test Pilot of Bristol Aircraft and Bristol Siddeley Engines Ltd, touched down quite sweetly; it then, ever so gracefully, tipped gently over onto its nose, hesitating momentarily before finally rolling over onto its back. Repaired and restored, Bulldog *K2227* took to the air again. However, its last fateful flight came at Farnborough on Sunday September 13 1964. Perhaps the Bulldog generally was a handful whether in the air or on the ground. I wonder how Sir Douglas Bader felt about it.

During this period in May 1968 the aerodrome relived a period of history in 1940, with the making of the film *Battle of Britain*. North Weald echoed again to the roar of the once-familiar Merlin and the Spitfire. In August 1979 the site was sold to Epping Forest District Council for the princely sum of £660,000. Today, London Transport and other drivers practice on the runways. The new M11 motorway cuts across the western edge of the airfield.

Orsett, Essex

177/TQ652824. North-east of Grays and just north of the A13 at Sand Pit Cross roads

This was a 1st class landing ground which was used by 78 Squadron while on home defence duties. It was located just south-east of the village of Orsett, after which it was named, and two miles from Stanford-le-Hope railway station.

The site covered an area of 80 acres and was in open surroundings. No permanent buildings were erected, the accommodation being tented. It came within the south-east area under 49 Wing. The landing ground operated from 1917-1919 and immediately after the war it reverted back to its former use.

Panshanger (Holywell Hyde), Hertfordshire

166/TL266126. East of Welwyn Garden City to the south of the B1000

Situated between Welwyn Garden City and Hertford this airfield originated before the war and was used as a landing ground for the Hatfield-based No 1 Elementary & Reserve Flying Training School. This use ceased early in the war and in 1940 the site became a decoy airfield for the de Havilland aircraft factory at Hatfield and was known as Holywell Hyde. By mid-1941 the need for decoys had largely passed and on June 16 1941 the site, under its original name of Holywell Hyde, was brought back into use as a relief landing ground for No 1 Elementary Flying Training School. It was a perfect training site for the surface of the airfield was as smooth as a billiard table.

On September 7 1942, No 1 EFTS moved in to Holywell Hyde leaving the

North Weald during May 1968 while making the Battle of Britain *film.*

Dummy airfield and factory that was built at Panshangar for the de Havilland factory at Hatfield. Photograph shows dummy hangars and imitation Oxford.

airfield at Hatfield free to concentrate on flight testing, and on September 13 1943 the airfield name was changed to Panshanger. The main task of the school was grading prospective pilots. This work continued until the end of the war. The EFTS then reverted to training reserve pilots and on May 5 1947 it was redesignated No 1 Reserve Flying School, still flying Tiger Moths. In April 1950 the school re-equipped with Chipmunks and remained with these until it eventually disbanded on March 31 1953. Since that time the airfield has been used by private aircraft.

Park Royal, London

176/TQ193828. West side of London between the Grand Union Canal and the A40 trunk road

This small piece of land, which was just north-west of Acton Aerodrome was first used for flying by Claude Grahame-White in April 1910. However, the grass was very rough and bumpy and very little flying took place from Park Royal. A few exhibition flights did take place but the site proved unsatisfactory and like Acton was overshadowed by Hendon. Park Royal closed in 1912.

The only military connection was that during the First World War Park Royal became a large mule and horse compound for the Army Service Corps. This was maybe the reason why Acton Aerodrome was not fully operational. The sight and sound of aeroplanes would have been a hazard for large numbers of mules and horses.

The site had no further use after the First World War and reverted to its former use.

Parlaunt Park (Langley or Slough), Buckinghamshire

See Langley

Penshurst, Kent

188/TQ522442. 4 miles north-west of Tunbridge Wells

Situated two miles north of Penshurst on the north side of the railway, this site, which measured 800 yds × 500 yds and covered 73 acres, was first used during the First World War and housed No 2 Wireless School, which formed at Penshurst on November 8 1917. The school was inaugurated to meet the demands for wireless work in co-operation with coast defence artillery, anti-aircraft guns and home forces for operations against hostile aircraft, and for wireless training in special work peculiar to home defence. The equipment of the school was 18 DH 6s. The course lasted one week for scout pilots and one week for wireless personnel. Two aeroplane sheds, each 130 ft × 60 ft, were erected, along with other buildings, for Penshurst was also the depot for wireless stores and repair and testing of apparatus. No 2 Wireless School disbanded on March 23 1919, the airfield closed and the buildings were dismantled.

During the 1930s Penshurst was used as a civil landing ground and one hangar was erected on the south side, but there were no repair facilities. It covered an area 550 yds × 320 yds.

The airfield was re-activated during the Second World War and it opened in 1942 in 35 Wing, Army Co-operation Command for the accommodation of air observation post squadrons. The first unit to arrive was No 653 Squadron whose Austers moved in during September 1942. The following year the airfield was transferred to No 83 Group. In October 1943 the resident unit was joined by a detachment from 658 Squadron who remained here until the following February. June 1944 saw the departure of 653 Squadron and the airfield does not appear to have had any more units until the arrival of 664 Squadron with Auster AOP IVs and Vs in February 1945, but this unit was only here for a few weeks and moved out again the following month. With its departure the airfield closed.

Radlett, Hertfordshire

166/TL155036. Just south of St Albans on the east side of the A5

Aviation folklore has it that in March 1928, J. Cordes, the assistant test pilot at Handley Page, had picked up an Avro Avian from Woodford, Manchester, and on the journey to Cricklewood ran into bad weather which forced him to land in a large field just north of Radlett, between the railway line and Watling Street. It was not very far from the former RFC aerodrome of London Colney.

Radlett aerodrome came into being a few months later and was ready for use by June 1929. By the end of the year a production flight hangar had been erected. On July 7 1930 the aerodrome was officially opened by Prince George, who later became the Duke of Kent. During the opening, Cordes demonstrated his flying ability with the HP 39 Gugnunc, when he began his take-off run from within the hangar and was airborne by the time he reached the open hangar doors.

At that time Radlett was a grass airfield which covered 154 acres with many of the buildings adjacent to the main A5 trunk road which formed the western boundary. It was rather a restricted site but it was adequate for the sedate aeroplanes of the time and many of Handley Page's machines made their first flight from Radlett. By the late 1930s civil aircraft gave way to military, and, as the war clouds formed over Europe, Handley Page geared up for bomber production. Extensions were made to the flight sheds in order to accommodate production of the Hampden bomber.

During the early months of the war, bomber production increased dramatically. Radlett was extended at the north end of the aerodrome at Park Street in order to house the Halifax bombers that began flooding out from the factory at Cricklewood, which was working under full pressure. Further expansion continued and new flight sheds necessitated the demolition of an entire farm. But this was still not enough, and, as production increased, more dispersal areas were needed. Stroud Wood became engulfed by the aerodrome and the new boundary almost reached the banks of the River Ver.

With the four-engined bombers came the need for paved runways and the standard wartime runways were laid to accommodate them. The prototype Halifax had been taken to RAF Bicester for its maiden flight on October 25 1940. Lord Halifax christened the Halifax, quoting the old Yorkshire prayer, 'From Hull, Hell and Halifax, Good Lord deliver us'. At peak production Halifaxes were leaving the production line at Radlett at the rate of 40 aircraft per month during 1944. Of the 6,116 Halifaxes produced, Handley Page turned out 1,539, English Electric 2,145, Rootes Ltd 1,070, London Passenger Transport 700 and Fairey Aviation 661.

During the war years a strip of land about 50 yds deep, bordering on to the railway embankment, was packed with scrapped motor vehicles. These could be dragged on to the airfield in the event of invasion and the landing area be effectively obstructed. The cars proved to be a useful spare parts department for visiting RAF personnel who frequently 'borrowed' large and small pieces for their private vehicles. The Ansons of No 109 Squadron were regular visitors during late 1940 and 1941.

After the hostilities, the need for bombers came to an end and Handley Page concentrated on Hastings and Hermes production. The Hermes story started badly, when, on December 2 1945, the prototype, *G-AGSS*, took off from Radlett on its maiden flight. The aircraft ran into trouble, and after a succession of dives and stalls it hit the ground in an inverted dive at nearby Kendall's Farm, killing the pilots Talbot and Wright. The wreckage was almost totally destroyed by fire. However, the cause of the crash was established as being the result of elevator overbalance. The next Hermes, *G-AGUB* did not fly until September 2 1947.

Aircraft production continued and the early 1950s saw Radlett enter the jet age. The first two postwar SBAC shows were also held here. In 1951 a high-speed wind tunnel and structural test facilities were constructed at the Park Street end of the airfield. That same year work began on the Victor prototypes. The first Victor, *WB771*, was taken by road to Boscombe Down for its maiden flight.

With the Victor programme under way the main runway was further extended in 1952 so that the Victors could be tested at Radlett. After it was ready the prototype came back on February 25 1953.

Victor production got in full swing and

Top *Photograph shows the 40-seat Handley Page Hermes 5, then the world's largest and most powerful turbo-propeller airliner, shortly after making its first flight from Radlett.*

Below *Hermes 4 aircraft, designed for BOAC service, on assembly line at Handley Page Radlett Aerodrome.*

Bottom *Society of British Aircraft Constructors Show held at Radlett in 1947. Some of the main aircraft in the photograph are, left to right: in the foreground a Desford, behind it a Gemini and to its right two Furies and an Auster. Behind that row a Lancastrian, behind it a Mosquito, to its right an Anson, a Hornet and a York.*

by February 1956 the first B 1s were in service with the RAF. In 1963 the last RAF B 2 came off the production line but work continued on converting Victors to tanker and reconnaissance versions.

Sadly, the end was in sight, for on April 21 1962, Sir Frederick Handley Page had died and the company ran quickly downhill. This was due to the founder's refusal to merge with other aircraft companies, but without doing so it could not compete. Handley Page, one-time builder of the first successful four-engined bomber in the Second World War, had to drop out of large aircraft manufacture and instead continued in the civil aviation field. The future of the company hinged on the success of the HP 137 Jetstream twin-engined feeder liner. It was to be manufactured at a new plant at Radlett and with orders amounting to nearly 200 aircraft the company looked set for a few more years. However, there was a big set-back for the development costs of the Jetstream tripled and eventually reached a point where to break even, orders for more than 1,000 aircraft were needed. The original estimate had been only 400 aircraft. The Treasury offered Handley Page some financial help but when no orders were placed by MoD, the Receiver was called in during August 1969. On August 16 Handley Page Aircraft Ltd was formed with the intention of continuing Jetstream production only. This was short-lived for the American-owned Cravens Corporation, which had backed the new company, withdrew its financial support after only six months and in March 1970 Handley Page was finally wound up. With the closure of the company the Victors awaiting conversion at Radlett were flown to Woodford and the airfield closed.

Reading (Woodley), Berkshire

See Woodley

Redhill, Surrey

187/TQ300475. South-east of Reigate, to the east of the A23 and south of the A25

Two miles south-east of Redhill, this small aerodrome first received a military presence in July 1937 with the formation of No 15 Elementary and Reserve Flying Training School operated by British Air Transport. The main aircraft types were Magisters and Harts and the school functioned until the outbreak of war in September 1939 when it was redesignated No 15 Elementary Flying Training School, retaining the Magister trainers. To relieve the congestion at Redhill a relief landing ground was used at Penshurst from March 1940, but events in Europe soon made southern England unsuitable for training aircraft, so in June 1940 the EFTS moved to Kingstown, the pre-war airfield for Carlisle, and Redhill Aerodrome and its buildings were requisitioned for use by the Royal Air Force.

No 16 (Army Co-operation) Squadron arrived at the beginning of June 1940, equipped with Lysanders, but it moved to Cambridge at the end of the month and Redhill had no resident flying units until

mid-September, when the Blenheims of 600 Squadron came from Hornchurch. They remained a month then moved to Catterick in Yorkshire. They were immediately replaced by 219 Squadron with its Blenheims and Beaufighters, which remained until December 10 1940.

A perimeter track was constructed round the airfield, which remained grass-surfaced, and from this led taxi tracks to eight Blister

hangars and a dozen double dispersal pens. The landing area was extended into roughly an 'L' shape, providing a main grass runway on a north-east–south-west axis with a shorter one running north–south.

From May 1941 to January 1944 numerous fighter squadrons flew from Redhill, all except six were equipped with Spitfires (see movement table). The airfield was used as an advance air base for the attack

Left *Squadron Leader L.V. Chadburn of 416 Squadron (RCAF) at Redhill on September 29 1942.*

Above *Two Canadian boys, LAC F.H. Morrell from Toronto, Ontario, and Corporal S.S. Crampton from Winnipeg, Manitoba, refuelling a Spitfire belonging to 416 Squadron at Redhill on September 29 1942.*

Right *Spitfires of 416 (City of Oshawa) Squadron sitting on the tarmac at Redhill, December 3 1942.*

on Dieppe in August 1942 and for this purpose housed Nos 350, 611, 303, 310 and 312 Squadrons.

After the departure of the fighter squadrons, Redhill housed No 83 Group Support Unit and various second-line squadrons. The Ansons of No 1310 Flight were here for a short period during 1944. No 116 Calibration Squadron moved to Redhill from Gatwick on September 5 1944. The unit was equipped with Tiger Moths, Oxfords and Hurricanes and its main task was calibration of radar used by AA units and checks of predictor equipment. On January 20 1945 it was joined by No 287 Squadron, also from Gatwick, and this was an anti-aircraft co-operation squadron flying Oxfords, Spitfires and Tempest aircraft. During the first week of May 1945, Nos 116 and 287 Squadrons moved out and the station then housed No 1 Aircraft Delivery Unit and No 49 Maintenance Unit. These two units remained until the end of the year.

Movement table for units at Redhill, 1941–1944

Date arrived	Date departed	Unit	Aircraft
2.5.41	1.6.41	1	Hurricane II
1.6.41	15.6.41	258	Hurricane II
15.6.41	2.7.41	1	Hurricane II
-.7.41	-.10.41	485	Spitfire II, V
21.10.41	17.3.42	452	Spitfire V
14.1.42	4.3.42	602	Spitfire V
23.3.42	31.5.42	457	Spitfire V
1.4.42	7.4.42	340	Spitfire V
-.5.42	-.8.42	402	Spitfire V
13.5.42	17.7.42	602	Spitfire V
1.7.42	7.7.42	308	Spitfire V
1.7.42	8.7.42	312	Spitfire V
20.7.42	27.7.42	611	Spitfire V
31.7.42	7.9.42	350	Spitfire V
1.8.42	23.9.42	611	Spitfire V
15.8.42	20.8.42	303	Spitfire V
16.8.42	20.8.42	310	Spitfire V
16.8.42	20.8.42	312	Spitfire V
-.9.42	-.2.43	416	Spitfire V
15.9.42	23.9.42	350	Spitfire V
23.9.42	1.11.42	412	Spitfire V
-.3.43	-.5.43	421	Spitfire V
-.4.43	-.8.43	411	Spitfire V
-.5.43	-.8.43	401	Spitfire V
14.7.43	7.8.43	412	Spitfire V
10.8.43	13.8.43	66	Spitfire V
14.8.43	19.9.43	504	Spitfire V
16.8.43	17.9.43	131	Spitfire V
15.10.43	15.1.44	231	Mustang I
15.10.43	2.11.43	414	Mustang I
15.10.43	17.2.44	400	Mustang I

Left *Olympia Eon 2*, G-ALLB, *photographed at Redhill on April 17 1949.*

Below *Cierva C 30*, G-ACUU, *at Redhill.*

Tiger Club at Redhill, August 9 1970. DH 60 Gipsy Moth G-AAKK in centre.

Soon after the end of the Second World War, flying schools were set up around the UK to provide flying practice for the RAF Reserve. On April 1 1948, No 15 Reserve Flying School formed at Redhill. Tiger Moths were used as basic trainers for pilots, and Ansons for navigational training. The RFS also used a few Oxfords and towards the end of its service life it received Chipmunks. The increasing complexity of modern aircraft resulted in the closure of the Reserve training programme in 1954 and No 15 RFS disbanded on June 20 1954. The airfield then became a busy helicopter and light aircraft centre and today is the base for Bristow Helicopters.

Rochester, Kent

178/TQ745645. South-east of Rochester between the B2097 and the A229

When Messrs Short Bros decided to include floatplanes in their aircraft manufacturing programme the airfields at Leysdown and Eastchurch, where their landplanes were flight-tested, were obviously unsuitable. They bought a piece of land above the bridge at Rochester in 1913 and the following year they built their Cuxton factory. Oswald Short supervised the works, which produced Short 184s.

After the Armistice there was a rundown of military contracts and Short's turned to the manufacture of buses, cars and other products in order to keep the firm solvent, until a successful venture in the 1930s resulted in the famous 'C' Type Empire flying boat. The construction of landplanes produced similar difficulties to those experienced earlier by the firm—lack of test-flying facilities. Until 1933, civil types were flown from Lympne or Gravesend and military types from Martlesham Heath.

In September 1933, Rochester Council purchased 105 acres of land between the Rochester-Maidstone and Chatham roads for the purpose of developing a municipal airport. A decision taken by Rochester Council on November 22 1933 granted Short Bros the lease for the land, provided it be available for use as an airport and that private and public landing rights be kept open. Unemployed men were given the task of levelling the ground under the management of Rochester Council. Short Bros moved in before any hangars were erected. The first hangar was erected in 1934. Throughout the winter of 1933/34, Short's four-engined biplane airliner *Scylla* was constructed in the open.

By the end of 1934 other firms had moved into Rochester. A site to the west of the aerodrome was purchased and a factory opened, which consisted of engineering shops, offices and test facilities.

Air services were established from Rochester on June 9 1934, when Short's

Short 830 Seaplane on the Medway at Rochester, 1916.

began a service from Rochester to Southend. The 12-minute flight cost 8 shillings single, 12 shillings return.

In 1934 a small hangar was built for a private aircraft owner/pilot, Miss G. Batcheler (the first woman in the country to have a pilot's licence). The RAF formed No 23 Elementary and Reserve Flying School at Rochester on April 1 1938 under the command of Flight Lieutenant R. Chambers in No 26 Group. An administration block and a hangar were built to accommodate the unit. A second hangar and admin block were built in July 1938 when the school was expanded to train pilots for the Fleet Air Arm. The Commanding Officer of the naval section was Lieutenant Commander Spencer Cooper, who had a staff of 16 instructors. Instruction was carried out on 504Ns, which were replaced by Avro Tutors and then by Miles Magisters. Intermediate and advanced training followed on Hawker Audaxes and Harts. With the coming of war, Nos 23 and 24 ERFTS were merged to form No 24 EFTS at Sydenham on September 3 1939.

During 1939 the factory was extended and Stirling production was started at Rochester. The first prototype flew in May of that year. From May 1940 Short's own Home Guard battalion (33rd Kent) carried out the defence of the factory.

On August 15 1940, the airfield was attacked by enemy aircraft, resulting in severe damage to Short's factory and the destruction of six Stirlings on the production line. Production was halted at Rochester and the work was dispersed to units at Swindon and other sites. Rebuilding soon got under way and Rochester was back in full production in 1942.

Whilst the aircraft factory was undergoing repairs the airfield was used as an emergency landing field for battle-damaged aircraft returning from raids on the continent. A decoy airfield was built at Lidsing a few miles to the south-east. The decoy was complete with dummy buildings and aircraft. It served its purpose and was bombed instead of Rochester.

Total production of four-engined Stirlings at Rochester was 536. With the war at an end, production ceased, and the Short Sturgeon prototype was constructed. In 1946 the production line was transferred to Belfast and the factory at Rochester then closed down.

In March 1946 the Flying School resumed its training role, assuming the title No 24 Reserve Flying School on May 1 1947. The school remained at Rochester until it disbanded on March 31 1953. During that period it flew Tiger Moths, Ansons, Prentices and Chipmunks.

Short's flying division continued to use the airport for several types of pilot instruction for the Admiralty. These included training to instrument standard. There was also an Admiralty flight for training pilots on ground appointments, an Army co-op flight for ack-ack and radar training, a maintenance test flight and a Fleet Air Arm ferry flight. In addition, there was a refresher flight for pilots trained in the United States.

Short Bros started up a small plant at Rochester in 1954 and here Beaufighters, Brigands, Mosquitoes and Sturgeons were reconditioned. In 1959 the plant changed

Cessna on the right and a Jodel on the left at Rochester Airport.

over to the production of Bailey Bridges and other equipment for the Army. It closed down in 1962. That same year the buildings were taken over by Marconi Avionics. The flying division moved to West Malling in 1964.

From 1960 to 1967 Channel Airways operated out of Rochester as part of its Channel Islands Service. Rochester Flying Club also used the airfield when civil flying restarted after the war. Civil flying is still carried out.

A variety of industrial companies has occupied the old Short buildings since the aircraft manufactures left the riverside, some of them turning out products for the aviation business. Marconi Avionics is the largest company involved and it continues Rochester's flying link by operating three private Piper aircraft from the field.

Rochford (Southend), Essex

See Southend

Romford (Maylands), Essex

See Maylands

Slough (Langley or Parlaunt Park), Buckinghamshire

See Langley

Smith's Lawn, Berkshire

176/SU973700. South of Windsor in Windsor Great Park

During the 1930s Smith's Lawn was used as a private landing strip. With the coming of the Second World War it was selected as a possible site. Towards the end of 1940 Vickers Armstrong of Weybridge built a Bellman hangar on the site and opened a production line known as VAXI (Vickers Armstrong Extension 1). Here were erected some of the special high-altitude Wellington Mk V and VIs. Only one production Mk V was turned out before the line was switched to the Mark VI. Sixty-four Mark VIs were completed altogether and of these 18 were re-engined and modified Mark Vs which were assembled and flown at VAXI, Smith's Lawn.

The airfield was situated in the southeast corner of Windsor Great Park and from July 14 1941 to February 1945 it was used as a relief landing ground by the Tiger Moths of No 18 Elementary Flying Training School at Fairoaks.

In 1944 Vickers Warwicks were stored at Smith's Lawn. The Americans used the site in a communications role with Piper Cubs and Sentinels but which USAAF units they belonged to is unknown. After the war the site reverted back to its former use and today many sporting events are held at Smith's Lawn.

Southend (Rochford), Essex

178/TQ872895. 2 miles north of Southend-on-Sea off the B1013

The War Office included Rochford in its 1914 listing of potential landing grounds and it opened that same year as a Royal Flying Corps home defence aerodrome, but flying did not take place until the following year. The first confirmed flying was on May 31 1915, when Flight Sub-Lieutenant A.W. Robertson reached 6,000 ft in a Bleriot, sighting the Zeppelin

LZ 38 above him. Robertson tried to intercept the enemy but was forced down after engine failure.

During August, aircraft of No 37 Squadron arrived at Rochford and the station took on a new role with night flying training.

After many months of night flying training which kept the Royal Engineers busy in recovering many machines, No 11 RS, the night training reserve squadron, came to Rochford at the end of January 1917. It was renamed 98 (Depot) Squadron on February 8 1917. To expand the training role No 99 (Depot) Squadron formed here in June 1917 and was tasked with training pilots for overseas duty. To avoid confusion with operational squadrons 98 and 99, No 98 (Depot) Squadron became No 198 (Depot) Squadron and No 99 (Depot) Squadron became No 199 (D) Squadron on July 7 1917.

To strengthen the home defence, No 61 Squadron was formed on August 2 1917 with an establishment of Sopwith Pups, most of which were mono-engined versions. Just ten days later they were airborne to intercept nine Gothas which bombed Southend, killing 32 people. One aircraft was shot down.

The Germans then turned to night bombing and used the cloak of darkness for their protection. This was in their favour, for night fighting was in its infancy. From December 1917 the 'Giant' bomber was used to supplement the Gothas.

Patrols from Rochford were usually carried out by four Pups, flying between 8,000 and 10,000 ft, 250 ft apart. They patrolled an area Rochford-Southend-Crouch End. However, the Sopwith Pups were not good enough to deal with the German bombers and the squadron re-equipped with SE 5As, and, later, Sopwith Camels. Unlike the Camels, the SE 5A was a difficult machine to land at night and was never a success as a night fighter.

On December 5 1917 a Gotha crashed almost on the aerodrome. It had been hit by gunfire near Canvey Island and on seeing the aerodrome flares had attempted to land. The German had fired a Very light and had chosen the right colour for the night. On being answered from the ground he came in to land but hit a tree and crashed on the golf course which was adjacent to Rochford airfield. The crew was taken prisoner. The wreckage was then inspected by many of the pilots. One found a Very pistol which was accidentally fired and within seconds the petrol-soaked wreckage

exploded in flames. By morning only the engines and charred framework remained.

On January 1 1918, No 141 Squadron formed from a flight of 61 Squadron under Major Sir Philip Bobington. The new unit had only a Sopwith Dolphin and on February 2 it moved to Biggin Hill. On June 1 1918, No 152 formed as a Camel night fighter squadron and that same month 37 Squadron moved out. Having worked up to operational status, 152 Squadron moved to France on October 18 1918.

Rochford played a defending role right up to the end of the war. Civil aviation returned to the area on May 10 1919, when a Handley Page 0/400 bomber, converted for peacetime use, dropped newspapers by parachute near Southend Pier. In June 1919, No 61 Squadron disbanded and that same month 199 Squadron moved to Harpswell. Three months later, No 198 disbanded and its facilities were handed over to Scampton. The last recorded RAF flying was on December 4, when a Bristol Fighter was flown from Northolt by Lieutenant Bromfield. On February 3 1920 he flew it to Eastchurch, after which it was stored and is now displayed in the Imperial War Museum.

Rochford was not included in the very small list of aerodromes selected for retention for use by the RAF and it was derequisitioned soon after the war. For a short time it was used for pleasure flying but soon the installations were dismantled and the land reverted to farming.

In the early 1930s Councillor G.E. Weber could see the potential with the build-up of civil air traffic, and after much campaigning it was decided to build an airport on the site of the First World War aerodrome. In 1933, Southend Corporation bought the land for that purpose. A club house and hangars were erected and flying recommenced, although it was not until September 18 1935 that it was officially opened as Southend Municipal Airport. It was declared open by the then Under Secretary of State for Air, Sir Philip Sassoon, who arrived in his DH 85 Leopard Moth. The airport was managed by the Southend Flying Club, which used the aerodrome with a Leopard Moth and five Cadets. Also, many privately owned aircraft were attracted to the airport.

From 1933 up until the opening of the airport, flying had taken place from a field just to the north and it was referred to as Rochford but known also as Holt Farm.

During the expansion period of the RAF, Rochford was established as an Auxiliary

Camp. In 1937 the RAF Volunteer Reserve formed and pilots joined this or the Civil Air Guard. The summer of that year, two Auxiliary Air Force squadrons came to camp—one being No 602 (City of Glasgow) commanded by Squadron Leader D.F. McIntyre, AFC. During this period, No 34 Elementary and Reserve Flying Training School formed, operated by Air Hire Ltd, with an establishment of Tiger Moths.

At the outbreak of war in September 1939 the Elementary & Reserve Flying Training School closed. The airport was requisitioned and the RAF took control. The airfield was renamed RAF Rochford for use as a satellite for Hornchurch. Southend's club and private aircraft were simply smashed up and stored in a derelict property in Westborough Road until taken to Newmarket and dumped in 1941/42.

The war was just eight days old when the Spitfires of No 54 (F) Squadron flew in from Hornchurch. They were joined on October 16 by the Blenheims of No 600 (City of London) AAF Squadron but after only four days they returned to Hornchurch. That same month No 74 (Tiger) Squadron made its first of many visits. It arrived on October 22 but had departed again by the end of the month, only to reappear on November 3. It was between Rochford and Hornchurch for the next nine months with a further five visits. The Tiger Squadron scored Rochford's first success—a Heinkel 111 damaged over the Thames Estuary on February 13 1940. This was followed a few days later by a Dornier 17.

Rochford's first escape 'gong' was awarded to Flight Lieutenant 'Paddy' Treacy of 74 Squadron. On May 27 1940, Treacy went down over Lumbres, France and after fantastic adventures returned via Spain and his native Eire in February 1941 to gain the DSO. Treacy then took over Bader's squadron, No 242, but was killed when one of his own pilots collided with him on take-off.

No 616 (South Yorkshire) Squadron flew in on May 27 1940, but remained only a few days and departed on June 6. On June 18, Flight Lieutenant 'Sailor' Malan flying a Spitfire of 74 Squadron from Rochford became the first single-seat pilot of the Second World War to destroy an enemy aircraft at night and first to get a double kill in one night. On June 25 the Spitfires of No 54 Squadron arrived. After a month they returned to Hornchurch. At the end of August, 264 Squadron arrived with its Defiants, but after only a couple of days it

moved to Kirton-in-Lindsey, Lincolnshire. On August 26 a Dornier Do 17 was attacked by Flight Lieutenant Saunders of 65 Squadron at 20,000 ft over the Channel. The badly damaged Dornier made a long diving turn towards Rochford and belly-landed on the airfield. Another battle-damaged Dornier crash-landed on the airfield on September 2.

After non-stop fighting the Battle of Britain was won by the gallant 'Few'. During the battle Rochford was used by the Hornchurch squadrons as a forward airfield, mainly by 54 and 74 Squadrons. The skies still belonged to the RAF but complete victory was a long way away.

On October 28 1940, the airfield formed as a separate station named Southend, still under the control of Hornchurch. December saw the arrival of two Spitfire squadrons; Nos 603 (City of Edinburgh) on December 3 and 611 (West Lancs) on December 14. Their role was to escort the bombers into Nazi-held Europe but 603 was soon on the move and on December 11 departed for Drem.

Wing Commander Basil Embry, DSO (later Air Chief Marshal Sir Basil Embry, GCB, KBE, DSO and 3 Bars, DFC, AFC) who had been station commander since October 1940 moved to the Middle East and Wing Commander J.M. Thompson assumed command as station headquarters moved from 'Greenways' Hall Road, Rochford, to Earls Hall school.

The station was made a forward offensive fighter base on January 9 1941. January 27 saw the departure of 611 Squadron and the arrival of 64 Squadron. Its Spitfires remained two months then moved to Hornchurch at the end of March. They were immediately replaced by the Spitfires of No 54 Squadron.

On May 11 1941 the station received a hit-and-run attack but the ground defences got one and Southend's fighters another of the Me 109 raiders, one of which crashed near the hangars. May 20 saw the departure of 54 Squadron and the arrival of 611 Squadron whose Spitfires were back once again, but it was a brief visit and on June 16 they departed. They were replaced the same day by the Spitfires of 603 Squadron.

On July 8, 603 Squadron departed and in mid-July No 222 (Natal) Squadron made its first visit to the station. It moved out in the middle of the following month and was replaced by the Canadians in the form of 402 Squadron. This unit had Hurricanes and it remained throughout the autumn.

On November 5, No 402 moved to Warmwell.

Over the winter months there was a lull in the station movements. No 313 (Czech) Squadron then arrived on February 7 1942 and after a month's stay moved out, only to be replaced by No 411 (RCAF) Squadron on March 7 but this moved out at the end of the month. It was replaced by 64 Squadron, which arrived on March 31. At this period No 1488 Target-Towing Flight formed here with an establishment of Lysanders. During April 1942, the Westland Whirlwinds of No 137 Squadron

arrived but this unit re-equipped with Hurricanes Mk IVs and the Whirlwinds went to 263 Squadron.

On May 1, Southend was transferred from Hornchurch to the North Weald Sector. During the first week of May No 403 (RCAF) Squadron arrived but on June 2 its Spitfires moved to Martlesham Heath. No 121 (Eagle) Squadron arrived from North Weald the following day. This unit moved to Debden in September and was later transferred to the USAF as No 335 Squadron.

During August, 19 Squadron made a

Left *402 Squadron personnel relax at Southend in 1941.*

Below left *A classic photograph—airmen sitting on the tail of a Hurricane to hold it down on engine run-up. 402 Squadron, RCAF, at Southend.*

Right *The Duke of Kent visiting 402 (RCAF) Squadron at Southend, late 1941.*

brief four-day visit. No 350 (Belgium) Squadron arrived on September 23 and its Spitfires remained until the end of the year. They were replaced by the Spitfires of No 453 (RAAF) Squadron which had previously been detached here for a week in October and had carried out offensive operations. The Australians swept between Ostend-Ypres-Dunkirk without loss. Their move this time to Southend meant they came back into line too late to join in the large-scale attack on December 6 against Philips' radio works at Eindhoven, Holland. During December No 453 was given only three sweeps to perform.

In a raid on Southend airfield on October 26 1942, a Dornier was hit by the guns of No 2830 RAF Regiment, Southend and it crashed into the dispersal area of 350 Squadron, killing Warrant Officer Dyon, a Belgian airman.

The onerous patrols maintained by all Fighter Command groups served the important purpose of restricting to a minimum enemy offensive and reconnaissance flights. Southend airfield was always a hive of activity and when the RAF turned to the offensive it proved a welcome sight for many crippled bombers and fighters, which kept Southend General Hospital very busy.

Throughout this period countless squadrons used Southend for refuelling and briefing. February was a month of low cloud and intermittent gales. The enemy made use of the poor visibility, and on February 9 1943 a single Dornier 217 sneaked in right under the noses of a section of Spitfires which was actually patrolling

over Southend, and machine-gunned the airfield at low level. The German raider escaped out to sea before it could be intercepted. The Spitfires of No 222 flew in from Ayr on March 27, only to move out to Martlesham Heath on April 1 1943. Southend reverted to the Hornchurch sector from June 1 1943 until that sector closed on February 18 1944 and it was again North Weald sector until September 1944 when Southend was reduced to Care and Maintenance.

Meanwhile, 234 Squadron arrived during the middle of September 1943 with its Mustangs, but stayed only three weeks. They were followed by the Spitfires of 350 Squadron which remained only two weeks and had returned to Hawkinge by the end of October. November saw the arrival and departure of 66 Squadron. It was replaced by the Spitfires of 317 Squadron, which arrived on December 2 for a 16-day stay.

By early 1944 the pace began to slow down and in February the station became the base for an armament practice camp. Between February and May, Nos 41, 122, 222, 302, 310, 312, 313, 331, 332 and 501 Squadrons had used Southend at varying periods. Each unit stayed only about a week and the last to leave was 122 Squadron, which moved out on May 28. The status of the station as at June 6 1944 was No 17 Armament Practice Camp flying Masters and Martinets for No 11 Group. The station continued in this role until September when it was reduced to Care and Maintenance.

As the Allies became established in Europe, No 287 Squadron moved in with

its Airspeed Oxfords, Beaufighters and Lysanders. Its role was co-operation with fighters and with ack-ack. The station was also used by squadrons of the RAF Regiment awaiting movement into Europe, but it was only for a short period and on September 1 the station reverted to the control of Hornchurch and remained its satellite for the duration of the war. By the end of 1945 the station was again placed on a Care and Maintenance basis.

The airfield was derequisitioned in 1946 and it returned to civil flying. The airport licence was issued to Southend Corporation on December 31 1946. Squadron Leader Jack Jones, who had operated his Puss Moth from a field at Herne Bay, flew in to establish East Anglian Flying Services and shortly afterwards the Municipal Flying School was formed. Jack Jones was joined by Captain H.A.M. Pascoe, AFC, and Captain Hugo Parsons, DFC. By 1948 his fleet had grown to five DH Rapides and Customs facilities were inaugurated at the airport, with services to the Channel Islands and Ostend having been established.

In January 1949, the Bovingdon-based company of Aviation Traders Engineering Ltd formed a base at Southend. It was set up to maintain aircraft then being used on the Berlin Airlift but it remained after the crisis and it has become one of the largest aircraft maintenance organisations in Britain. In 1956 Aviation Traders purchased all the 252 Hunting-Percival Prentice trainers after they had become obsolete with the RAF.

Aviation Traders had also branched into other fields, for in 1954, Air Charter Limited, an associate company, started the Channel Air Bridge carrying passengers, cars and freight to Calais, later to Ostend

Above *Viking aircraft on the apron in front of the control tower at Southend Airport.*

Above right *Loading Carvair G-ARSD at Southend, October 27 1962. The Carvair was a converted Skymaster and used for car ferry and general freight.*

Right *Douglas DC-4, G-ARVY, of Channel Airways, also at Southend on October 27 1962.*

and Rotterdam, using Bristol Freighter Mk 31s, later Mk 32s. In 1958, Air Charter combined with Airwork Transair and Hunting Can Airlines to form British United Airways. That same year Tradair Limited came to Southend with Vikings but in December 1962 it became a fully-owned subsidiary of Channel Airways (the new name for East Anglian Flying Services from October 15 1962). It now operated a fleet of DH 104 Doves.

During 1962 Channel Air Bridge had merged with Silver City to form British United Air Ferries and on October 1 1967 it was renamed British Air Ferries and headquarters moved from London to Southend. Since the 1950s, Southend had been a busy centre for cross-Channel car ferry operations but in the face of considerable competition from the sea ferries, British Air Ferries gradually ran down this type of service until by the mid-1970s it had ended. By 1978 BAF had reverted to purely charter work. January 1964 had seen the closure of the Municipal Flying School, which over the years had trained over 400 pilots.

Two paved runways were laid in 1955/56, the main one being 06/24 which is 5,265 ft

in length and 120 ft wide, with a tarmac surface and friction course. It has high intensity and low intensity approach and runway lighting. Following the removal of several cottages in 1981, which were obstructions at the south-west end of runway 06/24, the airport is now able to accommodate aircraft such as the B 737 which augurs well for inclusive tour business. The second runway 15/33 is 3,712 ft in length and 90 ft wide with a tarmac surface and has only low intensity runway lighting.

Today, the airfield houses a number of flying clubs and three of these undertake flying training. In 1981 two airlines had scheduled services from Southend; Air UK Limited to Ostend, Rotterdam, and Dusseldorf with Herald and Bandeirante aircraft and British Midland Airways to the Channel Islands with Viscounts. In addition, British Air Ferries operates an increasing number of charter flights.

Until recently, just off Aviation Way opposite the Airport Hotel was the Historic Aviation Museum, which had a collection of over 30 aircraft, now sadly dispersed.

Stag Lane, Middlesex

176/TQ200920. Just north of London to the west of the M1 motorway at Edgware

This small field in the countryside just north of London at Edgware was first used as an airfield during the First World War. It covered an area of 83 acres, dimensions 920 yds × 820 yds and it was used as a relief ground for nearby Hendon. The site was listed as a 2nd class landing ground in the south-east area. It came under 49 Wing and it was used by 44 Squadron and a training control squadron.

For a short period it was the home of the London & Provincial Company which ran its flying school from here with L and

P Biplanes. It remained until after the summer of 1920 when it forsook aviation and turned to chocolate and furniture making. Stag Lane then became the first home of the newly formed de Havilland Aircraft Company which began life in a collection of huts and sheds in a rented field in Stag Lane. Within two years Geoffrey de Havilland had erected several Bessoneau hangars and a permanent erecting shop. The work force had also grown from 50 to 200.

The airfield continued to expand and by 1926 more hangars and erecting sheds plus many other buildings had appeared. Additionally the work force had now risen to 1,000. The London Aeroplane Club and the de Havilland School of Flying were now established here, and it was a very busy aerodrome with the air space congested.

The rapid rise to fame, and growth of the airfield can be attributed to de Havilland's first really successful aeroplane, the Moth. The company's Moth series of light biplanes brought flying to the masses and is probably the world's best known biplane. On February 22 1925, Captain de Havilland took the prototype DH 60 Moth, *G-EBKT*, on its maiden flight. It was the first of many. Peak production was reached in 1926 when one Moth a day was being turned out. On Sundays the red DH 9Js of the de Havilland School of Flying would fly down to Southend and circle the pier in close formation, their Jaguar radials screaming attention at every turn.

However, by the early 1930s the days of the airfield were numbered as London began to spill out into the countryside and houses appeared around the perimeter of the aerodrome. De Havilland foresaw this and acquired a large site near the small country town of Hatfield in Hertfordshire. The company moved there during the early 1930s and in January 1934 Stag Lane was officially closed as an aerodrome. The last flight made out of Stag Lane was by Captain de Havilland in Hornet Moth *G-ACTA* on July 28 1934.

The open land was quickly snapped up by property developers and today there is little trace of the aerodrome which saw the birth of many famous Moths.

Stapleford Tawney, Essex

*177/TQ493970. North-east of London on
the A113 between Chigwell and Ongar*

Stapleford Tawney originally opened on
June 23 1934 as an operating base for Hillman's Airways. When it outgrew the small
field at Maylands, Hillman obtained 180
acres of land near the village of Stapleford
Tawney on a 25-year lease and laid out an
aerodrome. Three small hangars were built,
each with a concrete apron in front plus
an administration building and a small
passenger terminal, but the surface of the
landing area, which was not particularly
level, remained grass.

Hillman continued to expand and within
a few weeks of moving in, a Stapleford–
Liverpool–Isle-of-Man–Belfast service was
inaugurated. In December 1934 Edward
Hillman died suddenly at the age of 45.
However, despite the premature death of
its founder the company continued to
expand. Eight new DH 89 Rapides were
put into service as the daily schedules continued, but just after three DH 86s were
delivered at the end of June 1935 the company moved to Gatwick and was absorbed
into British Airways.

For the next two years Stapleford was
left empty with the exception of a few
private aircraft. In 1938, during the expansion of the RAF, the aerodrome was reopened for use by No 21 Elementary and
Reserve Flying Training School. It was
operated under contract from the Air
Ministry by Reid and Sigrist Ltd, training
RAFVR pilots. The school used Tiger
Moths for basic training, with Hawker
Harts, Hinds and Audaxes for the more
advanced training. One of the many pilots
to pass through the school was 'Johnnie'
Johnson, who later received no less than
five British decorations for gallantry and a
similar number of foreign awards.

At the outbreak of war the aerodrome
was requisitioned and No 21 E & RFTS
moved out. The aerodrome was then enlarged and a 2¼-mile concrete perimeter
track 18 ft wide was laid, plus six double
dispersal pens and accommodation and
administration buildings. The grass landing
area measured 1,000 yds north–south, 800
yds east–west and 1,150 yds south-east-
north-west, while the main north-east-
south-west direction measured 1,220 yds.
The landing area was camouflaged by
means of sooty black lines drawn across it
to represent hedgerows. The aerodrome
was now capable of handling one fighter
squadron, and early in 1940 it was handed
over to No 11 Group as a satellite for
North Weald.

The first recorded use was in March
1940 when Hurricanes of Nos 56 and 151
Squadrons were flown over from the
parent station for an overnight stop. This
procedure continued for the next few
weeks, the Hurricanes flying over at dusk
and back again to the parent station at dawn.

The first squadron to be permanently
based at Stapleford was No 151, which
moved in from North Weald on August 29
1940, mounting several patrols the same
day. On August 31 the resident squadron
was again in action when the Luftwaffe
attacked North Weald. During this raid
No 151 Squadron shot down a confirmed
Bf 109. On a second patrol, No 151 shot
down a Do 17 near Hornchurch and on
the third patrol they shot down a Do 215
over the Thames Estuary. No 151 Squadron lost two aircraft but both pilots, although injured, managed to parachute to
safety. On September 1, No 151 Squadron
changed places with No 46 Squadron at
Digby, Lincolnshire.

On September 2, No 46 Squadron
mounted a number of patrols and on the
last one of the day shot down a Bf 109,
but also lost Pilot Officer J.C.D.L. Bailey,
who was shot down in Hurricane *P3067*
near Eastchurch.

The squadron was now in daily contact
with the Luftwaffe and by the end of September five more pilots had been lost:
Flying Officer R.P. Plummer shot down
on September 4, who died in hospital ten
days later; Sub-Lieutenant J.C. Carpenter
shot down on September 8, Sergeant W.A.
Peacock shot down on September 11;
Sergeant G.W. Jeffreys shot down on
September 18 and Pilot Officer J.D.
Crossman shot down on the last day of
the month.

Bad weather restricted operations for
the first half of October. On October 15
No 46 Squadron lost two Hurricanes in
return for one Bf 109. Pilot Officer P.S.
Gunning was killed. A week later Sergeant
J.P. Morrison was shot down over Dunge-
ness. Then on October 25 Pilot Officer
W.B. Pattullo crashed into a house in
Romford after being in combat with a
Bf 109. He died in hospital the following
day. On October 29 Sergeant H.E. Black
managed to bale out of his burning Hurri-
cane, but he died of his wounds in Ashford
Hospital ten days later. During this period
Stapleford housed the Lysanders of No 419
Flight, later part of 138 Squadron, and it
moved to Stradishall on October 9. Two

nights previously a few bombs fell on the aerodrome causing many craters but no damage.

Operations continued from Stapleford Tawney but rainy weather had made the grass surface boggy and on November 8 the aerodrome was declared unserviceable. That same day No 46 Squadron moved to North Weald.

For the winter months the station was without any flying units, probably due to the poor state of the landing ground. On April 9 1941, No 242 Squadron arrived from Martlesham Heath with its Hurricanes. Eleven days later it was on its first operation but it ended in tragedy when three aircraft collided in cloud over the channel, all three pilots being killed including the CO, Squadron Leader Treacy. Three days later, Squadron Leader Whitney-Straight took command of the squadron and the month ended with two more pilots being killed.

During May, 242 Squadron carried out a number of offensive sweeps over France and Belgium until it moved to North Weald on May 22. The station was again without a flying unit for a few weeks until No 3 Squadron arrived from Martlesham Heath on June 23. Like its predecessor it was equipped with Hurricanes and carried out offensive sweeps and convoy patrols for a few weeks. During July and early August detachments were sent to Hunsdon on a nightly basis for night-flying practice with Turbinlite-equipped Bostons and Havocs of No 1451 Flight. On August 8, No 3 Squadron moved to Hunsdon.

Meanwhile, No 2 Camouflage Unit had moved in during June 1941. This unit had a few Tiger Moths, Oxfords and Dominies. Its role was to carry out aerial examination of camouflaged sites in the area.

On December 22 1941, No 277 formed with an establishment of Lysanders and Walruses. Its role was to carry out air-sea rescue duties in the sea areas between Northern France and south-east England. Stapleford then became the squadron headquarters and was responsible for major maintenance and pilot conversion. The New Year saw changes on the airfield when a number of new buildings, including billets and messes, were erected near the main hangar. Eight Blister hangars were also erected. In addition to machine-gun posts and pillboxes this airfield had a small number of retractable Hamilton Forts for defence.

In April, No 277 Squadron started to convert to Defiants, and by mid-May had

12 on strength. It also had some Tiger Moths, a Lysander and a Koolhoven FK 43 which had escaped from Holland in May 1940. The squadron moved to Gravesend on December 7 1942.

Again for the winter months the airfield was without a resident flying squadron. In March 1943 it was transferred to No 34 Wing Army Co-operation Command and became a satellite of Sawbridgeworth. During the middle of the month, No 656 Squadron arrived from Westley, Bury St Edmunds. This was an air observation post unit and was flying Auster Mk Is and Mk IIIs plus a few Tiger Moths. During the summer months the squadron carried out exercises and was then mobilised and left for India via Liverpool Docks on August 12 1943.

Meanwhile, No 34 Wing had been disbanded in June 1943 and the station transferred to No 12 Group, although still remaining a satellite of Sawbridgeworth. These moves were part of the build-up to the formation of the 2nd Tactical Air Force which formed on November 15 1943. By the end of the year a large number of ground personnel attached to the 2nd TAF had arrived at the station. These included RAF Regiment, signals, and repair and salvage units. These units left for the south coast advanced landing grounds in the spring of 1944 in preparation for D-Day.

During the summer of 1944, No 142 Flight, London Gliding Command, operated from the airfield. In September of that year No 2 Camouflage Unit moved out and this was Stapleford's last wartime powered aircraft unit.

On November 20 1944, a V2 rocket exploded in the centre of the airfield, making a crater 60 ft in diameter. Another hit the main camp on February 23 1945 during mid-afternoon, causing widespread damage and killing 17 personnel and injuring 50.

By the end of April 1945 the last of the few remaining ground units were posted away and on May 11 the station was reduced to a Care and Maintenance basis. For the remainder of the year and throughout 1946 the Wethersfield and Earls Colne Army units used the airfield as a drop zone for paratroops.

The airfield was then neglected and the American forces demolished all the southern pillboxes and defence works leaving the rubble piled on the perimeter track. Over the years the airfield reverted to agriculture.

In 1953, having sold their airfield at

Broxbourne, Herts and Essex Aero Club moved to Stapleford Tawney, renovated the hangars and certain buildings and began flying there with Tiger Moths and Austers. In 1955, Edgar Percival, the famous pre-war light aircraft designer, formed a new company under his name and set up a production line at Stapleford for his EP 9 crop-spraying aircraft. The first flight took place on December 21 1955 and nearly 40 aircraft were built before the company was sold and the production line moved to Blackpool in 1958. Thurston Aviation then used the airfield for its air taxis business before moving to Stansted at the end of 1978.

Today, although Herts and Essex still owns the airfield Stapleford Flying Club uses it for pilot training.

Stow Maries, Essex

168/TL835995. 9 miles south-east of Chelmsford

Stow Maries was built as a London defence landing ground in 1916 and it opened in September of that year when 37 Squadron moved in a detachment of two BE 2cs on September 15. Its headquarters was at Woodham Mortimer and similar detachments were also set up at Rochford and Goldhanger. The airfields were part of a grand design to provide a string of fighter airfields supported by searchlights stretching from Dover to Edinburgh in an attempt to prevent inland penetration. The airfields were sited near the east coast and were selected at distances of ten to 30 miles from each other.

The site had the usual equipment for a landing ground—one canvas Bessoneau hangar, an assortment of tents for living quarters, offices, stores etc, and the usual night flying equipment. As the home defence expanded, each squadron which was raised was split into three flights of eight aircraft and spread over three different airfields. In this way Stow Maries housed 'B' Flight of 37 Squadron while Goldhanger housed 'C' Flight and Rochford 'A' Flight. The idea was for each flight to patrol towards its adjoining airfield. No 37 Squadron covered the northern portion of the Thames estuary but a year later when home defence squadrons became more plentiful, 37 Squadron was concentrated on Stow Maries and Goldhanger.

In June 1918, No 37 HQ moved to Stow Maries and at the same time the resident squadron increased its strength with some Sopwith Pups and 1½-Strutters. The unit now became a night fighter squadron and in October 1918 some Camels were taken on strength, but the war ended before they could be tested against the enemy.

With the war over, the final detached flight of 37 Squadron was withdrawn from Goldhanger back to Stow Maries on February 20 1919, and for the first time in the squadron's history it was based as a complete unit on one airfield: the headquarters, three flights, 24 aircraft and 300 personnel. At Stow Maries the squadron was destined to keep flying for a little longer. Ironically the buildings and airfield facilities were not completed until December 1918. With the Royal Air Force rapidly dwindling, No 37 Squadron re-equipped with Sopwith Snipes and in February 1919 the unit's third commanding officer, Major J. Sowrey, took over from Major Honnett. On March 17 1919, No 37 Squadron moved to Biggin Hill and the airfield was abandoned. It had been thought that Stow Maries would be developed into a peacetime airfield, but within a few months it was under the plough, although many of the original First World War buildings survived for a good many years and were used by the local farmer.

Sutton's Farm (Hornchurch), Essex

See Hornchurch

Waddon (Croydon), Surrey

See Croydon

West Malling (Kings Hill), Kent

178/TQ680555. Five miles west of Maidstone on the B228

West Malling opened as a private landing ground in 1930, housing the Maidstone School of Flying. The site had been used during the First World War when it was then known as Kings Hill and was classed as a 2nd class landing ground. It covered an area of only 47 acres, dimensions 650 yds × 380 yds and was located in wooded surroundings 1½ miles from West Malling railway station. Kings Hill came under No 53 Wing and was used by 143 Squadron.

Kent Aeronautical Services began to operate from West Malling in 1931 with modified SE 5As and a Sopwith Dove. The Dove was owned by Mr Lowe-Wylde and after the owner's death it was rebuilt as a Pup in 1937/8 by R.O. Shuttleworth. It can be found today in the Shuttleworth Collection.

In 1932 the field became known as Maidstone Airport and was registered as a company. A new company called Malling Aviation moved in during 1934 with a varied collection of aircraft. The following year it purchased the airport and renamed it Malling Aero Club. Many displays were held at Malling and it had visits from Alan Cobham and Amy Johnson.

With the coming of war the RAF took over West Malling and a station headquarters was formed here at the beginning of June 1940. No 26 (Army Co-operation) Squadron and No 51 Wing moved in on June 8. The first fighter squadron here was No 141 on July 12 1940. This unit arrived from Turnhouse and was equipped with the Boulton Paul Defiant two-seat fighter. The squadron saw action on July 21 when it engaged the enemy over the Channel. Flying Bf 109s the German pilots' onslaught was launched from a position where there was no chance of retaliation. The Germans knew that the Defiant was very vulnerable when attacked from below—the gun turret of the Defiant did not move sufficiently for the gunner to fire down on the enemy. In the ensuing battle six Defiants were shot down—virtually wiping out 141 Squadron. The remainder of the squadron was immediately posted to Prestwick.

With the departure of the Defiants, Malling was left with No 26 Army Co-operation Squadron flying the very slow Westland Lysander. This unit carried out reconnaissance and photographic sorties in co-operation with anti-aircraft and searchlight units.

West Malling was designated a satellite for Kenley, to be used as an advanced airfield for both Kenley and Biggin Hill.

On August 10 1940, the Luftwaffe paid a visit to the airfield at 07.30 hours. This was the start of a series of bombing attacks which caused considerable damage. So intense were these raids that the station was out of action for many weeks.

The second bombing attack came on August 15 and again considerable damage was done and two airmen killed. The following day the Luftwaffe returned for another high altitude bombing attack. There were no casualties but three aircraft of 26 Squadron were badly damaged. Two days later they were back again, this time in a dive-bombing attack which resulted in further damage to new hangars and three Lysanders destroyed. The airfield was bombed another three times before the end of August.

On September 3 the station again came under attack and about 30 bombs were dropped. There were numerous craters and many unexploded bombs but only one civilian was wounded. However, it was the final straw for 26 Squadron and that same day it moved to Gatwick.

Repair work continued and by September 10 the telephone services had been restored. That same day a single enemy aircraft made a surprise attack on the airfield and dropped six anti-personnel bombs. One bomb scored a direct hit on an Army post, killing six soldiers and wounding three others. Three bombs were dropped on the airfield but the craters were quickly filled in. Five further attacks were made on West Malling before the end of the month.

October also saw further attacks but by the end of the month the station was ready to receive a squadron, and No 66 flew in with Spitfires. West Malling offered them a brief respite from the ordeal of constant battle. With No 66 Squadron came 421 Flight, whose role was fleet-spotting duties for the Swordfish units at Manston. No 421 Flight also took part in reconnaissance patrols to monitor enemy shipping movements in the Channel and interception of lone enemy aircraft crossing the south-east coast, known as 'Jim Crow' patrols. The Spitfires and Hurricanes of 421 Flight moved back to Hawkinge in November 1940 and on January 11 1941 it was re-numbered No 91 Squadron.

However, it was not until next spring that the station was up to full squadron status. No 264 arrived on April 14 1941, flying Defiants, but this time in the night fighter role. It was joined on April 27 by 29 Squadron, which arrived from Wellingore.

This unit was flying the new Beaufighter night interceptor and immediately began to notch up many kills. Serving with 29 Squadron at this time were two bomber pilots, Guy Gibson and Don Parker. The Air Ministry felt that the knowledge gained by bomber pilots of how to evade the German night fighters could be helpful to our own fighter pilots. Gibson, who later achieved fame as leader of the 'Dams' raid, and Parker were invaluable to the night fighter pilots.

At this period of the war one 'J' Type and 16 Blister hangars were in existence. The landing area was still grass-surfaced and Sommerfeld track had to be laid to give the station all-weather serviceability. The airfield measured 3,300 ft north-east–

south-west, 3,900 ft south-east–north-west, 3,600 ft north–south and 4,200 ft east–west. The north–south landing direction was later extended to 5,000 ft and the main east–west to 6,500 ft. Petrol storage totalled 72,000 gallons of aviation spirit and 5,000 gallons of MT fuel.

Throughout the autumn and winter, 264 Squadron was engaged on night patrols and interceptions. It was withdrawn to re-equip with Mosquitoes before being posted to Colerne on May 1 1942.

It was replaced by the Hurricanes of No 32 Squadron which arrived from Manston on May 4. This unit was in and out three times over the next few weeks, departing for the last time on September 9. During this period, 616 Squadron had arrived from King's Cliffe for a two week period during July and had then moved to Kenley. No 485 Squadron had also put in an appearance during August, and No 486 during October. Also visiting was No 1428 (Enemy Aircraft) Flight, which was at West Malling to give personnel a close inspection of the He 111, Bf 109 and Bf 110 and to enable the pilots to fly against them in mock battle.

On January 25 1943, No 531 Squadron disbanded. This unit had formed at West Malling from 1452 Flight (Turbinlite) on September 2 1942. It flew Hurricanes and Havocs. The latter were actually fighter

bombers and the noses of the aircraft were cut off and searchlights installed. The bomb bay was filled with batteries and the aim was for the Havocs to take off with the Hurricanes at night, pinpoint enemy bombers and turn on the searchlights. The Hurricanes would finish them off. However, this operation was not a success.

One of West Malling's strangest incidents happened on the night of April 16 1943. A single-engined aircraft was heard to approach the airfield. After circling twice it landed. Assuming that it was a Defiant, one of the ground crew climbed on to the wing to help the pilot out. Then he spotted the Nazi markings on the fuselage and hastily jumped off, meeting an officer coming from the control tower to arrest the pilot. The fire tender and crash crew also drove out. At the same time another aircraft came in to land, this also being German. The first pilot gave himself up but the second tried to take off again. Some shots from the fire tender must have hit the oxygen bottles in the pilot's cockpit for the aircraft exploded. A third German aircraft landed in the orchard having overshot the runway and a fourth crashed into trees at Staplehurst.

Apparently, about 15 Focke-Wulf 190s had been sent over on intruder operations and had mistaken West Malling airfield for occupied Europe. The ground crews were told that the reason the Germans had landed was that they were lost and were enticed in, in German, by the officer in charge of the control tower.

Mosquito 35 in a hangar at West Malling.

Flight Lieutenant M.A. Cybulski, Canadian night fighter pilot of 410 Squadron (right), beside the burned out rudder of his Mosquito in which he returned 250 miles to base at West Malling, after shooting down a Do 217 over Holland on November 5 1943. With him is his RAF navigator, Flight Lieutenant H.H. Ladbrook, who helped to pull the aircraft out of a 4,000-ft dive, and controlled the aircraft for six minutes when the Canadian pilot was blinded by burning petrol from the exploding enemy aircraft. A piece of flying debris knocked out his port engine, which was U/S all the way home.

On May 13 1943, No 29 Squadron moved to Bradwell Bay. During its stay at West Malling it had accounted for 49 kills. It was replaced the same day by 85 Squadron with Wing Commander John Cunningham. This was joined the following day by No 3 Squadron with its Typhoons which could carry bombs. However, No 3 Squadron remained only a few weeks and moved to Manston on June 11.

In July 1943, West Malling began to accept heavy bombers of the RAF and the USAF. During August, Nos 130 and 234 Squadrons arrived. Both were Spitfire squadrons and the following month they were joined by three more Spitfire squadrons, Nos 64, 124 and 350. However, by the end of September, Nos 64, 130, 234 and 350 had departed and were replaced by the Canadians by way of 410 Squadron which arrived on October 20 from Coleby Grange, Lincolnshire. This unit was flying de Havilland Mosquitoes but its stay was short and on November 7 it moved to Hunsdon. Its replacement was 96 Squadron from Drem which arrived on November 8.

During the summer months, Thunderbolts of the Eighth Air Force had used Malling during their escort duties for the American bombers. By now the tide was beginning to turn.

On March 18 1944, No 124 Squadron moved to Church Fenton and No 616 Squadron returned, but a month later it moved to Fairwood Common. It was replaced by 91 Squadron. This unit was engaged in *Diver* operations against the German pilotless aircraft or V1s as they were named. No 409 Squadron (RCAF) arrived on May 15 but a month later their Mosquitoes moved to Hunsdon.

West Malling became the main base for squadrons attacking the Doodle Bugs. During the latter part of June, No 96 Squadron moved to Ford and it was replaced by the Spitfires of 322 Squadron. The following month, No 85 returned, having been to Swannington for ten weeks. The first two weeks of July also saw four more squadrons arrive, Nos 80 with Spitfires, 157 with Mosquitoes, 274 with Spitfires and 316 with Mustangs. By the end of July, 91, 274, 316 and 322 Squadrons had moved on, leaving Nos 80, 85 and 157. These three units remained a few more weeks, then at the end of August, Nos 85 and 157 Squadrons moved to Swannington and No 80 to Manston. The station then closed for extensive reconstruction work, which included a new concrete runway. These alterations took until June 1945.

The station then reopened and West Malling became the main rehabilitation centre for PoWs returning from Germany to Britain.

On September 10 1945, No 287 Squadron arrived from Bradwell Bay with its Spitfires. Two weeks later 29 Squadron returned with Mosquitoes, but these it later changed for Meteors.

Vengeance aircraft then arrived with 567 Squadron at the end of April 1946 but this unit disbanded on June 15. That same day No 287 also disbanded here. It had been replaced by No 500 (County of Kent) Squadron of the Royal Auxiliary Air Force, whose Meteors had arrived on May 10. During September 1946 the Mosquitoes of No 25 Squadron arrived from Boxted. They were joined the following April by No 85 Squadron, which had been flying Mosquitoes, but later converted to Meteors which became a familiar sight and sound around West Malling. On February 28 1955, No 153 re-formed here with an establishment of Meteors and they flew alongside the three resident squadrons. However, the end was in sight for all the Auxiliary Air Force squadrons and on March 10 1957, No 500 Squadron disbanded. The three other units remained a few more months, before, in September 1957, No 25 moved to Tangmere, having re-equipped with Vampires, No 85 to Church Fenton and No 153 to Waterbeach. The airfield was then without a resident flying unit until No 85 Squadron flew in from Stradishall on August 5 1959 with Javelins. It stayed just over a year and moved out to West Raynham on September 8 1960.

With its departure, West Malling closed as an operational base and in August 1964 the station was placed on Care and Maintenance. In 1965 it reopened when a United States Navy facility flight moved in with communication and transport aircraft. Super R4Ds and Convair C-131s now used the airfield. The Americans remained for nearly two years before transferring to Blackbushe.

Silence descended upon the airfield and while its fate was being decided No 618 Gliding School arrived to give air cadets instruction. Also, Short Brothers, the commercial aero firm, moved in a maintenance section from Rochester for the purpose of servicing Varsity and Chipmunk aircraft for the RAF.

In 1970, Kent County Council bought the aerodrome and converted many of the brick buildings into offices. In 1972 it was used as a reception centre for the Ugandan Asians arriving in Britain.

Today the station is the location of the HQ of Tonbridge and Malling District Council. The airfield is still in a good state of preservation and in 1980 there were plans to turn it into a passenger and freight terminal but this proposal met stiff local opposition.

Lockheed P2V-7, 128382, seen at West Malling during a US Navy Open Day, May 13 1961.

West Pole Farm, Middlesex

176/TQ280950. To the east of Barnet

Situated a mile from East Barnet railway station, West Pole Farm was a 42-acre field that was listed as a 3rd class landing ground. It was light loam on gravel soil and it had a bad surface. The surroundings were wooded with many houses. It came under the south-east area under 49 Wing and it was used by 39 Squadron. There is no trace of it today.

Weybridge (Brooklands), Surrey

See Brooklands

White Waltham (Maidenhead), Berkshire

175/SU850785. South-west of Maidenhead to the south of the A4/M4 junction

Situated about two miles south-west of Maidenhead, the airfield at White Waltham opened on November 16 1935 and became home for the second de Havilland School of Flying. The school was formed to carry out *ab initio* training for pupil pilots and elementary and advanced training for officers and NCOs under the command of the superintendent of Reserve headquarters, RAF Reserve, Hendon. The school operated one of the most famous products of the parent company—the Tiger Moth— which served as a trainer in the RAF for many years.

During the build-up period of the RAF, the school became No 13 Elementary and Reserve Flying Training School on November 18 1935 and at the outbreak of war in September 1939 the unit was renamed No 13 Elementary Flying Training School. In 1940 it was allocated a Relief Landing Ground at Waltham St Lawrence, two or three miles to the south-west. During April 1940, the school began using Bray Court and Henley as Relief Landing Grounds but this ceased after a few months. In December 1940, No 13 EFTS moved to Westwood, the training airfield on the outskirts of Peterborough, where it became No 25 (Polish) EFTS on May 21 1941.

Although White Waltham housed a variety of RAF units during the Second World War, no operational squadrons were based there. For the remainder of the war, White Waltham was best known for its association with the Air Transport Auxiliary. This started in February 1940 when No 3 Ferry Pilots Pool formed on the first of the month with an establishment of nine aircraft and 40 pilots. Three months later sections 'B' and 'C' moved out. Section 'A' remained at White Waltham and on November 5 1940 it became No 1 Ferry Pilots Pool, ATA. The ATA headquarters was housed at White Waltham and from that small beginning the ATA carried out a total of 308,567 aircraft ferry trips in the Second World War; 78,500 were made in the year February 1944 to January 1945. The maximum in

Aerogypt IV at White Waltham in 1943.

Chrislea Super Ace, G-AKVB, and Chrislea Skyjeep, G-AKVS, photographed at White Waltham on May 29 1950.

any one day was on February 21 1945, when 570 deliveries were made.

The movement of such large numbers of aircraft called for considerable ground organisation. No 1 Ferry Pilots Pool at White Waltham played its part and was responsible for ferrying many thousands of aircraft throughout the war. Also housed here during the war years was the Air Transport Auxiliary Advanced Flying Training School and the ATA Air Movement Flight. The Technical Training Command Communications Flight was also based at White Waltham until it moved to Wyton in October 1945.

After the war, the airfield was used extensively by Fairey Aviation for test-flying its aircraft, particularly Fireflies and Gannets. Fairey's moved here in 1947 from Heston, and several flying clubs, including

HRH Duke of Edinburgh takes off in Harvard KF729 on solo flight, May 1953 at White Waltham.

Top *'B1' hangar that still remains at White Waltham (April 1980).* **Above** *Super Robin Hangar at White Waltham (April 1980).*

the West London, also moved in. The RAF maintained a presence, White Waltham being the headquarters of Home Command. With Mosquitoes, Ansons, Balliols and Chipmunks, it was also the base of several communications flights, with hangars, offices and housing on the south-east side of the airfield.

Home Command Examining Unit formed at Honiley in 1947 as Instrument Training Flight of Reserve Command and it moved to White Waltham in 1949, when it became a flight of Reserve Command's communications squadron. It then became

HCEU, an independent unit, in 1951. The staff consisted of the CO and six instructors. No airmen were on the unit and maintenance was carried out by Fairey Aviation. Aircraft used by the unit were two Mosquito T 3s, two Ansons, one Balliol and one Chipmunk.

In July 1958, No 6 Air Experience Flight formed at White Waltham where it was co-located with HQ Air Cadets. First-line servicing was done on contract by Short Bros. January 1959 saw the disbandment of the HCEU and the arrival of No 1 Air Experience Flight. The flight had now been reduced to six aircraft and the following year it moved to West Malling, returning to White Waltham in 1961, where it stayed until moving to Manston in 1963.

After Home Command disbanded the RAF gradually withdrew from the airfield in the early 1970s. The final unit to leave was No 6 Air Experience Flight. Its Chipmunks moved to Abingdon in 1973 and the station closed on August 31 of that year. White Waltham was then left as a light civil airfield with regular rumours of impending closure.

Wimbledon, Surrey

176/TQ220720. To the west of Wimbledon between the A3 and the A219

This was a 40-acre site, dimensions 600 yds × 350 yds, which was part of the north end of Wimbledon Common. It was not used during the day and it was listed as a 3rd class landing ground. Temporary canvas hangars were erected at the west side of the landing area. It was 1½ miles from Wimbledon railway station and it came under 49 Wing. It was used by mainly 141 Squadron but all manner of service aeroplanes used Wimbledon during the 1914-18 war. After the war the facilities were soon dismantled but the landing ground continued to be used for a few years.

First VC-10 lands at Wisley, June 29 1962.

Winkfield, Berkshire

175/SU912726. South-west of Windsor

This small grass airfield, close to the village of Winkfield, after which it was named, saw very little service. It was a field with very few facilities and could hardly be called an aerodrome. Its only role was as a relief landing ground for the Tiger Moths of No 18 EFTS at Fairoaks from May 28 1941 to July 9 1945. Winkfield closed as an airfield after the war and today the site is a radio and space research station.

Wisley, Surrey

187/TQ075575. East of Woking to the south of the A3 and east of the B2039

The airfield at Wisley originated in the same way as several other British airfields— by accident. An aeroplane flown by Captain Summers, the chief test pilot of Vickers-Armstong, had to make a forced landing and found an open space behind the woodland that fringed the A3 London to Portsmouth road. This was less than 20 miles south-west of London and only about three miles south of the Vickers-Armstrong factory airfield at Weybridge. Two or three years later the site was surveyed and work started to develop it into a relief airfield for the nearby factory. Wisley came into use in 1943 as a grass airfield and was used for the remainder of the war.

Tay-Viscount VX217, *at Wisley.*

Wisley was retained by Vickers-Armstrong after the war and additional accommodation was built. It became the main flight-testing centre for Vickers-built aircraft. Aircraft from Weybridge made their initial flight to Wisley and remained there for the flight-testing programme, even the Valiant V-Bomber. However, with the increase in size and weight of aircraft the grass runway became inadequate and in 1952 a single paved runway, 7,500 ft in length was constructed.

However, this did not solve all the problems, for the post-war boom in civil air traffic caused problems for Wisley, which was situated between London's two major airports, Heathrow and Gatwick. This factor influenced the British Aircraft Corporation, successors to Vickers-Armstrong, to close the airfield in 1973. After it had lain idle for several years a group attempted to reopen Wisley as a civil airfield but met with intense local opposition.

Woodley (Reading), Berkshire
175/SU780732. East of Reading just south of the A4
At the outbreak of war in September 1939, No 8 EFTS formed from No 8 Elementary and Reserve Flying Training School, which had been at Woodley since the mid-1930s. During that time it had trained some 680 pilots and 100 navigators. Now, with the outbreak of war, it continued the training as before, the only visual difference being the word Reserve which was obviously dropped from the school's title.

For some unknown reason this tiny grass airfield was allocated a decoy airfield. This was sited just north of Bracknell at Warfield. It is not known if it served any real purpose and its use was stopped early in the war.

Training continued during the early war years, but in 1942 the station had a change of role. On July 20 of that year No 10 Flying Instructor's School was formed and it gradually took over from No 8 EFTS until the latter disbanded on October 15 1942. During the period of change-over all but ten of the Miles Magisters were replaced by Tiger Moths. The school's complement remained Tiger Moths, Magisters and a single Anson Mk 1 for the duration of the war. Woodley remained a training station under No 50 Group throughout. During 1944 the circuit became very congested and Henley was used as a RLG.

With the war now over there was a period of uncertainty as the RAF raced downhill to civvy street, and Woodley immediately felt the effects, for, in addition

Miles M 14A Magisters ready for delivery from the factory, Woodley, 1938.

to the flying training, Miles Aircraft had a factory here and well over 5,000 Miles-designed aircraft, which were used for target towing, were built, test flown and delivered from this small grass training airfield. Throughout the war years many returned to be repaired and overhauled. In addition, there was a separate section for overhauling Spitfires. Miles was still producing the radio-controlled Queen Martinets at the time the war ended, but the new Monitor had also just gone into production for the Royal Navy. Miles had initial orders for 600 but the end of the war meant these were no longer needed and only a few were built. They were the last military aircraft to be built by Miles Aircraft.

For the time being, No 10 FIS survived, but the axe was about to fall and on June 1 1945 the Master Flight disbanded. Four days later the station received some Tiger Moths from a school that had disbanded at Theale.

With the increase in aircraft it looked as if the school was safe, but it was not to be and further changes were in the wind. On February 2 1946 Wing Commander Hooper arrived by Lancaster to take up his new post as Commanding Officer but by then the last course of instruction was under way and on May 7, No 10 FIS disbanded.

With the disbandment of No 10 FIS only a few Tiger Moths remained and from these No 8 EFTS re-formed on May 7 1946. It was then decided that schools should be formed so that wartime pilots could join the RAF Volunteer Reserve and keep their hand in at flying during their spare time. One of the schools was to be at Woodley and No 8 Reserve Flying School formed there on March 3 1947 from No 8 EFTS.

Initially, the school was equipped with 12 Tiger Moths and two Anson T1s which were later replaced by Anson T21s, which provided facilities for VR navigators and signallers. Most of the flying was routine refresher flying and for the next few years life continued at Woodley.

From 1946 until 1951 the Flying Training Command Communications Flight used the airfield with a variety of aircraft, which included an Anson C 19, Harvard T2 and a Dakota C4, *KK209*, which was the personal aircraft of the C-in-C. It had the Air Marshal's badge of rank on the nose and three stars on a small panel above fin flash. *KK209* had a silver finish with Type C markings and black lettering.

By the early 1950s the Tiger Moth had outlived its usefulness and the Chipmunk had been ordered as its replacement. No 8 RFS started to receive Chipmunks in the autumn of 1951 but the faithful Tiger Moth soldiered on until well into 1952.

In January 1953 it was announced that seven of the 20 reserve flying schools were to close down and Woodley was one of the seven. No 8 RFS disbanded on March 31 1953 and all flying ceased at Woodley.

Since the mid-1930s there had been flying at Woodley—now all is silent. Gone are the exciting days of Miles aircraft. Over the years the station had been visited by many aircraft, these included; Spitfire LF 16—*TE194* of the Central Gunnery School in 1946, Lancaster B3 *JA962* of the Empire Flying School the following year and two Wellington T 10s, *NA968* and *RP487*. Now, they are only memories and soon this little piece of history will be engulfed by a housing estate.

Wycombe Air Park (Booker), Buckinghamshire
See Booker

Other sites

Bentley Priory (Stanmore Park), Middlesex

176/TQ155933. North-west of Stanmore between the A4140 and A410

The grounds of Bentley Priory originally housed a small community of Austin Canons probably founded in pre-Norman times. In 1546 Henry VIII gave the priory to private owners. The estate was then sold to James Duberly, an Army contractor, in 1766. He pulled down the old priory buildings and in the 1770s built the present Bentley Priory on a higher point of the ridge some distance from the original site. In 1788 he sold the estate to the Honourable John James Hamilton, the 9th Earl and 1st Marquess of Abercorn.

In 1863 the estate was sold by the Hamilton family to Sir John Kelk, an eminent railway engineer, who spent lavishly on further improvements. In 1882 the priory was bought by Frederick Gordon, who converted it into a private residential hotel. Bentley Priory as an hotel was not a financial success, and in 1908, on Mr Gordon's death, it changed hands once again to become a girls' school. In 1922 the school closed and the property stood empty. In 1926 the priory estate was split up and one lot, comprising the priory itself and some 40 acres, was sold to the Air Ministry for a sum believed to be about £25,000.

Headquarters Inland Area, a part of the organisation of the air defence of Great Britain, moved to the Priory from Uxbridge on May 26 1926 and remained there until 1936, when it was renamed Flying Training Command and transferred to Shropshire. On July 14 of the same year Fighter Command moved from Hillingdon House, Uxbridge and established its headquarters at Bentley Priory.

In September 1939, Fighter Command consisted of three groups of 39 operational squadrons which were equipped mainly with Hurricanes and Spitfires. At the start of the Battle of Britain, the command had 52 operational squadrons, whereas the strength of the German squadrons actively engaged in the battle was approximately 2,790 aircraft. Yet during the Battle of Britain, in the period from July 10 to October 31 1940, the air defence destroyed 1,653 aircraft for the loss of 449 fighter pilots.

Fighter Command flew 11,000 offensive sorties on *Intruder* and *Ranger* operations, destroying over 500 enemy aircraft, provided fighter escorts for Bomber Command operations, destroyed nearly 2,000 flying bombs and made over 4,000 sorties against enemy rocket sites. All these offensive operations were in addition to its primary function of air defence, both over the United Kingdom and France. Throughout the war, Fighter Command claimed to have destroyed 6,751 aircraft and to have flown 4,864,867 hours.

On April 30 1968, Fighter Command was amalgamated with Bomber Command to form Strike Command. The Fighter Command headquarters at Bentley Priory became Headquarters No 11 (Fighter) Group. This is the operational air defence group in Strike Command, and, under the command of an Air Vice-Marshal, is primarily responsible for the air defence of the United Kingdom in wartime and the integrity of our airspace in peacetime. In addition it has the capability of rapid overseas deployment.

Geographically the group is widely spread from the far north of Scotland, along the east coast of the United Kingdom and across to the south-west of England and West Wales. The units vary in size from a score of personnel on a remote

Left *The operations room, Bentley Priory, 1940.*

Below *Supermarine Spitfire Mk LF XVI, SL574, outside Bentley Priory* (photographed October 4 1969).

radar site to 1,500 or more serving personnel on a major flying station.

Located 1½ miles away from Bentley Priory is Royal Air Force Stanmore Park. The station opened in 1938 on a 56-acre site previously occupied by a preparatory school, which consisted of a large mansion where the hangars now stand, surrounded on all sides by playing fields.

The station was commanded by a Group Captain Bald and was No 3 Balloon Centre of the Royal Auxiliary Air Force. Four large hangars were built to house the balloons and ancillary equipment. Two special hangars both 70 ft high, stood in the vicinity of the existing medical and dental centres. The two smaller Bellman

hangars were on the site of the junior ranks' restaurant.

Based here at that time were 906 and 907 Squadrons. The area occupied by the gymnasium and arena was a large instructional and gas storage area. The layout of the rest of the station was very similar to today, although the function of many of the buildings has changed. One major building, however, which was added around 1940 was Balloon Command Headquarters, sited where the officers' married quarters now are in Cherry Tree Way. This large complex of adjoining huts had approximately 70 offices. In the early 1940s this HQ passed over to No 43 Group of Transport Command and soon afterwards the station was incorporated into Fighter Command. The hangars were then used to store aircraft of historical importance, including Hess's machine. Barrack blocks replaced these hangars from the early 1950s and the station took on fully its role as a base support unit for the then Headquarters Fighter Command at nearby Bentley Priory.

RAF Stanmore Park now has a dual role. It is the base support unit for Headquarters No 11 Group and the home of the Joint Services Mechanical Transport Servicing Flight (JSMTSF).

Bushey Hall, Hertfordshire

176/TQ140950. South-east of Watford off the A411

Bushey Hall became USAF Station No 341 and was used by the 8th Air Force Fighter Command as headquarters from May 1942 until January 1945, under the command of Brigadier-General Frank O'D. Hunter. This HQ was within easy reach of RAF Fighter Command Headquarters at Bentley Priory from which much advice and assistance was sought in the early days. It moved to Belgium in January 1945.

Units attached to Bushey Hall were: 8th AF Fighter Command HQ; No 9 Bomb Disposal Squadron; No 887 Military Police Company; No 30 Postal Registry Section, Detachment A; No 151 Quartermaster Company Service Group; No 1073 Quartermaster Company Service Group; No 418 Signal Company; No 101 Station Gas Defence Unit; and No 75 WAAC Post Headquarters Company.

Bushey Park, Surrey

176/TQ150700. South of Teddington

Bushey Park, on the north side of the River Thames, housed the Americans during the Second World War. It was designated Camp Griffis, USAF Station No 586.

In September 1942 the Americans arrived and set up a camp in record time. Many spectators came to view their efforts since they were in a public park. About mid-September 1942 some equipment arrived, including six .50 calibre anti-aircraft machine-guns. These were immediately set up as station defence weapons. Camouflage training was conducted and three officers were sent to the Royal Air Force Camouflage School at Farnham Castle, Surrey. The rest of September was spent getting the camouflage school ready to travel. On October 1 the first of this

organisation's travelling schools was sent out to instruct the newly activated Twelfth Air Force in the latest camouflage methods. During the second week of October the Engineer Platoon Survey Section was sent out to lay out airfields for the Eighth Air Force. Travelling schools and survey parties were on the road for the rest of the month, coming in only when necessary to refit and to receive further instructions.

In November the camouflage platoon was engaged in work of great importance in connection with the African invasion. Fifty men were on detached service in Cornwall where they were employed in camouflaging aircraft. At that time the plans for the African invasion were top secret and since the aircraft were camouflaged as they arrived from the States the Enemy was prevented from knowing the air strength.

January 1943 featured a series of air raids. Luckily no damage was done to the camp area. That same month the organisation moved into its permanent quarters located in Warren Plantation, Bushey Park. This move was welcomed by everyone, for many had no tent stoves and they were hit by bad weather. The men now had latrines and showers on hand.

Work continued throughout 1943 and at the end of the year a mobile mines and booby trap school was formed for the purpose of instructing personnel of the Air Forces in the United Kingdom. Up until its disbandment the school instructed 25,000 officers and men.

In January 1944 some units moved from their old camp site in Warren Plantation to the Chestnut Avenue Camp, also in Bushey Park. The following month the United States Strategic Air Force in Europe established its Headquarters at Bushey Park, its duties were as explained under High Wycombe. The 8th Air Force Headquarters (this was the overall command) moved to High Wycombe. It had occupied Bushey Park since its formation in 1942. The Americans finally moved out of Bushey Park in June 1945.

Units attached to Bushey Park were: 8th AF Headquarters; USSAFE Headquarters; 8th AF Service Command; No 41 Altitude Training Unit; No 4 Bomb Disposal Squadron; No 55 Depot Supply Squadron; No 901 Engineer Company; No 952 Engineer Topographical Unit; No 301 Dispensary; No 1109 Military Police Company; No 2013 Ordnance Maintenance Company; No 1665 Ordnance Supply and Maintenance Company; No 635 Army

Postal Unit; No 8 Combat Camera Unit; No 802 Reconnaissance Group; 8th Tactical Service Area; No 423 Signal Company; No 951 Signal Intelligence Company, Radio; No 301 Station Gas Defence Detachment; No 1 WAAC Battalion; No 438 Army Air Force Band; and No 93 Machine Records Unit.

A plaque mounted on a concrete base was unveiled to the memory of American airmen who served at Bushey Park by General Ira Eaker on August 20 1945. Today nothing remains of the former camp site.

High Wycombe, Buckinghamshire

175/SU828910. Just off the A40 at High Wycombe

Bomber Command was born on July 14 1936, but was located at Uxbridge before moving to its present site, hidden among the Chiltern Hills at Walter's Ash, a few miles from High Wycombe, in 1939. Bomber Command was to operate in an area then chosen because of its remoteness, lack of features from the air and thickly wooded nature, all set in some 90 acres. It is close to Booker Aerodrome which is

also known as Wycombe Air Park.

Building started with 80 specialists and a labour force of some 800 men and it was estimated that over six million multicoloured sand-faced bricks were laid.

As the building got under way, some 200 tons of reinforcement, 28,800 cu yds of excavations and moundings and 8,800 cu yds of reinforced concrete were used.

It was here that Air Marshal Sir Arthur T. Harris took over as Commander-in-Chief of Bomber Command on February 3 1942. From High Wycombe, 'Butcher' Harris hatched his plots to destroy the industrial heart of Nazi Germany.

At the end of May 1942, against all odds, Harris put all his eggs in one basket. The sky became black with bombers. On a single night between May 30/31 the first thousand-bomber raid on one target left the city of Cologne a smouldering heap of rubble. Operation *Millennium* had been successful.

Operations Room, Bomber Command Headquarters at High Wycombe, 1943. Air Vice Marshal Saundby (standing, arms folded); Air Vice Marshal Graham (seated at desk).

'Butcher' Harris left Bomber Command at the height of its glory. It had ended the war in 1945 with over 1,800 operational aircraft. It had flown 392,137 sorties on all types of operations and dropped over two million high explosive bombs and 83 million incendiaries, equal to one bomb dropped every two seconds throughout the days and nights of the war. The cost in terms of life was high; some 47,000 aircrew were killed (67 per cent of the total RAF casualties).

Bomber Command and Fighter Command merged on April 30 1968, to become Strike Command, as Bomber Command became No 1 Group and Fighter Command No 11 Group, a role which still exists today. Around the same time Signals and Coastal Commands were absorbed and later Air Support Command was amalgamated to form a single multi-role operational command. These roles are concentrated into four groups. No 1 Group exercises a day-to-day operational control and training of strike/attack, air-to-air refuelling and reconnaissance forces. No 11 Group controls the air defence squadrons of Phantoms and Lightnings, the Bloodhound surface-to-air missile defences and the ground environment radars, including the early-warning system at Fylingdales. No 18 Group has maritime responsibilities, covering long-range maritime reconnaissance, anti-submarine warfare and search and rescue. No 38 Group controls ground attack aircraft, support helicopters, air transport and the RAF Regiment squadrons.

On April 10 1975, Strike Command became a major subordinate command within the North Atlantic Treaty Organisation (NATO) under Saceur to become Headquarters United Kingdom Air Forces (CINCUKAIR).

Looking to the future, the RAF is receiving the Panavia Multi-role Combat Aircraft (Tornado) which enters service in the strike/attack and air defence roles in 1982 and 1985 respectively. This swing-wing, twin-engined aircraft will give Strike Command the all-weather hitting power it will require to back NATO quickly and effectively in the future. A new generation of air-to-air and air-to-surface weapons is about to enter service, and in the field of logistic support the introduction of the Chinook heavy-lift helicopter will greatly increase lift capability.

During the Second World War the Americans were at High Wycombe, which became USAF Station No 101 Camp Lynn. Brigadier-General Eaker and his staff arrived in Britain early in 1942, with orders to establish a headquarters for the 8th Army Air Force, and to prepare for the reception of the main force upon its arrival from the States. For the first few weeks they were accommodated at Bomber Command HQ, High Wycombe, where they observed the methods of the RAF's planning staff at first hand. They moved into their own Command HQ, Daws Hill Lodge, on April 15 1942. The building was formerly in use as a private girls' school.

In February 1944, a new command was set up to co-ordinate the policies of the 8th Air Force in Britain and the 15th Air Force in Italy; named United States Strategic Air Forces in Europe, USSAFE, the command was set up at Bushey Park, replacing the original 8th Air Force Headquarters which moved to High Wycombe. In July 1945, the 8th Air Force HQ moved out to Honington, and the 8th Air Force Bomber Command HQ moved out to Okinawa, to continue its war effort against the Japanese. The 8th Air Force Fighter Command then moved into High Wycombe from Belgium and stayed until October 1945 when it moved to Honington. Daws Hill Lodge was then relinquished by the Americans and returned to its civilian role.

Units attached to High Wycombe, Camp Lynn were: 8th Air Force Major Command HQ; 8th Air Force Bomber Command HQ; No 41 Altitude Training Unit; No 5 Combat Crew Replacement Centre; No 8 Reconnaissance Wing; No 6 Replacement Training Squadron; No 942 Engineer Topographical Battalion; 8th Air Force Finance Detachment; No 2976 Finance Detachment; 8th Air Force Central Medical Establishment; 8th Air Force Dental Detachment; No 181 Medical Dispensary; No 302 Dispensary; 8th Air Force Medical Field Service School; No 10 Veterinary Detachment; No 1 Veterinary Detachment (Aviation); Nos 23 and 10 Veterinary Sections; No 896 Military Police Company; No 1283 Military Police Company, Detachment E; No 1119 Army Postal Unit; No 1132 Quartermaster Company, Detachment A; No 1153 Quartermaster Company; No 1245 Quartermaster Company; No 514 Quartermaster Car Company; No 2 Photographic Technical Squadron; No 1 Photographic Intelligence Detachment; No 19 Photographic Intelligence Squadron Detachment; No 161 Motion Picture Unit, 16mm; No 163 Motion Picture Unit, 16mm; No 3 Combat Camera Unit; No 417 Signal Battalion; No 322 Signal Company;

No 1025 Signal Company Service Group; No 95 Station Complement Squadron; No 1 Station Gas Defence Detachment; No 76 WAAC Post Headquarters Company; No 469 Army Air Force Band; No 739 Army Air Force Band; No 13 Special Service Company; and No 65 Machine Records Unit.

On May 15 1945, a victory flypast took place over the HQ at High Wycombe. Units representing all branches of the 8th Air Force flew in the aerial parade, led by B-24s and B-17s.

Kingston, London

176/TQ185705. West of London near the A307 at Kingston-upon-Thames

The Royal Borough of Kingston-upon-Thames has been associated with flying since the beginning of the century.

In 1910 Mr T.O.M. (later Sir Thomas) Sopwith was bitten with the aviation bug. He taught himself to fly and earned one of the first aviation certificates. He won many competitive flights and after experience in America he established the Sopwith Aviation Company at Kingston-upon-Thames in premises at Canbury Park Road, not far from the River Thames.

The first aircraft to be produced was named the Sopwith Wright Tractor. It was sold to the Admiralty for £900. These early machines were designed on the shop floor and took about six weeks to complete. Mr H.G. (Harry) Hawker, a young Australian flyer, helped with the flight-testing of the machines.

By the outbreak of the First World War the company had seven types of aeroplane in production, including the world's first triplane. The names of Sopwith aeroplanes became famous and have passed into history. The Pup, the Snipe, the Camel and the 1½-Strutter are but a few of over 40 Sopwith designs produced at Kingston. To cope with the increased war demands, additional factory space was built at Canbury Park Road and production was also conducted at a new site about a mile away on the Richmond Road—which is today's location. Nearly 16,000 Sopwith aeroplanes were built, some of the wartime production was sub-contracted to other companies in the UK, and some aircraft were built under licence overseas. Sopwith received the CBE in 1918.

By 1920 the scene had changed and for their peacetime role the Services were cutting down on new aircraft. The Snipe continued as the standard fighter for the Royal Air Force, but the Sopwith Aviation Company was wound up and a new company with more diverse engineering interests was formed. This new company was named H.G. Hawker Engineering Company Ltd.

In 1921 at the age of only 32, H.G. Hawker died when his machine crashed while practising for that year's Hendon Aerial Derby.

A young draughtsman named Sydney (later Sir Sydney) Camm joined the company in 1923. By 1925 he had become chief designer—an appointment he was to hold for 34 years till in 1959 he became the company's chief engineer.

Between the wars the H.G. Hawker Engineering Company produced many

Sopwith Pup, one of 30 built by Wm Beardmore & Co with skid undercarriage.

Hawker Hurricane PZ865 became G-AMAU. The world's greatest piston-engined aircraft, the brainchild of Sydney Camm. A historic aeroplane and seen here at Dunsfold Aerodrome in the mid-1950s.

aeroplanes but the best known were the Hart and the Fury biplanes of this period. These machines and others of their time were built using the Hawker patented light-weight tubular steel construction and this continued in use as a constructional technique on all Hawker aircraft up to 1943.

The year 1931 saw the Hawker Demon two-seat interceptor enter the production lists. The following year it was joined by the Audax army co-operation two-seater and the Osprey naval spotter.

By 1933 the company had entirely concentrated on aircraft design and production. Therefore the new name of Hawker Aircraft Ltd was adopted. At the same time Hawker purchased the Gloster Aircraft Company and the company went from strength to strength.

Further expansion took place in 1936 when Hawker purchased land at Langley, near Slough in Buckinghamshire, on which a factory and airfield were built. During this period various Hart developments went into production and Sydney Camm's ideas for a new fighter, a monoplane design, were taking shape. This was being built around a new liquid-cooled 12-cylinder Rolls-Royce engine (later to be known as the Merlin).

First flight of the Hurricane prototype took place in 1935 and following its trials at the Aircraft and Armament Experimental Establishment at Martlesham Heath in 1936 a production order was placed for 600 aircraft. This was a large order for peacetime but in fact the company had started planning, jigging and tooling for 1,000 airframes before receiving any Government contract. Its foresight ensured that by 1940 and the Battle of Britain several hundred urgently needed extra Hurricanes had been produced. At the outbreak of war in 1939 the Hawker factories at Kingston, Brooklands and Langley, employing over 4,000 people, were wholly engaged on Hurricane production. Five hundred had been delivered to the Royal Air Force and 32 out of the 52 interceptor squadrons were Hurricane equipped. Nearly 15,000 Hurricanes of many marks and roles were built at home and in Canada.

Other aircraft produced during the war were the Typhoon fighter/bomber and the Tempest. One Wing equipped with these accounted for the destruction of over 600 flying bombs during 1944. From the Tempest came the Sea Fury, the last of the long line of Hawker propeller-driven aircraft. It entered production in 1946 and saw service with carriers of the Royal Navy as well as with the Royal Australian and Royal Canadian Navies. It was a Sea Fury that was to become the fastest piston-engined aeroplane of all time when a cut-down version attained a level speed of 520 miles per hour.

Kingston moved into the jet age when the first prototype flew in 1947. The P1040 became the naval interceptor/ground

attack Sea Hawk and the first production aircraft was delivered to the Royal Navy in 1953.

During 1948 the main production operations were moved from Kingston town to the present site at Richmond Road. The company moved into the highly successful Hunter era. The prototype P1067 flew in 1951 and it entered service in 1953.

Hunters were sold in large numbers to Air Forces of over 15 nations throughout the world. Deliveries of refurbished Hunters continued a quarter of a century after the aircraft's first flight.

Kingston is recognised world-wide for its unique contribution to jet V/STOL. The P1127 (RAF) was the pre-production version of the world's first fully operational jet V/STOL ground attack and reconnaissance fighter—the Hawker Siddeley Harrier—which made its first production flight at the end of 1967. The first Harriers were delivered to the RAF in early 1969 and were fitted with the new computerised inertial navigation and attack systems (INAS). Designs for a naval Sea Harrier were accepted in 1976 when an order for 24 aircraft was received at Kingston. In the United States the McDonnel Douglas Aircraft Company is working on an advanced version of the Harrier.

In the late 1960s the HS1182 project was commenced to satisfy the anticipated need for a replacement fast jet trainer and weapons trainer for the Royal Air Force. It was selected by the RAF in 1971 and by the following year an order for 175 aircraft

Above *The Sea Harrier, whose extraordinary capabilities can be seen in this photograph. With all four nozzles able to rotate simultaneously, the powerplant's total thrust can be directed downwards for vertical (hovering) flight or rearwards for normal (wing-borne) flight. The Harrier V/STOL gives a new meaning to tactical support fighter operations.*

Top right *This excellent photograph shows the production of the Hawks at the Kingston factory.* **Above right** *The finished product—this line up of the Hawk trainer aircraft was taken at RAF Valley during 1978. The Hawk is a high technology aircraft and is an ideal replacement for both the Gnat and for the Hunter. The Royal Air Force Red Arrows aerobatic team has operated Hawk since the 1980 demonstration season.* **Right** *Aerial view of the Kingston site of British Aerospace (Kingston-Brough Division).*

had been placed with the Kingston Company. This elegant two-seater was named Hawk and the chosen powerplant was the Anglo-French Rolls-Royce/Turboméca Adour turbofan. In its trainer livery it entered RAF service in 1976.

During the progress of the Hawk design at Kingston, the Aircraft and Shipbuilding Industries Bill, which in part would effect the nationalisation of the British aircraft industry, was being formulated. It became law in April 1977. Thus Hawker Siddeley Aviation, Hawker Siddeley Dynamics, the British Aircraft Corporation and Scottish

Aviation were brought together to form a single nationalised aerospace enterprise—now, of course, de-nationalised again!

The new corporation was set up in two groups—aircraft and dynamics. Headquarters of the aircraft group is based at Richmond Road, Kingston-upon-Thames. This is the Kingston-Brough Division. The Kingston site covers an area of 78,000 sq metres and includes a major design centre and comprehensive research and development facilities. There is also a fully equipped training centre. Dunsfold Aerodrome is responsible for final assembly, production flight-testing and experimental flight development of all Kingston-built products.

The Kingston company will continue to produce aeroplanes and will play a leading role in the future. Kingston with its 3,500 employees has work well into the 1980s on the Harrier, Sea Harrier and the Hawk.

Stanmore Park (Bentley Priory), Middlesex

See Bentley Priory

Stevenage, Hertfordshire

166/TL225250. To the east of Luton, just east of the A1 motorway

Mention has to be made of Stevenage for it is part of British Aerospace, Stevenage Division of the Dynamics Group with 6,500 employees. The group has operated most successfully for more than 25 years and broadly speaking is responsible for all projects other than aircraft. This covers an extensive area but ground-launched weapons are the particular responsibility of the Stevenage Division. Weapons pro-

duced are: the Swingfire long-range anti-tank missile; the Rapier low-level anti-aircraft system; the tracked Rapier; and Milan, the infantry-portable anti-tank guided weapon which is built under licence from Euromissile. The Rapier system is in service with the British Army and Royal Air Force and is operationally deployed by both services in Germany with NATO forces. Swingfire is in operational service with the British Army and also in service with the Belgian Army.

Also, many types of component are made by the division and it is one of the largest manufacturers of gyroscopes in Europe, producing over 24,000 per year of all types.

The Space and Communications Division (site B) is also housed at Stevenage and it has 800 employees. This division, with another site at Bristol, is responsible for all British Aerospace space projects, and is the largest manufacturer of communications satellites in Europe.

The group designs, develops, supplies and supports a very extensive range of tactical guided missile systems. As well as the UK, British Aerospace Dynamics Group weapons are making a significant

Within the Dynamics Group, the Stevenage Division operates the largest factory complex located on a single site as seen in this aerial view. This includes design offices, development workshops plus a comprehensive environmental test facility. Note the helicopter pad in the centre. View taken looking south, with the main A1 road on the right.

contribution to the defence of many nations.

The Stevenage site opened in 1954 to replace the cramped Luton facilities and since then it has gone from strength to strength. Its future looks assured in this field.

Uxbridge, Middlesex

176/TQ063833. South-east of Uxbridge off the A4020

The present Royal Air Force station at Uxbridge comprises the house and land originally known as Hillingdon House and its estate. The house was built in 1717 by the Duke of Schomberg for use as a hunting lodge. Nearly 100 years later it was acquired, in 1810, by Richard Henry Cox, the heir to the banking business founded by his grandfather. In 1844 the house was extensively damaged by fire, but was rebuilt by Richard Cox on more or less its original lines. It remained in the Cox family until the death of Frederick Cox in 1913, when it was offered for sale. It was eventually acquired by the Government in early 1915.

To the consternation of the people of Uxbridge the Government's original intention was to use the house and grounds as a camp for the internment of German prisoners. To this end an elaborate system of barbed wire entanglements and guardhouses was prepared, only for these to be scrapped a few weeks later when the building was converted into a convalescent hospital for Canadian soldiers. It remained in this role until the end of 1917, when a special train transferred 394 patients and staff to their new base in the Manor War Hospital Epsom.

In the meantime, in June 1917, the Royal Flying Corps Armament School had opened at Perivale to train officers and NCO instructors in gunnery, together with armament officers, assistant armourers and gear fitters. However, its rate of expansion was so rapid that new premises had to be found, and subsequent to the Canadian evacuation of Hillingdon House, the Armament School took up residence in the house and its spacious grounds in December 1917.

The move of the school was to cause some concern to the local population, since houses in Park Road were commandeered as officers' quarters with effect from January 1 1918.

On a wider front, January 1918 had seen the formation of the Air Council.

Amongst its first tasks was the reorganisation of the training systems of the naval and military air services upon their amalgamation. One of the results of this reorganisation was that cadets, before being posted to a training squadron for flying instruction, attended the Armament School at Uxbridge. Courses lasted from 1–13 days for bombing pilots, and 1–27 days for single-seat fighter pilots. The monthly average of cadets passing through Uxbridge from April 1918 onwards was about 1,200, giving the camp an average population in excess of 2,500 cadets. To cope with such large numbers many new buildings, hangars and huts had to be erected.

On April 1 1918 the Royal Air Force was formed and the Armament School passed into the possession of the new service. After just over a month of Air Force service the school was honoured by a royal visit. On May 2 His Majesty King George V spent two hours visiting the camp, inspecting the various schools and workshops, showing particular interest in the Lewis gun which had been synchronised to fire through the revolving propeller of an aeroplane. It is believed that this was the first royal visit to a unit of the newly formed Royal Air Force.

During 1918 the Armament School had quickly settled into a well-regulated pattern of life. The leisure time of staff and trainees was catered for by concerts given by the school orchestra, by film shows in the camp cinema and by inter-section and inter-unit sports fixtures. The school cricket team was particularly strong, one J.B. Hobbs (later Sir Jack Hobbs) appearing regularly as one of its opening batsmen.

The end of the war and the subsequent dramatic reduction in the numbers of Royal Air Force units, squadrons and personnel brought major problems for the infant third service. Trenchard was convinced that a strong service could only be built on firm foundations at permanent bases. Uxbridge featured prominently as the location for many units and formations. Some were of a temporary nature whilst others were to have long associations with this station.

By June 1919 the Armament School was awaiting disbandment and by September it had gone. In the same month the School of Music had arrived from its previous home in Hampstead. On August 1 a detachment of the Royal Air Force Depot came from Halton and together with the Recruits' Training Depot, which was established soon after, formed the Uxbridge Depot. At about the same time, HQ No 2 Group (South East Area), which had previously been based at Oxford, arrived. Then in September, Headquarters Southern Area, which had been formed by the amalgamation of South East Area and South West Area, moved from Kensington to occupy Hillingdon House recently vacated by the Armament School. It was accompanied in its move to Uxbridge by two of its subordinate formations, Southern Area Medical Headquarters and Southern Area Barrack Stores.

By the end of October yet more units had arrived at Uxbridge. These included Southern Area Headquarters of the Air Construction Service together with SE Area Group Headquarters of the same service, a unit which was to cease to exist as a separate entity the following month. October also saw the arrival of the cadres of 4 Squadron which arrived from Northolt. By the end of the year they had been joined by the cadre of 39 Squadron.

The year 1920 was to prove an equally hectic one. In January the cadres of 3 and 207 Squadrons arrived from Croydon upon that unit's closure. February saw four of the squadron cadres moving, 1 and 3 reforming in India, 24 moving to Kenley and 207 to Bircham Newton. (39 Squadron cadre moved to Kenley in April.) The remaining Squadron, No 4, moved to Farnborough in March, a month which saw further arrivals and more administrative changes.

The arrivals were the Discharge Centre from Halton and a Records Office detachment from Blandford. The reorganisation involved the creation of Headquarters Inland Area which was formed by combining Northern and Southern Areas, Hillingdon House (previously used by Southern Area) being retained by the new formation. The rearrangement also involved the disappearance of Headquarters No 2 Group.

In April the School of Music was disbanded, making way for the creation of the Royal Air Force Central Band which has since served continuously at Uxbridge. In May the School of Physical Training and Drill was established at Uxbridge and in June the Officers Invaliding Board arrived from Hampstead.

Adding to the difficulties of the early post-war years was the fact that Uxbridge was also a major demobilisation unit. The extent of this task may be seen from a report in *The Middlesex and Buckingham-*

shire Advertiser and The Uxbridge Gazette of January 10 1919: 'The Armament School is used practically as the "University of Demobilisation", for not only are the men and cadets from Uxbridge demobilised at the rate of over one a minute, but staffs from other units had been sent to Uxbridge for instruction in demobilisation. The staff at Uxbridge is up to date and efficient in every way as regards any form of demobilisation'. A report in the same paper a week later estimated the camp size to be 'Some six or seven thousand men of all ranks'. Another article on September 26 1919 reported Uxbridge as '. . . the biggest Air Force Depot I have ever gazed upon. There are five main entrances on Oxford Road alone (now Hillingdon Road) and innumerable blocks of buildings which look as though they have been made for eternity . . . The place swarms with men and women in uniform'. Towards the end of the year, and concurrent with the rapid post-war reduction of the strengths of the Armed Forces in general and the Royal Air Force in particular, the depot was also discharging WRAF and civilian subordinates.

The main task of Uxbridge and its units during the inter-war years was the training and the forming of the characters of the young men of the service. The station motto *Juventutem Formanus* (We form youth) is a direct reflection of this early task of the unit. An impression of life at Uxbridge can be obtained from the book by T. E. Lawrence ('Lawrence of Arabia'), *The Mint*. Lawrence had assumed the name of John Hulme Ross during the autumn of 1922. Some historians believe that his true identity, known at very senior level, may also have been known to the permanent staff at Uxbridge, thereby explaining the harshness of the conditions he suffered.

Since the early days, the name of Uxbridge has been synonymous with Royal Air Force sport, a tradition which lasts to this day. The depot stadium was opened in July 1923 with an athletic meeting and PT display. It is interesting to note that Lawrence was employed on erecting the stadium fencing and he records this work as among his more pleasurable memories of life at Uxbridge.

A further task which Uxbridge acquired in its early days was the provision of highly trained airmen and military bands for ceremonial occasions in much the same way as presently undertaken by the Queen's Colour Squadron and Headquarters Music Services. Those original drill squads and the Central Band quickly established fine reputations and their services have since been in constant demand. The 'father' of drill at the RAF Depot was Flight Lieutenant Albert Wombwell, known affectionately as 'Stiffy', whose contribution to drill is now commemorated by a plaque on the headquarters building of the Queen's Colour Squadron. His skill and renown is summarised in this extract from an article which appeared in the magazine *The Aeroplane* on September 16 1925.

'For the high efficiency on parade and the fine spirit of the men of the RAF Depot today, thanks are primarily due to Flight Lieutenant Albert Wombwell, who, throughout the war, despite his most strenuous endeavours to get himself sent overseas on active service, was kept at home, as somebody has said, "teaching mechanics to walk". His particular genius has taken the direction of proving to mechanically minded men the aforementioned beauty of being a perfect part of a perfect machine.'

As for ceremonial functions, these are far too numerous to mention in detail, but it is worthwhile outlining two of the earliest occasions because they did much to establish the reputation which Uxbridge still retains. In August 1924 a torchlight tattoo was held on the camp on behalf of the local cottage hospital. This is believed to have been the first occasion involving Uxbridge in a function of this nature. A similar tattoo was held at Uxbridge the following year and that programme, devised by Flight Lieutenant Wombwell, was later included in a tattoo held at Wembley Stadium, in which the Royal Air Force was participating for the first time. The Royal Air Force was represented by 400 depot recruits, and their success can best be guaged from this extract from an article in *The Aeroplane* of August 26 1925.

'The Star turn of the evening was undoubtedly the Massed Physical Drill by the recruits of the RAF Depot. Their evolutions and revolutions with coloured torch-lights ran the PT show very close, but while every other item of the tattoo was greeted with a burst of clapping on the opening night, the RAF Recruits Display nearly took the roof off the stadium with a roar of cheers. Flight Lieutenant Wombwell and the Staff Instructors of the Depot are to be heartily congratulated.'

Throughout the 1920s and early 1930s then, Uxbridge quietly got on with its tasks. Recruits were trained and ceremonial duties were performed. At the same time, the camp, as envisaged by Trenchard, was being established on a permanent basis. 'A' Block of the new permanent barracks was entered in 1925, and the late 1920s saw further barrack blocks and officers' and airmen's married quarters being built.

In comparison with the immediate postwar years, the 1920s saw little in the way of unit movement at Uxbridge. The Discharge Centre, and the Inland Area Invaliding Medical Board ceased to function in 1921, as did the Inland Area Medical Headquarters in 1922. The year 1925 saw the arrival of the Royal Air Force Officers' Hospital from Finchley to begin its long association, in one form or other, with Uxbridge. In 1926 the depot, the School of PT and the RAF Officers' Hospital were transferred from direct administration by Headquarters Inland Area to Headquarters 21 Group, which had been newly formed at nearby West Drayton. The Central Band remained under the control of Headquarters Inland Area.

In June 1926, Headquarters Inland Area moved to Bentley Priory, its place at Hillingdon House being taken by Headquarters Air Defence Great Britain, which moved from its temporary home in the Air Ministry. It was joined soon afterwards by Headquarters Fighting Area. Also in the late 1920s Uxbridge became the venue for courses for short service commission officers. The officers spent a month at Uxbridge 'square bashing' and being fitted for uniforms, before moving on to Nos 2, 3, 4, 5 and later 6 Flying Training Schools.

Further administrative changes took place in the early 1930s. In January 1933 the Central Band was transferred from the control of Headquarters Inland Area to Headquarters 21 Group, whilst administrative control of the RAF Officers' Hospital passed from Headquarters 21 Group back to Headquarters Inland Area. A year later all Uxbridge units (excluding Headquarters Air Defence Great Britain and Headquarters Fighting Area) were passed to the direct control of Headquarters Inland Area when 21 Group was disbanded.

In the mid-1930s the British Government finally abandoned its policy of appeasement, and the Royal Air Force embarked upon a programme of expansion, a programme which was to have considerable impact on the RAF Depot, Uxbridge. In the four years from 1931 to 1934 inclusive, the depot had received just over 3,000 recruits at an average of just under 80 recruits per month. However, in 1935 the depot received nearly 8,500 recruits, the intake leaping from 338 in May to 1.279 in August. The pressure on Uxbridge was such that a sub-depot was opened at Orpington in August 1935, closing at the end of May 1936 when the initial problems had eased.

The year 1936 saw a radical change in the RAF command structure, when Headquarters Air Defence Great Britain was replaced by a number of commands organised on a functional basis. In April, Headquarters Fighting Area became Headquarters 11 (Fighter) Group and later in the year Headquarters Air Defence Great Britain became Headquarters Bomber Command (still at Hillingdon House). Headquarters Inland Area was renamed Training Command, and Uxbridge units administered directly by Headquarters Inland Area were transferred to the newly formed 24 (Training) Group. This same year the Central Dental Laboratory was established at Uxbridge.

Important as these changes were, they had no real bearing on the daily task at Uxbridge. From April 1936 to August 1939 the depot continued to receive an average of 600 recruits per month. In January 1937 a new sub-depot was opened at Henlow due to lack of space at Uxbridge. This was brought about by the implementation of a new policy requiring that all recruits should be accommodated on a scale of 60 sq ft per man. Records suggest that all recruits were received at Uxbridge for initial training, moving on to Henlow for completion of their courses. In the summer of 1937, Henlow sub-depot became No 2 Royal Air Force Depot with effect from September 1 of that year. Earlier in 1937 (April) the Royal Air Force Anti-Gas School had been established, being formed from the Anti-Gas Instructional Centre of the RAF Depot.

By 1938 Europe was gradually but inevitably moving towards war. Germany had occupied Austria, and had designs on Czechoslovakia. Between July and October of this year ten sub-depots were opened, presumably to deal with the increased numbers of people joining the expanding Air Force. A further reflection of the preparations for war and Uxbridge's future role can be seen in September 1938 when No 1 Mobilisation Pool opened on September 26, being ready to receive reservists on September 27. However, the implementation of this contingency was evidently postponed following the signing of the

'Munich Agreement' on September 29 1938.

The final months of peace in 1939 saw Uxbridge quietly carrying on its training commitments with little evidence of the turmoil that was soon to occur. On May 1 the School of Administration was set up and just over a month later (June 13) the Anti-Gas School moved to Rolleston Camp in Wiltshire. It was not until the late summer, following the signing of the non-aggression pact between Germany and Russia, that the full reality of the approach of war began to take effect.

At Uxbridge there was considerable reorganisation and last-minute preparation for the part it was to play. On August 23 the School of PT closed (to reopen just over a month later on September 29) and No 1 Personnel Transit Centre was opened. On August 25 the personnel of No 2 Base Area and other unspecified units began to arrive. On August 27 the short service officers' courses moved to Grantham. On August 28 Headquarters Bomber Command moved to Iver. Four days later, on September 1, the order to mobilise was received. The next day the Central Trade Test Board was formed, and the following day the Central Attestation Section opened. War was declared this same day, September 3, at 1100 hours.

The early days of war saw the intense activity that had marked the final hours of peace continue unabated. In September, Nos 4, 5 and 10 Central Medical Boards were formed, together with Nos 1, 2 and 3 Aviation Candidates' Selection Boards. The selection boards divided the recruits into aircrew and aircraft hands (ACH). The former were kitted and sent home to await recall for training. Such was the demand for clothing, kit and gas masks that the supply system almost collapsed under the strain during the month of September.

Other activity at Uxbridge in September included the closure of No 1 Personnel Transit Centre (closed September 6) and the formation of No 6 AA Division. Between September 8 and 12 No 2 Base Area moved to Northern France. September 22 saw No 1 AA Division moved into London. One week later the School of Administration moved to Gerrards Cross and the School of PT reopened.

After the initial rush of August and September Uxbridge settled down to its two main tasks, the receipt and despatch of recruits to training units, and the receipt and despatch of officers, airmen and

Operations-room at Uxbridge, 1940.

vehicles mainly to units in Northern France. From January to early May 1940 over 400 officers and 4,000 airmen passed through Uxbridge to various coded destinations. In mid-May, however, the outward movement of troops stopped as the position of the Allies in Belgium and France rapidly deteriorated and in late May Uxbridge began to receive people coming back from the British Expeditionary Force. Many of those returning passed through Uxbridge in May and June, the numbers being swollen in mid-June by personnel returning from the North West Expeditionary Force. The station handled more than 2,900 people in this short period, most of whom were quickly moved on to units re-forming in this country.

Throughout the summer of 1940 the station worked under immense pressure. Recruits were being dealt with at an average rate of about 2,500 per week. In addition, personnel were being received for drafts which were being formed for places as geographically diverse as Canada, Rhodesia, India, Malta, West Africa, the Middle East and the Far East. Meanwhile, across the river at Hillingdon House, Headquarters 11 (Fighter) Group, responsible for the aerial defence of London and the South-East, was engaged in the conduct of what was to prove one of the most decisive battles of the Second World War, the Battle of Britain. Many senior Service and Government officials were to visit Uxbridge at this time and it was fitting that Churchill should have decided to remain in the underground operations room for the whole of September 15, the day which is now accepted as the turning point of the Battle of Britain, the day on which Hitler made his final abortive effort to conquer Britain by air.

For the remainder of the year Uxbridge appears to have got on with its tasks, although with an easing of the pressure. During the summer the School of PT had moved to Loughborough college. A personnel administration course was organised and moved out to Denham. By the end of the year the Aviation Candidates' Selection Boards had moved to Weston-Super-Mare and the Recruit Centre had moved to Gloucester, resulting in the substantial reduction in numbers of personnel passing through Uxbridge to approximately 300 per month. The latter part of 1940 also saw Uxbridge undergoing the more traumatic experiences of war. On September 26 a delayed action landmine landed on a hut between the police school and the WAAF quarters. It was successfully defused the following day, and removed and exploded on September 28. Ten days later, on October 6, a bomb damaged the NAAFI shop and some airmen's married quarters.

The next three years were relatively uncomplicated years for Uxbridge. At the end of February 1941, No 1 PDC moved to West Kirby and No 3 PRC was formed at Uxbridge. In July the Junior Officers' School moved in from Loughborough, to move again 11 months later to Cosford. The only other items of interest in 1941 concerned administrative changes. Early in 1940 the RAF Officers' Hospital had become the Women's Auxiliary Air Force Hospital and by July 1941 it had changed its role again and had become the RAF Station Hospital. May 1941 had seen further administrative changes as Uxbridge and its units were transferred from 24 (T) Group to the newly formed 27 (T) Group. In November 1941 the RAF Service Police Headquarters and School split into two units, the School remaining at Uxbridge whilst the RAF Service Police Headquarters moved to Burnham, Bucks. The year 1941 saw only one change—with effect from 27 November, Uxbridge ceased to be known as No 1 Royal Air Force Depot, becoming instead, Royal Air Force Station Uxbridge.

January 1943 saw Uxbridge moving into yet another newly formed group, this time 28 (T) Group. In July, 5004 Airfield Construction Squadron moved from Romsey and, although on the strength of Uxbridge, it was actually housed at Coaxdene, a large house in Park Road, just outside the camp boundary. By the end of the year the police school had left, moving to Weeton.

Just as the late summer and early autumn of 1939 had seen the station heavily involved in the country's rush to prepare for war, so in 1944 Uxbridge had a part to play in the Allies' massive build up for the D-Day landings on June 6 1944. January saw the arrival of Headquarters 85 Base Group of the Allied Expeditionary Air Force and the headquarters of the 9th Tactical Air Force of the United States Air Force. These were joined on 1 February by the main detachment of Headquarters 2nd Tactical Air Force and Nos 150, 151 and 152 Mobile Dental Surgeries of 85 Base Group. All these Air Forces were to play important roles in supporting the D-Day landings. By late summer all these units had left, the 2nd Tactical Air Force leaving a rear Headquarters which itself had moved on by October. June had also seen the departure of 5004 Airfield Construction Squadron.

Having seen the build-up for the Allied landings, Uxbridge was now to see another change of emphasis in its role. In late August secret instructions were received for the formation of 100 PDC (Personnel Despatch Centre) at Uxbridge to meet dispersal requirements on the cessation of hostilities. The unit was officially formed on September 1 and tasked with receiving personnel for release, issuing released personnel with civilian clothing (from the Central Clothing Depot at Wembley), and returning these personnel to their homes. The unit was required to be able to handle 200 officers, 400 aircrew and 400 groundcrew daily and to be functional from September 15. Despite the urgency with which it was formed there was little work for this new unit, and until its establishment as a separate unit on May 15 1945 it had existed, overmanned and underworked, on a Care and Maintenance basis.

October 1944 witnessed the return of 5004 Airfield Construction Squadron to 'Coaxdene', where it was joined by 5025 Airfield Construction Squadron, which arrived from Launceston. Neither stayed long, the former leaving about one month later. December had seen the Continental Aircraft Control Unit being formed at

Uxbridge, to be operational with effect from January 15 1945. An indication of the relative peace that must have existed at Uxbridge, and indeed in the country, can be had from the fact that on November 30 1944, the Central Band went on tour to the USA, returning in March, in exchange with the United States Army Air Force Band which arrived at Uxbridge in December 1944.

The formal cessation of war appears to have made little difference to the tempo of life at Uxbridge in 1945. The latter part of the year had seen the arrival in September of the Overseas Distribution Centre, a new unit belonging to 46 (Transport) Group. In October 5004 Airfield Construction Squadron moved again, this time to Podington and the following month saw the establishment of Air Traffic Headquarters, another new unit. The year 1946 was to be an equally quiet one. The overseas Distribution Centre moved to Hendon in May and 100 PDC was disbanded in November, presumably on completion of its task.

In January 1947, No 9 (WAAF) Personnel Holding Unit arrived from Wythall and was added to Uxbridge's establishment. Its stay was shortlived as it moved to Halton in September of the same year. February saw the arrival of 12 Ground Control Approach Unit from Prestwick to install GCA equipment at Heathrow Airport. It moved to Leuchars in September on completion of its task at Heathrow. At about the same time Air Traffic Headquarters had moved to Stanmore Park. However, Uxbridge's link with air traffic was not broken, for in October the London Area Control Centre was established at Uxbridge. In addition to these movements of units to and from Uxbridge in 1947 there were two other events which are worthy of note. In January, a supply and transport unit was hastily assembled at Uxbridge. Its task was to help to meet the Government's request for service ministries to assist in the distribution of essential foodstuffs, the movement of which was being threatened by a strike of transport workers. However, the strike ended suddenly and the unit was disbanded after a life of only eight days. At the close of the year the station had received its establishment for the unit which was to man the station during the 1948 Olympic Games, when Uxbridge, together with West Drayton, provided accommodation for participants and officials.

Not unnaturally the first part of 1948 was totally dominated by preparations for the Olympic Games. The only other item of interest at this time was the retitling of the London Area Control Centre as London Air Traffic Control Centre (LATCC). By mid-August the games were over and the Olympic Games Committee had begun to hand back the buildings it had temporarily occupied. On October 1 Uxbridge was transferred from 28(T) Group to 22(T) Group and a week later the Recruits' Advanced Drill Unit had completed its move from Hornchurch.

In February 1949 Headquarters 28(T) Group arrived at Uxbridge as a lodger unit. It was joined later in the year by the School of General Service Training and the Recruits' Training Instructor course which, together with the Recruits' Advanced Drill Unit were ultimately to form Training Wing. Headquarters 28(T) Group's stay at Uxbridge was short, the group being disbanded in the spring of 1950. In the meantime the WRAF band had arrived from Henlow and in September the station hospital had become a separate unit, Royal Air Force Hospital Uxbridge, administered by 61 (Eastern) Group of Home Command.

In 1951 the RAF School of Education made the first of its two short visits to Uxbridge, arriving in May from Wellesbourne Mountford. However, the major concern of Uxbridge during this year was the training of officers and men of the King's Colour Escort Squadron which was formed at Uxbridge specifically to take part in the ceremony of the presentation of the King's Colour to the Royal Air Force in the United Kingdom by Her Royal Highness Princess Elizabeth in Hyde Park on May 26. The following year the Queen's Colour to the Royal Air Force in the United Kingdom was handed from the Royal Air Force Regiment Depot, Catterick, to Royal Air Force Uxbridge for permanent custody.

On November 30 1951 a helicopter landed on the parade square. The unit diary records this as 'the first event of its kind in the history of the station'. Whilst this may well have been the first helicopter landing at Uxbridge there is some doubt as to whether it was the first aircraft to land at Uxbridge. There is some evidence, as yet unconfirmed, that DH 6 aircraft landed at Uxbridge in early 1918 on communications flights. On May 11 1953 training commenced at Uxbridge for the entire Royal Air Force Coronation contingent, the Central Band and the Royal Air Force Guard of Honour duly taking up their positions at Buckingham Palace on Coronation Day, June 2.

The following month saw the Review of the Royal Air Force, and training commenced at Uxbridge on June 29 for all contingents from the commands in the United Kingdom. The review took place at RAF Odiham on July 15 with both the Central Band and the WRAF Band in attendance. The parade was commanded by Group Captain Ford, Station Commander, RAF Uxbridge. This was almost certainly the last major event and highlight of his tour at Uxbridge, since his successor arrived the following month. The final major ceremonial occasion of the year was the unveiling ceremony of the Commonwealth Air Forces' Memorial at Runnymede, which was performed by Her Majesty The Queen on October 17. Once again Uxbridge provided the Central Band and a royal guard of honour. Uxbridge's link with this ceremony has been retained to the present day through the unit's tasking to support the annual service held at Runnymede.

The year 1954 was marked primarily by more unit movements. Uxbridge lost the School of Education, which moved to Spitalgate in July, but gained the RAF Central School of Aircraft Recognition which arrived from Stanmore Park in September, the same month that the Inspectorate General of the Royal Air Force had arrived from Hendon. The following year saw the station personnel involved in an important local ceremony. On May 18 1955 Her Royal Highness The Duchess of Kent presented the Charter of Incorporation to the Borough of Uxbridge. The royal guard of honour was mounted by personnel of RAF Uxbridge. September/October saw the arrival of the Ground Officers' Selection Centre for its relatively short stay at Uxbridge. In September the unit diary carried the simple statement that No 1 Squadron of Training Wing carried out a display of continuity drill. This is the first reference to continuity drill at Uxbridge, and it may well have been the first occasion that continuity drill, for which the Queen's Colour Squadron is now justly famous, was performed in public.

On January 16 1957 Uxbridge Borough Council gave formal permission for the use of the Uxbridge coat of arms on the new gates to be erected at the St Andrew's entrance to the camp. Eleven months later, on December 16, the Mayor of Uxbridge, Alderman Meggeson JP, officially opened the new ceremonial gates which had been constructed by the trainees and instructors of No 8 School of Technical Training, Weeton. In February 1957 London Air Traffic Control Centre had been retitled Uxbridge Air Traffic Control Centre. The RAF Central School of Aircraft Recognition moved to West Malling in November.

The year 1958 was to be an important landmark in the history of Uxbridge. In February the NCO training school arrived from Hereford and was absorbed into Training Wing. Then, on April 14, RAF Hillingdon, ie, Hillingdon House, was transferred from Fighter Command to Technical Training Command and responsibility for its administration was given to RAF Uxbridge, which became the general title for all units on the Hillingdon estate. At the same time the South East Signals Centre was established in premises vacated by 11 Group as a lodger unit of 90 Group.

The move of 11 Group to Martlesham Heath was completed in May, thus bringing to an end two important eras in the history of the Royal Air Force at Uxbridge. It marked the end of the dual existence of RAF Hillingdon and RAF Uxbridge which had been created when the RAF depot was established in the park in August 1919. It also marked the end of the long and illustrious association with Headquarters 11 (Fighter) Group and its predecessor Headquarters Fighting Area, which began in June 1926. The empty Hillingdon House was taken over in November by the RAF School of Education which returned from Spitalgate for its second tour of duty at Uxbridge. The previous month had also marked an important date in Royal Air Force history, when, on October 19, St Clement Dane's Church had been reconsecrated in the presence of Her Majesty The Queen and His Royal Highness The Duke of Edinburgh. For this ceremony Uxbridge had provided the Queen's Colour Escort Flight, the Gate Keeping Party and the Colour Party.

The years 1959 to 1964 record further changes in the composition of RAF Uxbridge, but these were fewer in number than in any previous period of that length. In February 1959 the South East Signals Centre had become South East Zone Telephone Switching Centre, only to change again three months later to South East Communications Centre. Meanwhile, the hospital had moved from 61 (Eastern) Group to direct administration by Home Command and finally, in March 1959, to 22 Group of Technical Training Command, bringing it in line with RAF Uxbridge.

May 1959 saw the Ground Officers' Selection Centre move to Biggin Hill. One year later, in May 1960, Uxbridge Air Traffic Control Centre was absorbed into the Southern Region Air Traffic Service Centre. On November 1 1960 the new Queen's Colour Squadron (Royal Air Force Regiment) was formed at Uxbridge and took over those duties previously performed by the escort squadrons, the continuity drill team and the ceremonial drill unit of Training Wing. Two years later, on January 3 1963, the WRAF training courses were transferred from Uxbridge to the WRAF depot at Spitalgate, and on July 13 1964 the School of Education departed again, this time to Upwood. Of the many prominent occasions during this period, undoubtedly the most noteworthy were on March 19 1960, when Royal Air Force Uxbridge was granted the freedom of entry to the Borough of Uxbridge, and July 3 1964, when Her Majesty The Queen presented a new Queen's Colour for the Royal Air Force in the United Kingdom in the garden of Buckingham Palace. The parade was commanded by the Officer Commanding Queen's Colour Squadron.

In January 1965, Headquarters Military Air Traffic Organisation (MATO) arrived at Hillingdon House. At the same time Southern Region Air Traffic Service Centre (Uxbridge) was retitled MATO Southern Region Air Traffic Control Centre (Uxbridge), to be retitled again in July 1970 MATO Southern Region. On November 15 1966 RAF Uxbridge assumed responsibility for the functions of the Royal Air Force Headquarters Unit and was consequently retitled Royal Air Force Headquarters Unit (Uxbridge), a title which lapsed in mid-1970. The year 1968 saw the 50th anniversary of the Royal Air Force, and the Queen's Colour Squadron participated in the ceremony of changing the guard at Buckingham Palace. This was the first time that the Royal Air Force had taken part in this ceremony and the Queen's Colour Squadron has subsequently participated on an almost annual basis. On April 11 1968 Uxbridge was transferred from Technical Training Command to Maintenance Command. On January 1 1970 the Joint Airmiss Section was established in its present form and the same South East Communications Centre became South East Telephone Switching Centre and subsequently No 9 Signals Unit. In March 1972 the RAF hospital at Uxbridge closed, its task being transferred to

Halton, and in December the WRAF Band was disbanded.

The next three years were to see important ceremonies which revived memories of Uxbridge's past. On May 23 1973 Marshal of the Royal Air Force Sir Dermot Boyle, GCB, KCVO, KBE, AFC unveiled the plaque at the ceremony of dedication of the Spitfire which commemorates the important part played by Uxbridge units in the Second World War. On June 11 1974 a ceremony was held to commemorate the connection of Flight Lieutenant Albert 'Stiffy' Wombwell with Uxbridge. A commemorative plaque, sited on the headquarters building of the Queen's Colour Squadron, was unveiled by his grandson, Sergeant C. Inglis.

The Uxbridge story has been brought up to date by the formation in January 1975 of the Airspace Utilization Section and in July 1975 by the arrival of the Resettlement Advice Officers' Team from Bicester.

In January 1976 Headquarters MATO Southern Region disbanded and in April the Central Dental Laboratory moved to Halton to combine with the Dental Training Establishment to form the Institute of Dental Health and Training.

On January 1 1978, No 9 Signals Unit was disbanded and re-established as the Communications Flight of the Station Services Squadron RAF Uxbridge.

Through the latter part of 1977 and early 1978, RAF Uxbridge was the North West London Sector Fire Headquarters for Operation *Burberry*, when the Armed Services provided fire-fighting support at the time of the national industrial action of the civilian firemen.

After the war the operations room fell into disuse for many years. Then, Flight Lieutenant Michael Cooke took an interest in it and his No 9 Signals Unit restored the room, renovated the map table and rebuilt the tote board to its 1940 pattern. On September 15 1975 No 11 (Fighter) Group's Operations Centre was officially re-opened as a museum piece with access only by prior appointment. An exact copy of the room can be seen at the RAF Museum at Hendon.

Today, RAF Uxbridge is the base for No 219 Communications Squadron and The Queen's Colour Squadron. A memorial obelisk was unveiled by Lord Dowding on his visit to Uxbridge on April 22 1958.

Index of units referred to in the text

The church at Biggin Hill with its Hurricane gate guardian; on the other side is a Spitfire. (Photographed July 1981.)